Amani Haydar is an award-winning artist, lawyer, mum and advocate for women's health and safety based in Western Sydney. In 2018 Amani's self-portrait titled *Insert Headline Here* was a finalist in the Archibald Prize. Since then, her writing and illustrations have been published in *Another Australia, Admissions: Voices Within Mental Health, Arab, Australian, Other, Sweatshop Women Volume Two, SBS Voices* and *ABC News Online*. In 2020 Amani was a Finalist for the NSW Premier's Women of the Year Award and was named Local Woman of the Year for Bankstown in recognition of her advocacy against domestic violence, in her capacity as a victim-survivor and member of the board at Bankstown Women's Health Centre. *The Mother Wound* is Amani's debut memoir and received the 2022 Victorian Premier's Literary Award for Non-fiction, the ABIA Matt Ritchell Award for New Writer of the Year and the Michael Crouch Award for a Debut Work at the National Biography Awards.

THE
MOTHER
WOUND

AMANI
HAYDAR

PAN
Pan Macmillan Australia

Pan Macmillan acknowledges the Traditional Custodians of country throughout Australia and their connections to lands, waters and communities. We pay our respect to Elders past and present and extend that respect to all Aboriginal and Torres Strait Islander peoples today. We honour more than sixty thousand years of storytelling, art and culture.

First published 2021 in Macmillan by Pan Macmillan Australia Pty Ltd
This Pan edition published 2022 by Pan Macmillan Australia Pty Ltd
1 Market Street, Sydney, New South Wales, Australia, 2000

A catalogue record for this book is available from the National Library of Australia

Typeset in Adobe Garamond by Midland Typesetters, Australia

Printed by IVE

The author and the publisher have made every effort to contact copyright holders for material used in this book. Any person or organisation that may have been overlooked should contact the publisher.

The paper in this book is FSC® certified. FSC® promotes environmentally responsible, socially beneficial and economically viable management of the world's forests.

For Layla Shaikh Hussain Haidar & Salwa Haydar

bi-smillāhi r-raḥmāni r-raḥīm

PROLOGUE

A clock hung on the wall in the birthing suite at Bankstown-Lidcombe Hospital. I heard it pulse above my head, above the beeps, above the gurgle of the gas, above the cooing midwives.

I had opted for morphine instead of an epidural. I felt the sting of a needle sinking into my bare thigh. It surprised me that I could detect this among the other pains; the rising rumble and thrust of each contraction, the tug of a canula here, catheter there. There were waves of nausea, hot skin stretching and the dull force of baby grinding against bone.

Another pain, the unspeakable one, was present too. But the grief had to be held tightly, quietly. At least until my child was born.

I was falling asleep or passing out between contractions. Sweating and heaving through them. In my mind I began listing all the things that expand and contract; muscles, wombs, pregnant bodies, fruit when it grows and rots, concrete slabs, glass, metal, every molecule, and all the stars in the sky. Then I silently called upon *Al-Qabid, Al-Basit*. The One who contracts, the One who expands.

An obstetrician in a white jacket appeared at the foot of my bed. I watched her mouth open and shut as she explained that she needed to take a blood sample from my baby's scalp. It would indicate whether the baby was in distress.

I glanced up at the time and then down at my belly, which was swollen, almost translucent under the fluorescent lights. I had been in labour for eleven hours. Midwives in navy-blue scrubs shuffled around the room. Their shapes moved and voices spoke in short, quick strokes, as though there was an emergency.

The obstetrician asked me to hold still through a contraction while she found the baby's head with a piece of equipment I couldn't name or see.

'You mustn't push, no matter how strong the contraction is,' she said.

I nodded.

A kind senior midwife with a pixie cut sat beside me and chanted, 'Breathe in – hold – breathe out – good girl.'

My husband peered over her shoulder with furrowed brows.

Within minutes the obstetrician announced, 'Baby is not happy. You've got to start pushing. If you don't deliver soon, we'll have to perform a caesarean.'

'Okay, yep.' I huffed as another contraction surged.

'Push!' the senior midwife instructed.

I knew what I had to do but my arms were numb from gripping the metal bars of the bedhead. Grief mingled with physical pain at the crest of each contraction. I wanted to take it all back. I wanted to tell them I wasn't ready. That I was too sad to push.

Al-Qabid, Al-Basit, Al-Qabid, Al-Basit.

With every contraction, the room melted away and I was in a rectangular grave, at first only large enough to hold a person. Earth had been scraped away to reveal four walls, striped layers of sediment.

'Breathe in.'

I breathed in and the grave swelled into a cave, expanding, like a lung made of brown soil, like a uterus, its walls wet with mud. I was in it and it was in me.

'Breathe out.'

I breathed out and the walls collapsed inwards, pulling me back into my sticky skin. My pillow and tee-shirt were damp with sweat.

'Okay, now again.'

Pain burned through every muscle, but it felt like someone else's. Like my *ruh* had exited my body and was lying down beside it.

'Push, push, push! Almost there!' sang a second midwife in a navy-blue hijab, her face drifting in and out of focus.

Al-Qabid, Al-Basit, Al-Qabid, Al-Basit.

Relief arrived in three abrupt stages; the head, then the shoulders, then the warm gush of placenta. The midwife in the blue hijab placed a slippery baby on my chest.

'Oh my God, oh my God!' I laugh-cried out loud.

A dark-eyed child stared up at me, blinking, gulping, already trying to nibble at my skin. I didn't think to ask if it was a boy or girl until someone said, 'Don't you want to know? It's a girl!'

She was bigger and heavier and more purple than I expected, puffy from the vacuum suction that had helped her out. The hair on her head was thick and black but her eyebrows were faint and sparse. She stretched out her spindly fingers then rolled them into little fists before letting out a cry. My husband leaned in and whispered adhan in her ear, bearing witness, '*Ash-hadu an la illaha illaAllah*', as I searched her face for traces of my mother.

'You did so well!' Moey beamed, rubbing my shoulder.

'Everything hurts.' I smiled back.

The obstetrician in the white coat was still at the foot of my bed. 'We'll let Daddy hold her now. You'll need some stitches,' she said.

I sipped laughing gas and watched Moey rock our wailing baby back and forth on the other side of the room while my wounds were stitched shut. I counted nine needle-pricks. There was a little pain, the kind that didn't matter at all.

As I lay there exhausted but relieved and a little high, the senior midwife returned to the edge of my bed and asked, 'So, where is *your* mother?'

My neck stiffened and I felt myself returning to my body. She had not read my file.

'She was murdered in March by my father,' I answered.

The midwife's smile flattened, and her eyes widened. She patted my thigh and said, 'Oh, I'm sorry, darling.'

'Thank you,' I replied, grateful for the acknowledgement. 'I am so happy to have a daughter. I am from a family of strong women.'

ONE

Moey and I met in our first law subject during our first year of university. It was easy to spot the other Lebs at uni; the boys still grew mullets, wore caps and hung around in groups near the Uni Bros kebab shop. Moey had a habit of wearing his hat indoors which, at first, I thought was very rude. But he was friendly and funny and under the rim of his hat was a smile so generous it reached past his cheeks and into his brown almond-shaped eyes. His grin was underscored by a tufty goatee, which has grown into a lush beard in the time I've known him. It was the late 2000s so he added me on MSN, and we became friends. Our families were from different parts of Lebanon, and of different sects, but Moey wasn't trying to be my boyfriend and I wasn't interested in a partner. We got to know each other while living parallel lives until the final year of university when he started avoiding eye contact and I started looking forward to our classes together.

We each landed paralegal jobs at law firms on opposite ends of Pitt Street in Sydney and started meeting in the middle for lunch on workdays. Spotting Moey's face in the crowd at the mall was something to look forward to on days otherwise spent anxiously trotting to and from court registries and shuffling through files. After work we'd catch the bus to our evening classes at Haymarket. We explored the city together, spent evenings chatting by the Archibald fountain in Hyde Park or inspecting suits, silk ties, art galleries and hobby stores. As we made the transition from study to work, our interests and futures seemed to fold into each other.

One evening Moey and I went up to the Sydney Tower Eye with a brown paper bag full of fancy chocolates. We stood shoulder to shoulder pointing to the clusters of light we each called home and I realised I could never grow tired of him. We look back at this now as our first real date and we knew that if we were dating then we were dating for marriage – this was an unspoken thing. So it came as no surprise when, with only a couple of months of university left ahead of us, Moey asked, 'So, when can we get married?'

'My parents are strict,' I replied, 'so I think we should speak to them after our admission ceremonies. I don't want them complaining that we're young or unemployed – on top of the Shia-Sunni thing.'

Our differing sects had never been a barrier between us, but as we began contemplating the future, we feared it would be a problem for our families. Neither of us had been in a serious relationship or lived away from our parents before so there was no way to guess how they would react. We'd each memorised anecdotes about inter-sectarian relationships that ended with aunties and uncles saying, 'See what happens when you marry outside your community!' or 'See what happens when you don't take your parents' advice!' But had those relationships really failed for religious reasons? Weren't couples more likely to fight about finances or raising children or lack of fulfilment?

I didn't want or aspire to any of the relationships I had seen modelled; certainly not my parents' relationship. I hadn't yet found the language of abuse, but it was clear that my parents' *incompatibility* (as I understood it then) and my mother's unhappiness hadn't been mitigated by the fact they shared a cultural heritage or religious school of thought. The way people behave in relationships must stem from factors deeper and more complex than that, I concluded.

I struggle to put into words what made me feel so sure about Moey. I certainly knew what I *didn't* want and, when I was with him, I felt at ease; it washed over me like cool water. Moey and I agreed that we would make things halal and speak to our parents as soon as we were admitted as solicitors.

*

I was admitted to the legal profession in February 2012 at a ceremony at the Supreme Court of New South Wales. Mum and Dad watched from the audience as my surname was called out. My 'mover' formally requested my admission to the profession. I went up to the front of the courtroom to accept my certificate. Chief Justice Thomas Bathurst wore traditional red robes with a white curly wig and gave a speech about law, justice and our responsibility as lawyers to help make society better. I felt proud to be welcomed into this meaningful work. I also felt relieved; this was the culmination of many tears cried into textbooks and endless hours hunched over desks.

After the ceremony, we filed into the foyer of the Law Courts Building to sign the roll. The roll is a big book with lined pages where lawyers place their signatures upon admission. All around the foyer, young lawyers in smooth suits and tailored dresses took photos with their families and colleagues ('Tell your guests to dress conservatively as though they are going to church,' one blogger advised). There were 'legal families' where several generations of lawyers were present. They claimed the space with ease, standing straight and tall, dropping names – barristers, judges, schools, yacht clubs. I had just become the first lawyer in my family. My parents stood to the side and spoke in hushed voices, strangers to this space and its nuances, Dad in a suit and Mum in a neatly wrapped silk hijab. I ushered them around and introduced them to my 'mover', who was the partner I was working for at the time and one of Australia's leading shipping lawyers. I beamed as he told my parents I was a quick learner and a hard worker. Dad kept moving his hands like he didn't know where to put them.

Afterwards I took my parents out for lunch at an Italian place on King Street Wharf, where I planned to tell them about Moey. *Here, in the city, I have home ground advantage.* I spent the first two courses summoning the courage to tell them while they talked about my siblings and Moey sent me texts asking, 'Have you told them yet?' and 'Is everything okay?' Finally, after a mouthful of sour gelato, I blurted, 'Okay, so I have to tell you something.'

They both looked up. Mum clasped her hands together apprehensively and said, 'So tell us.'

'Well, um, it's about a boy who is interested in me, and I want you to meet him,' I said, pushing a ball of pink gelato around my bowl. This scoop tasted like liquor but there was no point sending it back. I tried to eat around it quickly as it dissolved.

They were both silent so I continued, 'It might be easier if you ask questions and I'll answer them.'

Mum glanced at Dad then down at her lap. Dad wove his fingers together in front of him and asked, 'What's his name?'

'Muhammad,' I answered.

'Is he from a family we know?' Mum asked.

'No. His family are from a different part of Lebanon – and they're Sunni.'

I held my breath, awaiting their disapproval.

It was common knowledge: a girl from the village marries a boy from the village. This is underpinned by a couple of assumptions. The first is that men from families your parents know are a safer choice than complete strangers because they are accountable to your family. The second is that marriage is easy if you share the same religion, sect and politics. If only things were that straightforward.

Mum looked down again and swirled her spoon through the froth of her cappuccino. Dad blinked a few times. I tucked a stray curl behind my ear and decided to keep talking.

'We met at uni and we'll be graduating together. I want you to meet him and his family before graduation. He works at a firm not far from here.' I gestured towards some buildings that towered over nearby streets.

Then I added, 'He's serious and I'm sure.'

I looked back and forth between them, holding my breath. The liquor-flavoured gelato was now a puddle.

Dad spoke first. 'Is he a good person?'

'Yes, well, I believe he is – he's kind and responsible and I think you'll both like him.'

'Okay, we'll meet him,' he said with a stiff nod.

Mum stayed silent as we finished our dessert. After we left the table and Dad was out of earshot, she pursed her lips then smiled. 'We'll need to find a good dressmaker.'

Relieved to hear excitement and not disappointment in her voice, I finally took a breath. 'Just meet him first, Mum.'

*

I introduced Moey to my parents over coffee and cakes at Sweet Fantasy, a Greek cake shop in Bankstown. Moey smiled as Mum and Dad asked him questions including, 'Did you attend Arabic

9

school?' (Yes) and 'What do you like most about our daughter?' (Her curly hair). The conversation flowed smoothly between them; I ate my profiterole and drank my coffee quietly. I didn't dare interrupt.

'*Subhan Allah!*' Mum said as we drove away afterwards. She turned to face me from the passenger seat, beaming. 'It's true what they say – when you meet someone and it's *naseeb*, you feel it right away.'

'He is perfect for you,' Dad's reflection said in the rear-view mirror.

Over the next few weeks, our parents met, and we organised a *Fatiha* where our other family members would be introduced. It would be held at our house in Bexley, which my sisters and I had always affectionately referred to as Four-One-Six. On the day of the *Fatiha*, Moey, his parents and a long line of oiled beards, pressed shirts and colourful hijabs arrived at Four-One-Six with a bouquet of red roses. Uncles, aunts and cousins from both sides sat in a wide circle around the border of our backyard, heads bowed, palms upturned, as we recited the opening chapter of the Quran, *Al-Fatiha,* symbolising our intention to get married. Then the men handed out crispy-sweet *znoud el-sit*, which Mum ordered from a local Lebanese pastry store. I wasn't so naive as to believe everyone approved of our union but, on this day, Quran and food were enough to silence any prejudices and doubts. Within the same few weeks, Moey and I attended our graduation ceremony together and set a date for our wedding. *Alhamdulillah, Alhamdulillah, Alhamdulillah.* Things were falling into place like beads on a *masbaha*.

TWO

One year later, Moey and I had a typical Lebanese wedding reception. It was an evening of *dabke* and Jagged Edge at the Grand Royale in Granville with 350 guests (both our parents had complained that this wasn't enough). We entered the hall accompanied by a *zaffet* of six drummers in shiny costumes, a *zamoor* player who wiggled his head from side to side as he blew the instrument into the air and even a firebreather who twirled a flame above our heads.

On the dancefloor, my eldest male cousin led a group of young men in the *dabke*, as he had done at a lot of the weddings I'd been to. We'd known each other all our lives but I'd only spoken to him a few times because our families hadn't been close. He'd once spied one of my older girl cousins getting a ride with a male colleague and dobbed to all our uncles. I was about twelve when this happened, and Mum had taken me aside and told me to be careful because men like him would ruin girls' reputations over small *mistakes* like that. His footwork was low and loud, leather shoes slapping the floor to the beat of the drums. Sweat twinkled above his eyebrows, which remained furrowed even as he danced.

My dad and his four brothers – my amos – joined the *dabke* line, side by side, hand in hand. Stiff and upright, they marched in unison, round and round and round the dancefloor.

Mum and her sister, Khalto Jinan, took photos with their cousins and friends on the side of the room. The rest of Mum's siblings – my other khaltos and khalos – lived overseas so Khalto Jinan was the only immediate family Mum had in Australia. They'd stayed extra close since Khalto married Dad's younger brother, Amo Abbas. Mum half-joked that her mother-in-law had been so impressed by her she'd gone back for her fourteen-year-old sister. 'They'd have come back for my other sisters too if they weren't already married!' she'd said.

Khalto was sixteen by the time she arrived at my childhood home in Arncliffe dressed in white, and I was four years old when I laid eyes on her, thinking a real-life princess had walked into our house. Khalto and Amo moved in to live with us and Khalto became like an older sister; together we completed every page in my *Beauty and the Beast* colouring book. Now *I* was in white watching Mum and Khalto as they posed, holding hands then wrapping their arms around each other and tilting their heads so their temples touched. Mum wore a long champagne-coloured lace dress that was fluted at the bottom. Khalto was in a black gown. For a long time, Khalto had almost always worn black.

I danced with my friends, sisters and new sisters-in-law until my dress felt too heavy for my ribcage, then I fell into the chair beside my husband at the bridal table. 'I don't know how I'm going to have the energy to catch a plane tomorrow,' I yelled into his ear, competing with the music.

'We'll figure it out.' He smiled, taking my hand.

Once cake and *ahweh* had been served, the music stopped and a white Lexus pulled up at the doorstep of the reception lounge. Our families gathered around for awkward goodbyes.

My sister Nour wrapped her slender arms around me first, then took the heavy bouquet from my hands. She had her hair pulled into a bun at the nape of her neck in a way that made her look older than twenty. Even though I was four years older, she'd always had a way of moving and speaking that was so smooth and contained that people had often asked whether she was the eldest.

'Do I need to keep this?' Nour asked.

'Nah, chuck it if you want, we got plenty of photos,' I replied.

Ola, sixteen at the time and the baby of the family, came in next for a cuddle. My makeup smudged into her rose-pink hijab as I pressed my cheek against her head. 'Wish I could sack school and come with you guys!' she said to Moey with a laugh.

I must have said goodbye to my brother and Dad next. However, there are holes in my memory where their embraces would have been. I remember Dad shaking hands with guests, thanking them for coming and politely saying *'Inshallah b'tof-raho b'awladakum'*, which means 'May you find joy in your children', which *really* means 'May your children get married'. I also remember my brother loading my luggage into the boot of the getaway car. Being only two years younger than me, he'd shared more of my life than anybody other than my parents, but by the time we were adults our parents were all we had left in common. I'd bought him a suit and invited him to be a grooms-man thinking, *Maybe this will be a fresh start.*

When I turned to say goodbye to Mum, her eyes were wet but her cheeks were dry. I felt a lump in my throat like I'd swallowed the bouquet. My face and her face pleaded with one another: *Don't you dare make me cry!*

'Bye, Mum, I'll see you in two weeks. Love you,' I said as casually as I could.

'Okay, take care, love you.' She smiled in return, clutching my hand and pulling me towards her for a quick hug.

I had seen brides cling to their mothers on their wedding nights, sobbing until their eyeliner had run and their eyelashes peeled away. But Mum and I were never sentimental. I resented that when I was younger and wished that I could be more vulnerable with her. But, as I tumbled into the car that night, sinking into layers and layers of silk and tulle, I was glad I hadn't cried in front of everyone.

Mum waved goodbye, and her smile said it all: *Go ahead, you're going to be fine.*

*

The driver talked the whole way from the Grand Royale to the Westin about how he drove cars to make enough money to keep his wife happy and that marriage is hard. Moey and I rolled our eyes in the back seat.

It felt weird to be in that car driving away from our parents in the middle of the night when, until then, we'd been so sheltered. The city we found each other in shimmered like a row of chandeliers as we crossed the Anzac Bridge and the dum-dum-dada-dum of the *zaffet* continued to beat in my chest. I dropped my shoulders and closed my eyes.

I had done what had been asked of me: graduated, got a stable job, married without bringing shame to the family. Through each stage, I'd factored in my parents' sacrifices: the family they'd left behind, the hope they'd put into settling in Australia, the labour they'd put into providing for us, the unhappiness they'd tolerated so that we'd grow up with both parents. I was relieved to be free of this debt. I could build whatever life I wanted now, do whatever I liked.

With our parents' help, Moey and I had bought a house in Chester Hill. There were two spare rooms. One I could use – eventually – as a nursery. The other could be a study, or an art studio. I could paint a big abstract for my dining area, maybe something floral for my bedroom, maybe even a few pieces to sell.

Happily ever after.

THREE

I've only visited the village on two occasions.

The first was when I was four years old, making it one of my earliest childhood memories. I recall Mum – her hair wavy and wild, her eyes still sleepy – folding clothes into a suitcase and explaining that my two-year-old brother and I would be catching a plane with her and Dad to visit relatives in Lebanon. I thought of the tiny white triangles I'd seen drift through the sky and wondered how we'd fit.

It was the Lebanese summer of 1992. Beirut was all tangled wires, washing hung out on balconies and bullet-holes in concrete. I don't know if I remember those details because I saw them back then or because I've seen them in photos and news reports so many times since. Hot and nauseous, we bounced in a leathery van as it transported us from the smoky, sweaty capital to the south. After four hours on the road, a vomit and a change of clothes, we arrived in craggy, war-ravaged Aitaroun; a place that lives in me more than I have lived in it. This was where my parents were born and raised. Mum cried as she hugged the people she'd missed, while my toddler brother yanked at her skirt.

The houses in the village were surrounded by gardens and open land. They had squat toilets that didn't flush and mosquitoes pinched me in my sleep but, to me, this place was a playground that I could run around in for days. At Mum's childhood home, I darted in and out of bright turquoise doors, picking white and yellow snapdragons in the garden before tossing them into the *berkeh* – an open above-ground cistern commonly found in the village. I cried when I was stung by a bee one morning and again when I fell down some concrete steps into a chicken yard. Hens scattered and flapped as I landed, grazing my knee.

This region had been occupied by Israel since 1982 and was technically still at war. Oblivious, my cousins and I crouched under gnarled olive trees, collecting their fallen fruit in old tins. Harvest was an arduous chore for the adults, whose backs and arms ached from years of agricultural labour, but I was delighted to play a role. The blue tarpaulin used to capture the bruised olives was dappled with sunlight and crunched underfoot as I happily filled my tin.

I had no idea what horrors those olive trees had hunched over, or that blood might have stained the ground beneath the blue plastic.

About a month later, our grandparents said goodbye through sloppy kisses, and we came back to Australia. Home had never been far from the airport but now I had a sense of how vast the world was. Growing up in backyards in Arncliffe and Bexley – Gadigal Land – playing with Barbies and plastic cricket bats, I'd watch planes arrive and depart, conscious of my parents' displacement. They spoke endlessly of loss and regret. Every now and then, Mum pulled out a silver rectangular cassette player and we would record ourselves mispronouncing Arabic greetings and singing nursery rhymes on tapes to send back to the relatives we had gotten to know. We were connected by blood but, in the days before WhatsApp, Facebook or even phone cards, we could only witness each other age in photos and cassettes sent with relatives on planes. They came few and far between.

Like most second-generation Australians, I understood that there were oceans separating us from family. At the same time, I sensed that those oceans were like a moat, protecting us from the violence we witnessed through television screens. No one changed the channel or covered our eyes in September 2000 when Mohammad al-Durrah was shown shot to death in his father's arms, trapped against a wall and a barrel. He was twelve and I was twelve. What was I to do with this image? I lay in bed that night, the picture floating above me, telling myself I had mis-understood something. That it was war and war is like an accident that happens to other people, far away. That we lived in Australia because the Middle East was dangerous. Here, girt by sea, we must be safe.

FOUR

My father fled the village in the 70s. He wasn't the only one. When civil war broke out in 1976, the Lebanese Shia Muslims of south Lebanon joined a third wave of Lebanese migration to Australia. They settled in Arncliffe, taking up factory work alongside Macedonian neighbours who had fled a different civil war. They established the Al-Zahra Mosque in 1980, and by 1985 it was the biggest mosque in Australia. They prayed for the end of the occupation and for families they left behind, believing it would only be a matter of time before they could return to their villages.

Dad, aged about twenty-one at the time, his father and a few of his brothers were part of this growing community. I've picked Dad's stories apart in the years since he murdered Mum, trying to sift truth from embellishment.

Like many of Aitaroun's inhabitants, Dad's parents were tobacco farmers, and he was brought up between the tobacco fields and aged sandstone of village streets. He was one of eleven children, born somewhere in the middle (I can never remember the exact order). In the tales he told me and my siblings, as we sat cross-legged and wide-eyed before him, he cast himself as a boyish hero. His square face, broad shoulders and hazel eyes would twitch with excitement as he described himself as stronger and more cunning than the other boys. Tears of laughter would form in the points of his eyes as he told stories of stealing nectarines and broad beans from neighbours.

'There was an old lady in the village and we all knew she was a witch,' he would say about one of the victims of his childhood schemes.

Mum would frown with disapproval in the background. She probably thought he was talking shit. But to me and my siblings, these escapades were thrilling and hilarious.

'I would've liked to be a General in the Lebanese Army,' he'd lament.

Dad had been conscripted to the Lebanese Army at some point.

'We had to sleep on the floor in our boots,' he'd recall, telling us about the time that he deserted post by sneaking away in the middle of the night. Now, when I picture him sleeping on the ground with combat boots on his feet and a rifle by his side, I can't help but wonder if he had killed before.

At other times he spoke bitterly about someone duping him out of an opportunity to study medicine in Romania.

'Please don't talk about him, I feel like I'm going to vomit,' Dad would say, his Arabic heavy with loathing whenever that person's name came up in conversation.

When he finally arrived in Australia as a young, single man, Dad dabbled in English literature at university. I don't know if this lasted months or only weeks; he spoke boastfully yet mournfully of the experience. I remember him saying he worked at the old brewery in Chippendale and then on the train lines at Central Station. Later, he found work as a product control officer at the

Streets Ice Cream factory in Arncliffe, inspecting Paddle Pops and Bubble O' Bills.

Dad eventually settled into a long career as a taxi driver, but he was perpetually dissatisfied. Even though he later earned a diploma in travel services and two master's degrees in linguistics, he stuck with taxi driving until sometime in 2013 when he started a casual role teaching English as a second language at a college in Hurstville. The students wrote him thank you notes for being a good teacher and one gave him a tin of moon cakes for Chinese New Year. He showed us the gushing notes and passed the tin of moon cakes around. It was endearing to see Dad enjoying his new role. I'd believed him to be a victim of his circumstances, driven away from his homeland, encumbered by the responsibility of taking care of his family, forced into mediocre jobs, dragged away from his true potential. He'd made sure we understood this sacrifice and said, 'It will all be worth it if you all turn out *shatriin* – good and smart.' There had always been immense pressure knowing that his self-worth hinged on the marks I got at school and the success of my career. Finally he'd found some satisfaction in *his* work.

As this memory comes to me, I realise I loved the person my father was in this moment; he had his own thing to be proud of and it didn't depend on what Mum or us kids were doing.

I wish he'd continued to grow in that direction.

*

I'd always looked up to my father. I liked that he was smart and hardworking; things I was raised to value. I liked his nostalgic village stories and political anecdotes. I liked the fact that he was into words and books, pulling out a copy of the famous *Al-Mawrid* dictionary whenever I used an English word he didn't know or when I asked for the meaning of an unfamiliar Arabic one. To be unconditionally devoted towards one's parents was a strong part of my religious and cultural context and no one had ever outlined the boundaries or exception to this. For all her complaints against him, even Mum encouraged my siblings and me to be polite and respectful of Dad's authority.

I remember Dad taking my siblings and me to parks, libraries and swimming pools when we were really young. If there had been a fight, we'd go without Mum. If Mum came, they would likely fight afterwards. I was too young to know what these fights were about. Dad could be aloof, but he wasn't absent from my childhood. As I grew older, our relationship became more like teacher and student than father and daughter, to the extent that when a counsellor asks me about it now, I find myself describing it as 'professional'. Whereas Mum took care of our everyday needs, immersing herself in the details of what my siblings and I wore and ate, the time I spent with Dad had the tone of a history lesson or a performance review. With the flinching lines of his face or a slight rise in the volume of his voice, or his teeth brought together to hiss 'tsk, tsk, tsk', Dad had the power to make me feel ashamed for small failures such as bad marks or silly behaviour.

For the entirety of my childhood, I accepted his parenting as valid and loving. He was rarely violent but there were moments when his ego surfaced, fragile against failure or insubordination. On one occasion he made my nose bleed when I failed to solve a maths equation. I was almost twelve years old, preparing to sit selective high school entrance exams, and struggling with the maths homework set by an intensive coaching college I'd only been attending for a few weeks. We were sitting on the rug and Dad was talking me through each question. When I got stuck on a fraction, I began to cry and Dad suddenly lashed out. I wrote about this moment in the 2019 anthology *Arab, Australian, Other*:

'I felt the force of Dad's palm across my face. When he pulled his hand away, my cheek felt hot and tingly from the blast. My nose pulsed and began to bleed. I didn't know where to look. The lesson was over. Blood and tears dropped onto the page of my exercise book.'

When I wonder why it was so easy to forgive this incident, I realise the power Dad had to make me feel sorry for him. In hindsight, I see this as his most manipulative trait. He didn't socialise often, and when he wasn't at work his head was buried in a book. He pitied himself for a wide scope of reasons. He could have been more than a taxi driver. He didn't like driving the early shift. He never got enough sleep. He had to iron his own shirt sometimes. His wife nagged. His brother ripped him off. He'd never permanently return to his homeland. When I search my mind for answers as to how I viewed my father with pity while simultaneously respecting his authority, the only explanation is this: I simply believed in the way he saw the world.

*

There is a pressure on second-generation kids in migrant families to somehow fix the past. Our parents made sacrifices. We're supposed to reach back across time and space and make it all worth it. I don't think anyone feels this burden like the eldest daughter does.

On the day I married Moey, I felt I'd done everything Dad expected of me. I carefully pinned a buttonhole rose to his stone-coloured suit and he kissed me with the bristles on his cheek. I hoped he was proud.

FIVE

Mum was also from Aitaroun, the seventh of nine children born to my teta. She grew up in a modest house, in the shade of a modest mountain called Kheil on the outskirts of the village.

Kheil is red earth patched with green grass and wild herbs. In a certain light it glows pink. I know this because I watched the sunrise from Teta's flat concrete roof during my second and last trip to the village.

When Mum was a girl, Aitaroun was in the midst of a twenty-two year long occupation. Villagers of her generation were raised under the constant threat of violence. There was poverty and hunger, disappearances, and disruptions to schooling. Mum sometimes described hiding in the basement of her parents' home, listening to the sounds of artillery and rocket-fire above. At other times she would reminisce fondly about girlhood in the village.

'I used to climb the tree in the garden and make dolls out of paper with my friends,' she told me once.

'Your parents let you hang out with your friends? But you're so strict with us!' I rolled my eyes.

'Amani, they were other children from the village – the neighbours, cousins – our parents always knew who we were with. And *we* didn't throw answers back at our mum. If we did, our dad would only have to snap once and we would freeze! He would take her side, unlike *your* dad . . .'

We always ended up here. Talking about Dad. About how he didn't set boundaries, that he never helped, never had her back, that the only person he ever snapped at was her.

'Mum, maybe you shouldn't have married him.' I threw in the words and it was too late to retract them.

'Yes, *kent ktiir zghiiri*, what would I have known at that young age! If I knew he was like this, I would not have married him,' she said defensively.

'I know, Mum, but you realise you can get a divorce?'

'Do you think he'd actually leave me alone?' she said. 'He would never accept that. He'll destroy my reputation. *W'elness b'tehki alayna* – people will talk and make life hard for you and your sisters. You don't know him, Amani.'

'I don't care what people say, Mum, and nor should you,' I added flippantly, knowing that it wasn't that simple.

*

Mum was in her final year of school when Dad came back to the village in search of a wife and found her.

In one of the photos I've salvaged from that time, Mum stands in a rose garden, wearing bright clothes, dark bangs and a slight smile. The sky is blue and endless, but I know it has been punctured by bombs and bullets. She has her hand on her hip and looks straight into the camera. She's wearing a boxy fuchsia *abaya* with white embroidery around the collar, but I think she looks trendy anyway.

'I was shy and pretty. But I didn't know I was pretty because I wasn't as white as my sisters, and I didn't have blue eyes like some of them did. I used to hear the older ladies say as we walked past how pretty my sisters were with their fair skin and coloured eyes,' Mum would recall whenever we talked about her early teenage years.

War and occupation restricted everyone's options, but especially the options available to girls. Despite being the daughter of a skilled and literate woman, and despite the potential she had displayed during high school, Mum was not able to continue her studies. Attending university would have meant moving to Beirut during an unsafe and uncertain time, in a society where it was frowned upon for a single woman to move away from her parents.

'I was really good at history and philosophy.' Mum beamed whenever she remembered school. 'I loved to read and write. If I found a poem I loved, I would copy it down in a notebook so that I could look back at it later.' She would have liked to have become a reporter or writer, given the chance.

Mum was just seventeen and Dad was thirty when they married. In the village, it was not unusual for adult men to marry girls in their mid-teens. Mum didn't question this herself until she was much older and then she started to say, 'They wanted young wives so that we didn't yet know how to say no! That way they could always be in charge.'

A couple of my amos had married their wives when they were barely fifteen. Mum was good friends with one of them, and together they would lament the time and opportunities they lost. One time she told Mum, 'I was still playing with the little children when they came and said, "You're going to get married." All they showed me was a photo of him!'

Then she explained to me that – out of social expectation, selfishness, convenience or a thirst for authority – grown men of my dad's generation often married girls who could have been their daughters. It's hard to spot a red flag in a man who is simply doing what everyone else is doing.

My mum confronted her own mother about it once. I was seventeen years old myself by then, sitting on the couch and listening to them converse in Arabic.

'*Lesh?* Why did you let us marry the first men who asked?' my mum demanded.

Teta looked confused and defeated. 'We worried you'd fall in love with some stranger and ruin your lives,' she answered. Her tone dropped towards the end of her sentence, signalling to me that she no longer felt convinced that strangers were the problem.

'*Shu be'arefni*, what would I know?' she added. Then she said, '*Mesh b eidi*', which means 'It wasn't in my hand'. 'There was war and it's what everyone did, and you girls were no different, and I know some of you have had bad luck, but you also got to live well overseas, in beautiful countries. Maybe we're cursed with the evil eye – people get jealous you know.'

Mum stood her ground. 'You rushed us,' she said. I was impressed.

They fell silent, and it was the kind of silence that comes at the end of so many conversations between mothers and their grown daughters. The type of silence where you forgive each other and understand that you tried your best. The type of silence that says, *I'm sorry, I know better now.*

*

When Dad came to Mum's parents to ask for her hand one afternoon, they saw an exciting prospect, not a life sentence. Being from the same community, Dad's family weren't strangers to Mum's parents. They were already loosely related and even shared a surname. But Mum would've been about seven when Dad migrated so she didn't know him at all.

'He knew my older brother and came with him to pick me up from school,' Mum told me. 'They met me at the gate. Then he wanted to come over straight away, and he brought his parents to speak to my parents that same afternoon. They told me that he had been living in Sydney for ten years and was from a family in our village. I thought, *He has lived overseas and maybe he is open-minded and maybe he is well-established.*'

Her family thought it was a good match. Timid and unable to find a reason to say no, she had nodded.

'I went to bed that night and thought, *Uh-oh, I think I made a mistake!*'

'Why didn't you just say no?' I asked.

'Because everyone else got married that way, including my sisters,' she answered. 'I felt like it would be *'ayb* – shameful – to change my mind without a reason.'

One week later they had their *kateb al-kitab,* a ceremony that rendered them a married couple in the eyes of God and by the tenets of Islam. In practice, it signalled the start of an engagement period and would give them the opportunity to get to know each other unchaperoned while they prepared paperwork for Mum's migration. Mum wore an off-white tea-length dress of organza, with ruffles and pearls, which she later donated to my primary school to use as a drama costume. I wish she had kept it. Her fringe was swept across her forehead into an updo.

'No one had even bothered to brush my hair before that day,' she joked. 'And they finally let me fix my bushy eyebrows! These days, girls start plucking them when they're twelve!'

'Oh, come on, Mum. Your parents let you get married and move whole countries at seventeen!' I teased. 'You'd freak out if I tried to do that! So, don't tell me about eyebrows.' She frowned at me.

Dad wore a black suit to the *kateb al-kitab*. In the scheme of his life, I don't think that day had mattered much to him because he never spoke about it. I don't remember him saying anything about what kind of relationship he had hoped for, or what he specifically liked about Mum. He rarely even spoke about the ten years he had spent in Australia as a single man.

Mum, on the other hand, spoke about her *kateb al-kitab* like it had happened fifteen minutes ago, like she had just stepped out of the photos we were looking at.

'If he'd waited until after Ramadan,' Mum said, 'we could've at least served sweets and tea! But he wouldn't wait. I don't know why he was always in a hurry. We had all his family over and it was a hot day and we were all sweaty. It wasn't nice at all.'

'Well, you looked pretty hot!' I said as I flipped through her photos. They were posed against a backdrop of large oleander bushes bursting with baby-pink blooms. Grey-green olive trees kept watch from a distance. With rings, bangles, manicured fingernails and big bows in her hair, Mum looked like a dark-haired Madonna. 'Look at your bling!' my sisters and I would remark.

She was adorned with bridal gifts: one long gold chain with a twinkling heart pendant and another with a filigreed letter *H* for Haydar. Haydar is Dad's first and last name. There are Ali Alis and Muhammad Muhammads in villages like ours. It is normal, but my siblings and I teased him anyway.

'Did your parents run out of ideas by the time they got to you?'

'Maybe you should just write *Haydar²*,' we'd giggle, and Dad would laugh along.

*

Dad returned to Australia to prepare for Mum's arrival while Mum shared a few final months with her family. In August of 1987,

Mum sent letters to Dad. She called him *habibi* in neat Arabic handwriting and said she missed the time they had spent together. When we think of arranged marriages in the West, we imagine that they are dull, predictable and transactional. But these letters are passionate and affectionate, brimming with hope and longing. They are uncomfortable for me to read.

On another piece of paper, Mum listed the dates she was anticipating; on 4 October 1987 she would farewell her family, on the 6th she would fly and on the 8th she would arrive in Australia. Her neat and steady hand disguises how emotional and terrifying this big move was for her.

When Mum arrived in Australia, she found that Dad had already furnished an old apartment in Arncliffe to his own taste.

'Everything was old and ugly!'

Had he not considered that it might be important for her to be involved in the making of her new home? Didn't he think that she might need to lay down roots in a new and foreign place? Didn't he want her opinion? She was offended by his disregard and I could hear the hurt in her voice whenever she retold the story.

Her swift marriage and sudden move abroad must have been more traumatic than I can grasp. She never came to terms with the disappointment. That disappointment doubled when Mum realised Dad was not interested in celebrating their marriage with a big wedding reception. She had agreed to be his bride. She had left those she loved and travelled all this way. She believed she deserved a white dress and a proper welcome. But she was forced to compromise.

'I was shy, and your dad made it sound silly, so I just said okay to everything,' she lamented.

Instead of celebrating with their new Australian friends and family, they hired a gown and took staged photos in a studio, with no one else in sight. Mum resented that compromise and the long series of compromises that came after it.

When I was a child, Mum narrated these events time and time again with raw regret. I think she wanted me to understand the importance of choosing a partner carefully. She wanted me to know that it was okay to wait and to want, to make demands and to have a say in a relationship. She lectured me on these things before I was old enough to fully understand.

*

For a time, Mum blamed herself for going along with what was arranged for her. As she got to know Dad better, she found that he was highly critical of the way she carried herself, berating her if she said or wore the wrong thing, or if she laughed too loud or at the wrong time. Mum had cousins she'd shared a childhood with who now lived in Western Sydney, but Dad disapproved of their lifestyles and prevented her from building a relationship with them, so Mum only saw them on rare occasions.

Internalising his judgment and criticism, Mum assumed that Dad was right and accepted the role of the good wife; always agreeing, always trying to please. She did not feel she could complain or demand, even when something embarrassed or inconvenienced her. She complied with unwritten rules: first you obey your parents, then you get married and obey your husband.

Believing that she should be ashamed of her expectations, she learned not to vocalise them. There was no point fighting over petty, girlish things like wedding parties and furniture. After all, her new husband was thirteen years older and had travelled, studied and worked. She had only just finished high school, having spent her whole life in the village.

Young and hopeful, Mum believed the difficulties she encountered in the early days of her marriage could be overcome. He *could* become a better husband with time. Besides, as an unemployed migrant – soon to be a mother – with no English, no qualifications and limited access to support in a country growing increasingly hostile to Muslims, there were other roads to cross before she could confidently challenge the man she depended on.

One year after leaving home, alone on unfamiliar soil, Mum gave birth to a girl.

I try to imagine what her first few months with me might have looked like. I hope I was a consolation in the long nights. I hope I was a comfort when she was missing her mother in all the ways her husband couldn't begin to understand, in ways he didn't care to know.

SIX

I was about to start my final year of high school when we made a second family trip back to the village. No one recommends visiting Lebanon in the winter, but my paternal grandfather, my Jedo, had been sick with cancer for a while and Dad was desperate to see him. He had sputtered at the dinner table, trying to hold in a sob after telling us he would be going to say goodbye to Jedo. It was, and remains to this day, the only time I've ever seen him cry. I felt sad for him; it must be tough to lose a parent.

He left immediately and it was soon decided that my mum, brother (who was fifteen) and I would join him. Nour, who had started high school, and Ola, who was still in primary school, would stay with Khalto Jinan and Amo Abbas while we were away because we couldn't all afford to go at one time. Despite the sombre reason for the trip, the idea of an overseas adventure excited me.

'We leave tomorrow!' I told one of my closest friends over the phone the night before our hurried flight.

'Okay, stay safe and don't get blown up or married!' she joked. I forced a laugh. I might have made the same joke myself (I didn't know any better), but still cringed to hear it from someone else.

I had internalised too many stereotypes, been too self-deprecating around my non-Muslim friends, to blame them for laughing at the idea of my violent death or early marriage.

I was conscious that I was making this trip at the same age Mum was when she married Dad and left Lebanon. I was in my final year of high school. I had friends, university and a career to look forward to, so the prospect of getting married didn't capture my imagination the way it may once have captured Mum's when it was her only path out of the village. Still, I flirted with the idea that I might meet a handsome Lebanese boy with the right personality and interests, and come back to Australia with a ring on my finger, transformed from an awkward teenager into a glamorous fiancée. Would it be so different to the time my blue-eyed, fair-haired friend got a promise ring from her boyfriend?

*

When we landed in Lebanon in December 2005, I was struck by its contradictions. The new and polished sat side by side with the old and derelict. From the airport, we rode south-bound along the coast in a rickety van with no seatbelts. It smelled like men, leather and fuel; the same smell that made my head spin when I'd been there in 1992. My amto, one of Dad's sisters, had met us at the airport. She was chatting quietly with Mum, but I was too embarrassed to contribute to their conversations with my clumsy Arabic. They spoke with the urgency of years spent apart – 'How's so and so?' and 'Did you hear about this?' – while the driver talked loudly on his phone. My brother was asleep and I tuned out, trying to ease the nausea by focusing on the road, studying fixed points in the distance. I remember the shapes and the colours of the landscape more clearly than the conversation.

As we made our way out of Beirut, dark-eyed models on large billboards flashed luxurious jewellery and watches at us; products only tourists and the affluent could afford in a place with such a high unemployment rate. Further south, citrus trees dotted with yellow and orange fruit stood either side of *el-autostrad*. Street vendors pushed wooden carts of round bread, shouting '*kaak, kaak*' above the beep-beeps and toot-toots. Blue signs announced the name of each coastal town we passed in Arabic, English and French, but I only recognised the names of two famous cities, *Saida* (Sidon) and *Sour* (Tyre). My memories have since blurred them into one place, even though there's about a thirty-minute drive between them. Eventually we turned inland, and the roads travelled over undulating hills and placid valleys, passing trees coated in gold leaves left behind by autumn. We stopped for sticky, sweet *mshabak* at a pastry shop before heading further south. The terrain became more ragged, and silver olive groves stood in neat rows on every slope. The trees reminded me of old people, of soldiers, of ghosts. Gnarled trunks clambered out of the rust-coloured soil, branches drooped with late harvest *zaytoon*, and leaves glistened as the sun went down. Split, twisted, hunching, they clung to life.

The pretty landscape was disrupted by refuse; abandoned plastic here, a broken-down car there, the smell of something burning. I knew from my dad's stories that the Israeli forces once occupied and controlled the entire area we had just traversed. At the entry to each town, large green billboards displayed the photos and names of young men – boys – who were killed fighting the occupation. Each town took pride in its *shuhadaa*, a name given to people believed to have died in a state of innocence or in the pursuit of a just cause. Their frozen faces made the little hairs on my arms stand on end but I couldn't look away. I noticed evidence of war everywhere. Innocuous-looking parcels of land were cordoned off with skull-and-crossbones signs warning of land mines. White vehicles like space rovers marked with large black letters, UN, signalled the presence of United Nations peacekeeping forces.

It was almost dark when we arrived in Aitaroun, but we had to stop at Jedo's place anyway to see Dad and reacquaint ourselves with his family. My brother and I were welcomed with hugs and kisses and exclamations of '*Mashallah*, how tall they are!'

I tried not to stare at my grandfather. He was gigantic in my memories and here he was skinny and sad and wrapped in blankets like a baby.

*

In Aitaroun, people hung pictures of a bearded man in a black turban in their lounge rooms next to photos of their grandchildren. They asked Allah to bless him and create long-lasting peace in the land. In the first few days of our trip, I couldn't work out how the people we were visiting were all so intimately related to the same man. As I pieced things together from the adult conversations taking place around me, I understood that the bearded man was Hassan Nasrallah, the leader of Hezbollah, who was popular at the time for the role he played in liberating the region from Israeli occupation. Every time he was scheduled to give a speech, people would gather around the television to hear what he had to say. It was hard for me, a cynical teenager who hadn't grown up in the occupation or experienced war, to relate to this devotion. I know now that poor people, wounded people, find hope in ways that other people will struggle to understand.

'The Blue Line marks out the area from which the Israelis withdrew in May 2000,' Dad narrated as we explored the neighbouring villages in a hire car over the next few weeks, sometimes bringing one of my amos along for the ride. I wondered why they called it a blue line when it was really a wide strip of long grass, fencing and barbed wire. In some parts, the road ran right along the border fence. I sensed that it wasn't necessarily right to call it the Lebanese–Israeli border as it was still contested. Villages near ours, which were part of Palestine in the 1920s and 1930s, had either been occupied or destroyed on the other side.

I later read that seven predominantly Shia villages are documented to have been 'depopulated as a result of the war' in the region just south of the Blue Line. One such village, Malkiyeh, is documented to have had 360 Muslim residents as of 1949. I try to imagine what 'depopulated' meant for each of those people. In the space where they lived sits a *kibbutz*, a type of agricultural Israeli settlement, called Malkia with about 450 residents. As I looked through the car window, across the fencing and barbed wire, I noticed modern houses in neat rows on the other side in stark contrast to our meandering villages. I observed aloud, 'They're only metres away, but it's so much greener on the other side.' Someone in the car answered back, 'They have more water.'

Towards the middle of our trip, we drove back to Beirut to visit more relatives. While we were there, Dad took us on a quick tour of the city, stopping at the resting place of former Prime Minister Rafic Al Hariri who had been assassinated earlier that year. His grave was covered in a mound of white roses and hidden in a large tent with security guards stationed in each corner. On Dad's instructions, we stood around the memorial, hands cupped, and read *Al-Fatiha*.

For another one of our outings we travelled slightly north of Aitaroun to the village of Arnoun to see Beaufort Castle, which I was introduced to by its Arabic name, Qala'at al-Shaqif. The castle sits at the top of a mountain, high above the Litani river. I was unimpressed at first. No one had preserved the site; there was no entry fee or cafe out the front, barely any information to read, no tour guide and no proper paths to follow. Dad said the castle was ancient and of military significance, but I didn't feel like something important would be left so neglected. As an adult I read that, in fact, the site had been captured and recaptured multiple times throughout history by sultans and crusaders and was also the site of a battle between the Palestine Liberation Organisation and Israeli soldiers in 1982. In late 2005, Lebanon was still celebrating Israel's withdrawal. Before the war in Syria, before new calls for a revolution, a yellow Hezbollah flag swayed at the top of the castle, above a mound of rubble. When I finally stood still and looked out, I saw more of the Earth than I had ever seen before – or since – and the land stretched out until it bled into the sky like watercolours.

On the way home, we drove past a huge house with a long driveway lined with palm trees. 'Those trees are not native,' Dad explained. 'They import them from the Gulf to show off.' Houses like these were springing up at the outskirts of every village. Families who had fled twenty or thirty years prior had returned from diaspora and built mansions where there had once been tobacco fields. These palaces were shrines to lost childhoods, trophies on reclaimed land. The new houses boasted migrant success but stood eerily empty in the winter. Years abroad had cemented their owners to other places, schools, jobs and debts. Even though people like my parents had promised, 'We'll move back when the war ends,' they visited for holidays every other summer, and only when they could afford it. While settlements flourished on the stolen land south of the border, on this side of the Blue Line, safety and economic security remained scarce and unemployment high. Neighbours and relatives who had found a way to return to their homeland in the early 2000s would soon find reason to leave again.

*

It was cold and dreary in Aitaroun. I looked for excuses to avoid the misery and grief of my father's family as they attended to my dying grandfather. The house where Dad and his ten siblings were raised smelled like antiseptic and tobacco. A woodfire heater ensured that the house was always hot because my grandfather's body could no longer keep him warm. Despite his daily deterioration, the family refused to tell him the prognosis: he would not live through the winter. It was suffocating being there, smiling politely as they lied, 'You are not dying, you are a healthy, strong man.' He'd look back at them already vacant, afraid. One day he burst into tears and cried, 'Why do I feel like you're all going to leave me soon?' No one told him that he would be the one leaving and they justified this, saying they were giving him hope. This made me feel depressed for them all.

When I had to be there, I tried to befriend Sudiva, the domestic servant. Sudiva was from Bangladesh like some of my school friends, but Dad's family called her 'the Sri Lankan'. All the domestic servants in the village were called 'the Sri Lankan', even if they were from Ethiopia or the Philippines. Sudiva and I were both super awkward in the crowded house – we'd smile at each other across the room. Sudiva was always invited to sit with us and my uncles said they considered her 'a sister'. They tested Sudiva's Arabic, cheering or laughing when she said something clever or funny and bragging about how much Arabic they had taught her. I sat next to her on a day when no one was around and asked about her family. With just enough English and Arabic between us, and holding up our fingers to represent numbers, I understood that she was only a little older than me. She was the eldest in a large family and was sending all her earnings back to them. I don't know where Sudiva is now but she's the only 'aunt' from Dad's side I miss.

There was no domestic servant at my mother's childhood home. I stayed there, hiding from death and sickness and getting to know my maternal grandmother, Layla Haidar, who we called Teta Em Hussam because her eldest son was named Hussam. Khalo Hussam lived next door to my grandparents with his daughter, Zaynab, and wife, Tante Insaaf – we used the French word for aunt since she was neither a khalto nor an amto. Khalo Hussam's two older children had moved to Beirut to attend university. Zaynab was still in school and we got along like sisters; she was the same age as Nour. Like me, she loved to draw so we showed each other our sketches and talked about art.

Teta's house was even prettier than I remembered. It sat across the road from a servo called Ghazar's Station. An adolescent cedar stood by the front gate and speckled terrazzo tiles led to the same turquoise front door I had skipped through as a four-year-old. In the lounge room was a huge kitschy blue wardrobe, an intricate Persian rug and a lounge where my grandfather smoked Marlboro Reds from when he rose for *fajr* 'til he prayed *isha* while shouting bitterly at the news, 'Everything is America's fault! Even if I sneeze, I blame America!'

The most important space – the kitchen – was at the back of the house. It was filled with light and air. The back door, built to face Mecca, opened to a courtyard filled with roses and a tall pine tree. There was a row of beehives right at the back and, beyond that, the most definitive feature of our village, Kheil. To the side of the yard, there was a granny flat with a proper toilet. Or at least it looked like one until I realised it had to be cleansed manually by pouring water into the bowl with enough force to simulate a flush. That and the frequent power outages were enough to keep my privilege in check over the next few weeks.

Teta made me feel valuable and strong. She listened to every word I said, and that made it hard to stop speaking. At home, I'd survived by getting the necessary marks at school and retreating to my bedroom when confronted. My relationship with Mum was strained because we were both pre-occupied and unavailable. She was busy managing a family while building a career, and I was facing my final year of school while navigating the challenges of being a teenage girl. With Teta I felt loved for no reason other than that she seemed to delight in my existence. I watched her closely, fascinated. She had tanned skin and tied a white square hijab in a knot at the nape of her neck while she pottered around the house. She was big and warm and had a hearty laugh. Her belly jiggled when she laughed at her own jokes about her size. She dipped Lebanese bread in home-pressed olive oil and ate it just like that even though the doctor had told her to watch her weight. She gave me the cuddles I had been too embarrassed and angry to want from my parents. She laughed at the things I said in broken Arabic.

Unlike many other women from her time and region, Teta had been taught to read and write. She was a talented seamstress and could embroider *tatriz*. She taught me to crochet in one night and praised me as a quick learner. She gave me her crochet needle and said, 'Start with one simple stitch and build on it.' By the time I got back to Australia, I had almost finished making my first doily, having learned only a few stitches from her and improvised some of my own in the plane.

One morning, Teta handed me a stash of pinecones from her tree and led me into the garden to a makeshift nut-extraction area, which was simply a small mat placed on the ground, in front of a tile and a heavy hammer. I sat there legs crossed in my pyjamas watching the neighbour turn his soil with a horse-led plough as I gathered pine nuts into a bowl with a bang, crack, scrape. That afternoon, Teta tossed the nuts into her favourite old pot with some hot oil. Her two gold bangles clanged as she stirred and she reminisced about her mother and how lonely it had been caring for her towards the end. She said it was important to learn to accept death.

'*Kel shi byeblash sgiir w ba'den bysiir kbiir . . .*'

Everything starts out small and grows bigger over time.

'*Ella el-mawt! El-mawt byeblash kbiir w ba'den bysiir sgiir . . .*'

Except death. Death starts out huge but it gets smaller. Grief shrinks over time.

*

My grandmother was a healthy, fat woman in her early sixties when our trip came to an end. At the gate she looked into Mum's eyes and said, '*Ma'alsalemi benti.* Go with peace, daughter, I do not think that I will see you again.'

My mum told her not to cry, '*Os-hik tebkay!* I will see you again, you are still so young!'

I held my sadness in my belly. As the van carried us away from the people and things I had just learned to love, I turned back and looked through the window at the house where my grandmother raised nine children and nursed her dying mother. Teta stood under the cedar with tears streaming down both cheeks, palms facing the sky, and lips moving in prayer for us; *Allahumma yassir.*

I remember the mood and aesthetic of that goodbye so clearly. Like if I were to turn and look over my shoulder again right now, I'd find the whole scene still there; my grandmother, her house, her trees and Kheil in the background, swelling into the sky with the expanse of our goodbyes.

I have not seen that place since. I prefer to think of it as I left it, but I asked about Teta's pine tree when Khalto Jinan came back from a trip one year.

'Is it still there?'

'No, it was burnt in the war.'

42

SEVEN

Moey and I were alike in many ways. We were the eldest children in our respective families, accustomed to carrying a lot of responsibility, argumentative and opinionated, albeit inexperienced in relationships. Marriage started as a chance to revive some of our childhood. We rode bikes around our honeymoon resort in the Maldives. When we moved into our new home, we played chess and Scrabble and ate too much ice cream because there were no *real* adults around to tell us no. On weekends we visited our families and poked around the garden. Moey grew cabbages and chillies and even a crop of *mlokhieh*. I took his produce into the kitchen and taught myself some of our favourite dishes, calling Mum every now and then to ask things like, 'How long do you boil the *malfoof*?' In the nights, Moey and I stayed up late watching Quentin Tarantino films, hating ourselves the next morning as we stumbled out of bed and back along the trainline to our respective firms.

Barely a month had passed after our honeymoon when I got a call from my brother telling me that he had been arrested. I was sitting at a desk on secondment to an insurance company when he called from the police station to ask for advice. I lowered my voice so my colleagues wouldn't hear, 'You should call a criminal lawyer, and you don't have to do an interview until they get there. I don't know what else to say.' I sighed, put down the phone and typed an email to my supervisors: I need to leave work to attend to a family emergency. Kind regards.

I'd never had an easy relationship with my brother and was always baffled by his recklessness. The first time I felt sorry for Mum and ashamed of my family was when he had a tantrum in the school playground before the morning bell one day. He was about six years old and I would've been eight. He wanted fifty cents for the canteen, but Mum said no; she had packed our lunch boxes with *zaatar* sandwiches and Lebanese cucumbers and Arnott's Shapes. My brother lay on the black bitumen kicking and screaming while Mum – heavily pregnant at the time – tried to get him off the ground before anyone noticed. She pleaded with him quietly, embarrassed that he would do this over a fifty-cent piece. As Mum was bent down, he began kicking her in the belly. I clutched the straps of my backpack as I watched the scuffle, anxiety bubbling in my tummy. I worried that the baby would be hurt and said, 'Stop, you'll hurt the baby!' He couldn't stop until the teachers came running across the grass and the hopscotch to help Mum get him under control.

We weren't much older when he shoved me and I fell into the sharp corner of a dresser at home. I had been playing with a bouncy ball – the small marbled kind we used to get from a vending machine at Amo Ali's corner shop in Arncliffe. My brother grabbed me from behind, wrapped his arms around my waist and flung me to the side, claiming the ball was his. It may have been. I cried out as the room spun and my head hit the *toilette* (the word Mum used for 'dressing table', a hangover from back when her French was better than her English). My parents came quickly and were horrified to see blood trickling down the side of my head. Dad took me to the medical centre and I lay across two chairs in the waiting room watching *Australia's Funniest Home Videos* with him. The doctor said the wound would be okay without stitches and sealed it with glue and strips.

My parents were relieved to discover that I had only suffered a superficial cut to my ear and reminded me not to provoke my brother: 'You know what he's like.' I defended myself. I hadn't done anything to provoke him.

These incidents remained a regular occurrence throughout my childhood, occasionally increasing in severity, but each time, Mum would say, 'Just stay away from him', and Dad would say 'It's just a phase', 'All boys are like this', and 'He will grow out of it'.

During the year I was engaged, my brother had become more volatile. I am not sure what was going on in his life at the time, but he had fallen behind with his studies and was having regular fits of rage. One afternoon, while I was out with Moey, he fought with Mum and threw his mobile phone during the fight. It hit Mum's eye, cutting it open and bruising her socket. She needed surgery at Sydney Eye Hospital, and he was charged with assault. All the while he swore, '*Wallah*, I didn't mean for it to hit her face.'

Moey and I visited Mum after her procedure. She lay in a dimly lit, curtained space under white hospital sheets. One eye was red and blue, swollen shut. The doctors weren't sure if her vision would be permanently damaged. My brother was in the visitor's chair, his head drooping below his wide shoulders and cheeks resting in his hands.

A policewoman called Donna or Daphne stood at the foot of the bed with some papers. She berated my brother in a low but serious voice. 'You've seriously hurt your mother,' she said, 'and you need to accept help before you end up in prison.' My brother nodded and shrugged and hung his head lower in response. It was impossible to know what he was thinking. The policewoman sighed, turned to me and said, 'I've seen a lot of women go through this. The next time I see them, their injuries are even worse or they're dead.'

Dad was nowhere to be seen. Later, Mum sobbed and said, 'He didn't bother to visit, and he hasn't said a word to your brother.' Mum worried that her eye wouldn't heal in time for my wedding – or ever. When she went back to work, she told her colleagues that she'd had an accident, too ashamed to admit that she'd been assaulted by her own son. She made a decision to stop wearing a hijab in the bleak aftermath of these events. 'I don't feel like I'm in control of anything,' she'd said.

An AVO was put in place to prevent my brother from inter-fering with Mum. This left her feeling conflicted and let down that her only choice, in the absence of non-judgmental support, was to turn to the law. She never stopped wanting the best for her son, and he remained welcome at Four-One-Six. We tolerated this assault and then forgot about it in the busy lead-up to my wedding, like it was just another hole in the wall.

*

When my brother had found himself in trouble with the law again, Mum and Dad were devastated. They couldn't believe that their only son, who was now a university student with a promising future, had taken up drug-dealing. Dad blamed Mum, accusing her of being too strict and emotional in her parenting. Mum said Dad had failed to set boundaries for my brother and 'always put ideas in his head, teaching him things I didn't want to teach him'.

This added a strain on their already volatile household and Mum decided to take tangible steps towards separating from Dad.

Having resolved that she could no longer live with him, she put Four-One-Six on the market. The five-bedroom house was 'too big anyway', she said, now that I had moved out and my brother was in prison awaiting trial. Under considerable pressure to play peacemaker between my parents, I mediated some uncomfortable negotiations. They had lived together a long time and did not have any significant assets apart from the family home, plus they both worked and contributed an income. I convinced them that it would be pointless to fight and waste money over a property division. Dad reluctantly agreed that the proceeds of Four-One-Six would be split roughly in half, allowing each of them to put a substantial sum towards a new place to live. I couldn't believe they were actually going through with it!

Mum bought a villa, right up at the end of a long driveway. We called the villa 'Valda', after the street it was in. It was dark and small compared to spacious sun-filled Four-One-Six.

The air there felt stale the few times I visited. Everything about Valda was a downgrade when compared to our childhood home. My sisters detested the move and I had tried to cheer them up, denying that I, too, ached for Four-One-Six. Not wanting to make Mum feel bad about the hasty sale of the family home, I called the new house 'cute' and 'cosy' and said I liked the floorboards.

Dad bought an apartment but, instead of moving in to it, he leased it out and followed Mum to Valda, convincing her that he would be different and that they ought to try again. 'He promised he'd be better but he's already refusing to pay the bills,' Mum complained. Mum, despite being trained to identify controlling behaviour and gaslighting in her role as a counsellor, wanted to see opportunity instead of danger when her husband made promises of change. If there was a way that she could salvage the relationship into which she had invested her body and soul for twenty-eight years, she would have taken it. I can't help but wonder what lies

Dad told her in private, what threats and accusations he used to imprison her when she was, in every way, the more successful and confident of the two.

When Mum first told me Dad was moving to Valda, I was unsurprised but fatigued. I was tired of trying to be a good daughter to both parents. Now that I was married, I could see the difference between my relationship and theirs. With maturity and insight, it became more and more apparent that Mum was the one who had drawn the short straw.

My brother would spend the next four years in prison and I would try to be there for him – first as an older sister, then standing in as a mother. I reviewed his brief, organised lawyers, provided him with a character reference and helped him get back into university. We haven't spoken in a long time, and parts of his story are not mine to tell, but I will always remember my brother's phone call as the precise moment that my happy month or so ended. I was mad at him and hurt for him. This was entirely his own fault and yet the adults and institutions in our lives had also failed him. Some had even told him that this was who he was meant to be.

Life keeps happening even when something is deeply broken. I took one day off from work, keeping the arrest mostly to myself, before returning to routine.

EIGHT

My glass cubicle was dense with paper and stale air as I flipped through a pile of reports about a crane collapsing at a mine somewhere in rural New South Wales. Level thirty-one of the building on Park Street was musty and grey. Sometimes it smelled like someone's instant noodles or tuna sandwich. I was struggling to concentrate; it had been over a year since my brother's arrest and he was being held on remand. He'd been moved to Lithgow, and every few weeks, Moey and I would go with my sisters or parents to visit him. I hated the way gaol felt sterile and dirty at the same time but enjoyed driving through the Blue Mountains as the seasons turned. I loved the poplars that fluttered like they were covered in yellow butterflies in the autumn. Sometimes we took the Bilpin way so that we could stop for apple pies and listen out for the bell birds in the bush.

I had been working there over four years since starting as a summer clerk during my penultimate year at university.

I made the decision to study law in high school. I'd loved and excelled at visual art but never considered it a career option. 'Don't waste time drawing and painting,' my parents had warned when I was younger, realising that I would lose touch with reality while I was creating. I developed a habit of keeping my art projects secret, working on them before sunrise or late at night to avoid scrutiny, hiding dirty paint palettes on the balcony and airing out my bedroom to rid it of the smell of turpentine. I'd insisted on studying visual art in year 12 but when I began to excel at legal studies, I realised a career in the law was a way to make my family proud while doing something I was passionate about. When I really think about it, I cannot separate this choice from the ways in which my life and community had been affected by war overseas and policies in Australia. As a young person, I saw the law as a remedy for some of the wrongs I had witnessed, not as an instrument that was complicit in them.

A part of me also gravitated towards the law, perhaps, because of the illusion of order that it provides. One day in kindergarten I lost my hat. Realising that this put me in breach of the 'no hat, no play' rule, I felt a dreadful sense of doom, like there was a hole where my stomach should be. Not a single person noticed, but I was so law-abiding I voluntarily sat on the silver seats in the dark shadow of a massive Moreton Bay fig. I was too embarrassed and ashamed to tell anyone I'd lost my hat, and berated myself the entire lunch hour, isolated in the shade, while other children ran in the sun. I don't remember what ended up happening after that. Did I find my hat and get away with it? Did I confess and get a new hat? Whatever the outcome was, it was not as memorable as the sense of doom that came before. I was well into adult life when I began to realise the ways in which catastrophic thinking and a fear of breaking rules had characterised my childhood. I was an anxious child but excelled at school and behaved well enough at home that nobody noticed. This is precisely the type of thinking that is rewarded in legal practice;

the ability to anticipate consequences and understand the ways in which facts can work both for and against you.

My goal, initially, was to work in human rights or public policy, so I'd studied social sciences alongside my law degree. But the opportunity to do a paid clerkship at a commercial firm was highly sought after and hard to come by. When I applied (at my mum's insistence) and got through, it was impossible to turn down.

As a commercial litigation lawyer, my work was mostly about accidents and disasters. A kid fell off a train, a truck ran into some cars, a silo spontaneously combusted, a ship dropped tonnes of cheese into the sea, a drunk woman fell from her friend's pool deck and broke her hip. My job was to help work out what happened, who was to blame, and how much they should pay. I was good at this and enjoyed appearing in court, beaming when a partner referred to me as the team's 'new star advocate'. Another told me I could be partner someday – unintentionally reminding me that I had drifted from what I had set out to do. In between the interesting bits, I mostly churned out letters and emails and worried about whether I had made any mistakes. The pressure crept up; my suits pilled where my elbows rubbed against desks and at a spot on my hip where binders sat as I carried them like children. I started waking up with a tightly clenched jaw and sore teeth most mornings, head cluttered with emails and documents I had relived in my sleep. I felt ready for a change and had started tossing up between looking for a new job or trying for a baby.

I looked up from my crane file just as an email notification appeared on my computer screen. The email was from one of the partners. She was offering a chance to undergo training in the investigation of war crimes with experts, as part of a pro-bono project. I thought of Teta and all the things I'd hoped to do as a lawyer.

'Please let me know if you are interested in this opportunity.'

My fingers twitched over the keyboard with excitement.

I tapped out a reply, 'I would be very interested in participating in this training.'

*

A cold wind whipped up Pitt Street from Circular Quay and frizzed my curls as I looked for the entry to the building where our training would be held. When I arrived at the cool, clean offices of the top-tier firm, I found a group of young lawyers sitting around a long board table. I quickly chose a spare seat close to the front. I was missing Eid celebrations for this. My family had never done much to mark religious festivities because school and work were more important and most of our attempts at fun would end with my parents fighting anyway. But all the Eids in the calendar were special in Moey's family. This Eid, his grandmother was serving a feast of our favourite dishes. I kissed Moey goodbye that morning and told him to enjoy the day without me, promising I'd never prioritise my work over sentimental occasions again. I've broken that promise a couple of times since.

Over six days of intensive training, lawyers and investigators who had worked at the Hague Convention taught us about how they prosecuted terrible men like Charles Taylor, the former president of Liberia who was found guilty of war crimes and crimes against humanity, and General Gallic for his role in the siege of Sarajevo. A barrister took us through various human rights instruments, explaining the difference between different types of crimes and what it takes to prove them. Another trainer, who had been a prosecutor, explained that it was very hard to track down war criminals, but prosecution was important for peacebuilding. We were taught how investigators went to painstaking lengths to collect evidence of torture and other atrocities, and how they would usually have to wait for a change of government before they could start the process, often relying on testimonies from survivors, refugees or defectors. We were told that this work was important because criminal accountability had the power to bring healing to communities. It could help nations recover from genocide. Justice could bring peace.

We drank unlimited Nespresso as we studied images of bodies in streets and mass graves. I dug a fingernail deep into the side of my thumb as a teacher explained the horrific ways in which people are subjected to sexual violence during war. It was easy to hide this nervous habit with my hands in my lap or tucked under a table where I could press the swollen sides of my thumb like a panic button. I'd tried to protect my thumbs with bandaids or by keeping my arms crossed, but every time the skin healed, I found myself peeling it away again.

'Sexual violence disproportionately targets women and girls but is sometimes also inflicted upon men in ways that may be more taboo,' the teacher, an expert on sexual- and gender-based violence, said.

The figures in her handout made me nauseous. Up to half a million women raped in the Rwanda conflict of 1994, an estimated 60,000 rapes in the Bosnia-Croatia conflict between 1991 and 1995, and around 64,000 in Sierra Leone. Projected onto the screen, these numbers seemed so silent in place of the unspeakable pain and trauma they represented. I thought about how numbers can't scream or cry or beg for mercy. I was troubled by the presentation but couldn't articulate my discomfort. Was it the detached way in which these atrocities were conveyed? The assumption that everyone present was privileged enough to have never been touched by them? The pressure I felt to keep my proximity to these stories quiet because I didn't want to appear *emotional* when it was important to be *objective*? Besides, if you speak up when portrayals of violence make you uncomfortable, everyone *else* in the room gets uncomfortable. If you say that it hits too close to home, you'll have to explain. If you explain, they'll blame you anyway: 'Your people are uncivilised! Undeserving! That's the way it is!' I knew this because I had shared some of my experiences before, in school and later in university tutorials, and, when you're young, speaking up and being denied compassion feels a lot worse than saying nothing at all.

The trainer clicked to the next slide. 'In modern warfare it is estimated that eighty per cent of casualties are civilians, and seventy per cent of those civilians are estimated to be women and children.' My toes went numb in my pointy shoes as I listened. Under the desk, I continued to pick at the cuticle around my thumb, burrowing further under the nail.

The training ran through business hours for six days, back to back. In between sessions we were fed Danish pastries and fruit platters. I chatted with some of the girls about how crap boyfriends and husbands were at doing their share of the housework; a white girl with big glasses was on the brink of moving out because her partner had been utterly unhelpful. We debated the merits of hiring a cleaner because it was so hard to be on top of your billable hours and on top of your laundry. We admired the enormous view and commented that the course was 'pretty intense' but 'very interesting' and a 'good change' from the usual workload. When we ran out of small talk, I went back to flipping through my investigator's manual, which contained diagrams of guns and battle tanks and a page on 'how to conduct an exhumation' – all harmlessly printed in greyscale. Towards the end of the week I started having nightmares that I was walking through a high-rise building made entirely out of glass. The glazed panels were joined so loosely that the structure swayed, threatening to collapse. Through the thin transparent floors, I could see straight to the ground but the faceless figures around me just kept on working.

One of the trainers, former military, was a tall white man with a buzz cut and athletic figure. He taught us how to identify chains of command and different types of weapons and artillery. He explained that the acceptable collateral in a military operation should be proportionate to the importance and proximity of a legitimate target. Other trainees were surprised to hear that, in war, it's totally legal to kill random people while trying to get one bad guy. I didn't feel surprised.

'A study was undertaken with commanders from armies across the world to see what they considered acceptable collateral. Guess how many commanders thought that the only acceptable collateral is zero?' He gave this anecdote in a cheerful British accent.

We looked around at each other, none of us brave enough to guess and some of us probably still idealistic enough to think it would be all.

'Only one! Only one country said there should be zero collateral. And guess which country it was – it was Germany!' He smiled.

I got the impression that there was a joke in there somewhere, so I smiled back, even though there was nothing funny about it. The more this charismatic and intelligent man (who I imagined could kill six men in one manoeuvre) continued talking about guns, the more I started thinking about being collateral. It's weird being the only Arab in the room when everyone is discussing war and learning about drones from a manual. I turned the next page of my manual and spotted a diagram of something called a field gun captioned:

'Artillery has also been used to punish civilian populations. It has been so used in south Lebanon, where Israel and her proxy militias shelled villages as punishment after attacks by local resistance groups.'

With each word my ears grew hot. I thought of Teta. A scene – half imagined, half remembered from stories and news articles – forms as though I am hovering over it.

What would have happened if I had been there? I imagined some polite lawyers in a nice building somewhere grabbing a file with our names on it. They'd say, 'Let's take a closer look at Lebanon 2006.' They'd flick through pictures of our bodies long after we had screamed for help, long after we were buried, and try to determine whether there was enough evidence to prosecute someone.

As the next facilitator flashed through a presentation on vicarious trauma and self-care, I wondered whether anyone else in the room could feel the data in their body. Whether their arms felt heavy, whether their hearts raced, whether they ached in old scars and invisible wounds. My thumb throbbed as I dug deeper into the cuticle.

*

My war crimes training triggered more than grief. It spoke to something I had always known about my gender, my Arab-ness, my vulnerabilities. I had believed those vulnerabilities would resolve once I worked the right job, married the right person and started my own household. Oppression wasn't supposed to follow me into my happily ever after. It wasn't meant to follow me into the places I had worked towards: into heels and suits, barristers' chambers and conferences with articulate white men who hung fancy artworks in their offices. Hadn't I done enough?

But, more and more, I felt compelled to watch what was happening locally and abroad. I followed Destroy the Joint's 'Counting Dead Women' project on Twitter. When I look back now, their names ring like sirens and my ears burn: Leila Alavi aged twenty-six and Nikita Chawla aged twenty-three, both murdered by former partners in early 2015. Again, and again, the count went up. On 4 February 2015 I re-tweeted:

> lydia_shelly
> 9 WOMEN DEAD SINCE 2015 FROM DOMESTIC
> VIOLENCE. @TonyAbottMHR will U reinstate funding
> 2 community services? #domesticviolence #auspol

The more I learned, the more I felt like I had missed an important conversation and still I wasn't sure what contemporary feminism could do for me. When Clementine Ford's hashtag #questionsformen went viral, I chatted to my work friends about her work with a mix of admiration and skepticism. 'Look, I agree with what she says but I don't agree with the *way* she says it,' I said to Gumneet, my Sikh friend with a Masters in International Law, who had very happily decided to marry her husband the day she met him; they got engaged an hour after meeting and were married a few months later. Where did our lives fit within these questions, and to what extent could we benefit from these conversations? How were women like us meant to get on board when mainstream feminism had often silenced us? Why did feminists sound so angry?

My friends and I had never been given permission to sound angry. And *radical* feminism? We weren't allowed to be radical! We were the subjects of *deradicalisation*. My education, my jobs, my role within my family – they all needed me to be a likeable Arab woman; not an angry one, and certainly not a radical one. I appreciated the privileges I had acquired by learning to say the right thing at the right time. I didn't want people to stop listening to what I had to say because I was too honest or direct when they said something racist or sexist or hurtful. Besides, I was raised to never swear.

I didn't know for sure if I was a feminist but had always believed vehemently in equality. I wasn't sure what that looked like or how it should be achieved. Potty-mouthed, topless feminism seemed inaccessible to me and my peers with our complex ties to tradition and culture; it challenged us but also alienated us. At times it even blamed us. Corporate feminism didn't approve of the willingness with which we were prepared to abandon our work for our parents, husbands and babies. Scholarly feminism spoke about issues far away and different from the ones we faced, and *Sex and the City*'s designer-brand, runway feminism was too Western and just plain *haram*.

I didn't realise it at the time, but I was slowly carving out a feminism I could shelter in. I hadn't yet discovered terms like *intersectionality* or embraced the power of rage and rebellion. Through my own research and reading, I did, however, discover Muslim feminists and feminists who worked within Islamic frameworks, online bloggers and Facebook communities where lively discussions around gender and Islamic jurisprudence took place. They challenged things I had taken for granted. That, along with the work of the local anti-violence campaigners I would later meet, became my gateway to re-thinking my own assumptions about gender – and just about everything else.

NINE

My final year of high school had started so well. But, in mid-July, war had broken out in Lebanon and I was feeling jumpy and distracted. At first, I told myself that the media was probably exaggerating, but this denial was unsustainable when the casualties took on familiar names from familiar places. Four days into the war a family known as bet Alakhras, who lived near my father's childhood home, were killed when an Israeli missile hit their house. As the adults talked about what had happened, I imagined the blast booming through the valley like the evening adhan. Twelve people were dead, mostly women and children, seven of them visiting from Canada. The event would later be investigated by Human Rights Watch and a woman who lived nearby would describe the way 'people ran towards the house to try and save them, but they only found parts . . .'. Whenever neighbours neared the site, she said, 'a helicopter would appear in the sky and a warplane would fly around. So we got scared and stayed away.'

With my trial exams fast approaching and my major art project due in a few weeks, I tried to remain focused on my studies. My trip to the village had left me feeling recharged by my grandmother's love and comforted by the unconditional sense of belonging she'd given me. I'd put my goals up on my bedroom walls, made a study calendar and monitored my progress carefully. But as they say, we plan and Allah plans. My dad explained that, after what had happened to bet Alakhras, people who could get out of the village weren't taking any chances. Any amos, amtos and cousins who were also Australian citizens were on their way from Lebanon to Sydney, having been evacuated by the government. Other relatives had nowhere to go and no government obliged to evacuate them, even after Israel declared that they would 'turn Lebanon's clock back twenty years'. Others still no one had heard from at all.

I absorbed the war in an abstract way – in my imagination and in my chest. Adults around me had seen worse and I could tell they were tense, feeling this new war in old wounds and memories. We dreaded phone calls but hoped for a word of reassurance. We dreaded the news but we were fixated on it anyway.

*

I was thinking about my upcoming exams and bombs when I got home from school on 19 July 2006. Mum and Dad were still at work and my siblings were still at school so there was no one at Four-One-Six when I arrived that day. I trudged upstairs, dumping my overstuffed schoolbag on the couch and loosening the candy-striped necktie we had to wear as part of my school's winter uniform. I turned on the television and it was already set to Al Jazeera. Carnage gazed back at me. I turned it off and decided to study instead.

At dusk, I was still at my desk while my parents watched the Arabic news and drank *shay* in the lounge room. Political talk and bomb sounds ratted down the hallway and through my wooden door where I'd stuck a hand-made sign: 'STUDYING – DO NOT

DISTURB.' I was lost in calculus when a horrible, unforgettable cry cut through Four-One-Six. A thing we'd been dreading had happened. When I got to the lounge room, I found Mum smacking her palms into her thighs and sobbing. Dad was standing in the middle of the room, his face grim.

'What is it?' I asked.

'It's Teta. Your grandmother has died,' Dad answered.

The report had aired Teta's full name, hometown and the location where she had been killed. I looked over at Mum who was shrinking into the armchair, inconsolable. I couldn't imagine how she felt hearing her mother's violent death announced over the airwaves without any warning. No one else from our village shared her name, so we knew it was *our* Layla who had become a *shahidi* – a martyr – while fleeing in a convoy near a town called Bazoureyeh. But how had this made it to the news before we'd even heard from our family? We hadn't spoken to them in a couple of days. Mum's eldest brother, Khalo Hussam, had warned us not to call because they would have to come out of the basement and up into the house to answer the phone. We did not know they had left Aitaroun. We did not know where they were. We did not know how many of them had been with Teta when she died or if they were dead too. We were so far and we couldn't do anything about it.

I don't remember where Nour and Ola were at the time. Ola tells me she was in the lounge room when the news report aired but was too young to understand it immediately. Nour says she was in her room and ran out when she heard Mum crying. I remember finding my brother there, hunched over, sobbing. I recall comforting him briefly – automatically – with a hug and a few words before retreating to my room. I draped myself in my *salat* clothes and prayed *maghrib* while my insides shook with rage and grief. I found comfort in the motions of prayer; standing up, bending, falling to the ground. I had once attended a lecture

61

where the sheikh compared prayer to the rhythms of life and death. I struggled to rise from my last *sajda*. Teta was my favourite person; I did not want her to be dead.

*

News spread quickly through our local community, and relatives who lived nearby turned up to comfort Mum. Through rushed telephone calls, we were able to start piecing together what had happened. Teta had been fleeing the village in a car with Jedo, Khalo Hussam, Tante Insaaf and Zaynab when they were set upon by Israeli drones. Teta had died at the scene. The survivors were at a hospital being treated for their injuries; Jedo had lost a finger and Tante Insaaf was receiving surgery for her arm. They'd all suffered shrapnel wounds.

The next morning, I walked myself to school and no one stopped me. Mum interpreted this as indifference and would later label me a 'wall' for not showing my emotions. This hurt because I was devastated. I figured Mum must have been too upset to see that I was my own kind of sad. I've long forgiven her for that assumption – we were different in that way. At school, I went straight to the deputy principal's office and told him that my grandmother had been killed. The deputy principal was a kind man and one of my English teachers. He took his glasses off and turned them over between his forefinger and thumb. He said he was sorry and I could have my first exam – which was about a week away – rescheduled. I didn't feel entitled to be accommodated in any other way. I was determined not to have my plans derailed, so I sat the remainder of my assessments as originally timetabled. I think I even topped two of my classes. There was no way I was adding academic failure to the trauma my family was already going through.

I saw the school counsellor but felt anxious the entire session. Maybe she, like Hillary Clinton, supported Israel taking 'whatever steps are necessary' to achieve its objectives, without regard for what that would mean for bodies like my grandmother's; the one that had birthed my mother's body, that had birthed mine. She advised me to apply for special consideration in case my final grade was impacted. War wasn't an excuse for bad marks in our household, but I took the forms and filled them out anyway. I didn't pursue any other counselling. I didn't feel that my quiet grief qualified me for treatment I thought was intended for students whose parents were going through a divorce or those suffering panic attacks before exams. My loss lacked the immediacy and urgency I associated with *needing* support. It concerned overseas events and people I had already been separated from for long periods.

My parents *lived through* war and turned out fine, I thought.

*

The next few days were a blur. Almost all the Lebanese families in our Sydney community were either grieving or searching for relatives. Normally, an *aza* is held to mourn a death. But that week we attended an *aza* at Al-Zahra Mosque to mourn Teta along with over one hundred other war casualties from our community. Afterwards, I sketched what I'd seen; rows of women draped in black, sitting in the overcrowded mosque, one of them with her head bowed, the glint of a teardrop on the tip of her nose.

A television crew came to interview us at Four-One-Six. Khalto, who was Teta's youngest child, didn't cope well at all. She had thrown the entire phone – handle, cord and dial pad – across the room when Mum called to tell her the bad news. Then she shut down completely. Back in Aitaroun those who were too elderly or frail to flee were cut off from the world. Roads in and out of south Lebanon were too damaged for anyone to get in or out and there were reports that the remaining families were running out of food.

When no one was paying attention, I went to the computer to read more about what had happened.

There was one article in which the BBC had interviewed Zaynab in her hospital bed. There was a photo of her in a blue hospital gown, looking pale but brave. I read the text:

'Zeinab Haidar smiles sweetly but nervously as she sits up in bed and points to where she has shrapnel wounds in her chest, arms and legs.'

The article explained how Zaynab had 'survived an ill-fated civilian convoy' escaping 'one of the most bombed areas in south-east Lebanon'.

There were three cars in the convoy; the other two cars contained neighbours from our village. As the first approached Tyre, it was hit by an airstrike, killing all the occupants. A second car was hit as they tried to escape. Terrified, Zaynab and her family leaped out of their car and fled to a nearby orchard, where another two bombs fell. It was here that she was injured, along with her parents, her grandfather, and her grandmother – my teta – who died.

I swallowed hard and read on.

'Ambulance drivers say two charred bodies still remain trapped in the first car, and two days later dogs and cats have started eating their remains.'

I closed the article and returned to my homework.

*

Dad's youngest sister, her husband and four children were among those evacuated from Lebanon. When they arrived in Sydney, they moved in with us at Four-One-Six. Mum was grieving but she made them comfortable at our place. Dad and I took Amto straight to Big W while her husband and children settled in. They had arrived with nothing but the clothes they'd been wearing since they fled the village a few days earlier.

Amto was frantic. 'The kids need clean pyjamas,' she said.

I could smell sweat through her long black *abaya*. She was a conservative woman, with sharp black eyebrows. She couldn't wait to get back to Lebanon, worried that the kids would miss too much school and lose all their manners here. I loved her children and wanted them to stay as long as possible. My cousin Hady would sit on my lap while I was studying. I fed them Cornflakes – which they pronounced 'Con-fleks' – for breakfast and helped them with their homework once they enrolled in school. The youngest was only two years old. Each time a plane flew over, he'd point to the sky and ask, 'Is that the plane that drops bombs?'

'No,' his mother would explain, 'that's the plane that brought us here.'

*

A ceasefire came into effect on 14 August 2006 – with both Hezbollah and Israel claiming victory. An estimated 1300 civilian deaths had been recorded in Lebanon. After the war ended, we began receiving news of the old people who had remained bunkered in the village, living off stale bread and water. Three older women were found trapped in a house with the decomposing bodies of two of their relatives; they'd been there for eight days. Relatives returned to their homes to find that they'd been bombed or even inhabited by Israeli soldiers before their retreat.

My eighteenth birthday came and went. I don't remember it. I was struggling to communicate how the war had left me feeling.

Not even five years had passed since 9/11 and only eight months since the Cronulla Riots. To much of the world, my relatives and I were indistinguishable from the *terrorists* who had *provoked* the war to start with. The troublesome *Lebs* who were trying to take the beach for themselves. I tried to talk to a school friend about how angry I felt about what had been done to my family. She replied, 'I'm sorry, but isn't that just what happens in war?' I hesitated to talk about my grandmother at school after that, for fear of reliving the pain that those words had inflicted.

During the same few weeks, I finalised my art project; fourteen small paintings, reminiscent of Islamic miniatures. I'd started working on them before the war, but they evolved after my art teacher encouraged me to express my distress and grief through them. I incorporated sketches I'd done after my visit to the village and those depicting the women mourning at the *aza*. I included reflections on war and peace, quotes from Islamic texts and news paper clippings about the 'War on Terror', carefully documenting the light and dark I'd witnessed that year.

Mum was cranky and short with me and I didn't have the skills to cradle her trauma or reason with it. Our shared wound over losing Teta did not bring us closer. I remember arguing with her constantly. I blamed her for my loneliness, because she was a counsellor and I thought that meant she should be able to read my mind. I don't remember my siblings during this period at all; I must have been too immersed in my studies.

I also don't remember many of the conversations I had with Dad that year. We must have talked about how my studies were tracking. I told him that I had decided to study law because I wanted to fight injustice, and he said that a career in the law was too demanding for a female, maybe I should consider teaching instead. This was totally inconsistent with the ways in which he'd always pressured me to work harder, to be the best I could be, to 'aim for the moon'. Perhaps he wanted the daughter who could get the marks he could brag about, not the one who would take the stand against him. We talked through this with the mutual respect and professionalism that had defined our relationship. I insisted that I'd be studying law and he didn't press any further.

I had promised myself that one day I would tell Teta's story, get some kind of justice. I believed that perhaps as a lawyer I could figure out how to do that.

*

That October, only days before my final exams, a large, multi-denominational service was held at Sydney Town Hall for the victims of the war. Ahead of the event, Mum gave an interview to Elizabeth Jackson and Jennifer Macey on ABC's AM radio show, alongside Professor Ghassan Hage, who was the chairman of Friends of Lebanon-Australia. I remember listening to the interview on the way to school.

'They ran on foot into the lemon grove to hide between
the trees. So it was my father, my brother, his wife and his
daughter, and my mother. So, they got bombed a few times,
which, one of them killed my mother.'

Professor Hage explained the intent behind the service, his words echoing the ways in which – as a teenager at a school with very few Lebanese students, in a family where other griefs were much bigger than my own – I had experienced the war in a private and lonely way.

'And so there were lots of funerals happening, but they
were all private. It became quite obvious in some ways

that other Australians should know that their fellow
Lebanese-Australians were suffering on a massive scale
as a result of this.'

Two things struck me when I found a recording of the interview online as I was writing this book. The first is that Mum was only thirty-seven when Teta's life was taken – a few years older than I am now. The second is that, as a teenager, I hadn't appreciated the strength it must have taken for Mum to speak her mother's story so soon after losing her. Despite the devastating content, this artefact – this treasure – gave me a way to relate to Mum in a way I'd never related to her before. I shook my hands in the air to calm my jitters before clicking play for a second, third, and then fourth time.

Listening to the interview as an adult, I encounter Mum in a similar phase of her life as I am now, telling a similar story.

'My mum didn't deserve to die this way. I would never
[have] imagined that she would die this way, and we're still
in shock until now. And we have to live with this memory
for the rest of our lives.'

I meet my mother in the words she speaks as the interview ends. In this liminal space she passes me the baton. Her words have become my words and I understand, again, that our fight is timeless.

*

In 2007, Human Rights Watch published a report titled *Why They Died: Civilian Casualties in Lebanon during the 2006 War*, which includes an investigation of the attack on my family – among many others – as suspected war crimes. The report contains a statement by Khalo Hussam in which he describes the inexplicable:

'There was nothing around the area where we were
attacked, only fruit orchards – no people and no fighters.
It was an empty area . . . Until now, I try to analyze what
happened, and I still don't have an answer. We were clearly
civilians, we had white flags.'

Despite the investigation, Israel never provided a satisfactory explanation for the attack on my family, and no one has ever been held accountable for the war crimes that are alleged to have taken place during that period. A total of six had been killed in the attack on my family and their neighbours, the youngest of them, a girl named Sara Wasef Abbas, aged one.

All these years later, I contact Zaynab, initially over Facebook where we've remained in touch, loosely. I tell her I am writing about Teta and the war. Lebanon is in the middle of the Covid-19 crisis, a state of political uncertainty, calls for a revolution and a crashing economy.

Zaynab is keen and her email comes a few weeks later:

There is no way to get justice for what war does.
War just happens to you and you can do absolutely nothing about it.
I have always looked at it in a not so earthly way, but instead in a metaphysical way. I mean, can we really bring world peace anyway? Can we end all wars?

I understand this hopelessness, even as it makes me uncomfortable. We want trauma to create revolutionaries; we look for the heroes who refuse to give up hope. We want to feel better about it all. Those feelings are about us, not about the victims. Zaynab seems to feel the same:

> I couldn't find any explanation for what happened. What good could possibly come from this to anyone? Are we, my family and I, the people, so unimportant that we were brutally attacked and killed and all we can do is accept it as a fact?
>
> Sometimes I think that in tough situations I get to look back and say 'look what you've been through and what you've overcome'. If I survived a war, I can survive anything, right? But I still do not completely understand the meaning behind what happened besides that life can carry unexpected shocks and we should always be prepared. Horrible things can happen, and we've got to find a way to deal.
>
> I do a lot of introspection. I write in a journal almost every day, but I haven't done any writing about war yet. As a 13-year-old, I didn't think much about what war is. All I remember is thinking that war is a fact. I had feelings of helplessness, the kind that you don't even know that you have. It's one of the worst and most harmful feelings a person can have; as if whatever feelings you are left with are not real nor valid. You start to question whether you have the right to these feelings at all.
>
> I didn't complain. No one really did. You just know it is how it is and it's no time for complaining. Fear becomes the master. Thirty days of war, running between shelters and hospitals and bushes . . .
>
> Amid all the fear, the child in me, in us, could find some serenity and unintended mindfulness. In one of our attempts to escape to more secure areas, and on our way from Sidon up to the Jabal (Mount Lebanon), we had to take routes that pass across villages we've only read about. My parents and I were no more than observers. We knew that the worst has already happened. In moments like that we felt that everything is pretty normal

and that nothing really matters as long as the rest of us are alive. We sat in a car being driven through the Chouf region, silently watching the trees, the greenery. It was a hot summer day, and it almost felt like we're on a field trip. Almost.

The driver stopped for gas, and there was a spring just across the road which for some reason left us in awe. We walked to it to fill up some water for the road. It was so sparkly, and the water was so cool and refreshing. Something tasted different in that water. I believe it was us, not the water. It was our first moment of peace since the attack.

During the beginning of the war we hid in a shelter beneath our neighbor's house with about four other families. Women kept their calm way better than men did. They would sneak to their houses to cook and pray. I remember Teta like she had always been. A smile on her face, a colorful scarf on her head, she was calm and full of hope and life. They say I look like her, and some say I look like Amto as well.

I smile at this mention of my mother. I see the resemblance too. Zaynab continues:

Women of a bright face and a brighter smile! You could easily feel their energy filling up the room. I will always remember tiny details about Teta, like the smell of her kitchen, her gold bracelets wrapped around her arm, the plants she placed all along her stairway, her blooming garden. You can feel her house dancing as she waters her plants, makes arabic 'ghar' (laurel) soap and washes her white linen in the backyard boiling them in a huge pot.

Zaynab's observations about Teta comfort me, reassuring me that my memories were not embellished by my nostalgia. Teta's house truly had danced.

Her house was never the same, neither were the family gatherings after she was gone. It's not the same thing to die and to have your life taken from you. A death is never as painful as an unfair death.

For Zaynab, the aftermath of the war felt worse than the war itself. Her mother had survived serious injuries but lost a finger and, according to Zaynab, 'was not the same person anymore'. When they returned to the village, they found that their house had been destroyed. She remembers this phase as a 'gloomy, silent time . . . I could feel my parents dragging themselves'. Zaynab tells me that no one even mentioned therapy, given that it was still largely taboo in the village. She says the psychological scars, 'the images, the smells of blood and gunpowder, the taste of metal, the emptiness that comes after' are not as bad as the physical scars, which have faded but remain 'printed' on her body. Yet, there is an optimism in her final reflections that seems to defy reality.

The memory of war is a million little pieces of shattered memories from the sweet life you had before, the moments of terror throughout the time of war, the deaths and tragedies you had to witness, and the life you have to carry on after, a life with no sense of security.

But one day it ends and the calm takes over, and you can see clear again. Life becomes a little bit more valuable. Seeing so much darkness can make you easily spot the light when it's there. It's the contrast that gives meaning. It gives you new eyes to see.

*

Six months after we said goodbye to Teta, Mum inherited one of her gold bangles and Khalto received the other. Now Mum's one is mine. I take it out sometimes just to hold it. It is too big and hangs hard and heavy on my wrist as I think of how it came to me. It feels like a moment since I watched it glint on my grandmother's solid arm. A moment since I stood on the flat roof of Mum's childhood home watching Kheil turn pink then copper in the sunrise. A moment since I clicked my disposable camera trying to capture the scene, hoping to hold on to that peace forever.

TEN

I experienced unanticipated grief around my brother's arrest and the sale of Four-One-Six, a sense of innocence lost that I hadn't felt since losing Teta. The antidote, it seemed, was to cling firmly to the rhythm my husband and I had established in our daily lives. Some nights, when we felt like a home-cooked meal, Moey and I would stop by his parents' sea foam–green fibro house in a grassy Granville cul-de-sac. The family next door is Iraqi, next door to them is an elderly Lebanese couple, and next door to them is a Turkish family with chickens and a rooster that free range across the dead-end street. Across the road there are more Lebs whose kids dart recklessly onto the road like the chickens. Some of the houses in the street, including my in-laws' place, are still housing commission.

My mother-in-law would greet us with warm dinners: *fassoolyeh* or *bemyeh* – stews with sides of rice. Sometimes she'd offer a creamy potato bake or a tangy stir-fry. It was all welcome after a long day's work. No cooking, no washing up.

On Monday evenings my husband would head out for Oztag, and I'd spread my art supplies out on my lounge room floor to experiment while watching *Q+A*. One evening, I drew two scenes on two large pieces of paper. One was a lifeless body, childlike in its proportions and swaddled in a white sheet with charred and crumbling buildings in the background. The other was a landscape with a lemon tree in the bottom righthand corner, ghostly shapes in the foreground and a long black road winding past a ruined town in the distance. The two images felt like memories but they could not be. My mind conjured them from things I had seen and read in the news, and stories I'd heard from my family. They seemed too morbid to hang on a wall, and I felt ashamed that I had produced something so dark.

What right did I have to be haunted by such images when I had never suffered direct injury or lost a home? I packed them away, deciding to keep them to myself.

*

Moey and I started planning for a family, and in late 2014 I found out I was pregnant. I sensed it when the taste of my morning cappuccino changed and confirmed it shortly afterwards with a test. The timing seemed perfect; we were at a comfortable stage of our careers and would have the support of our families. Looking back, however, I can't help but associate my pregnancy with the period leading up to the Martin Place siege. A couple of months before the siege, then Attorney General George Brandis came to Bankstown for a special episode of *Q+A*. I sat in the audience with another female Muslim lawyer friend while Brandis was questioned about metadata legislation and foreign fighters. Muslim audience members were sick of being told that we were simultaneously the problem and the solution. My friends and I joked that we already worked full-time jobs and couldn't afford to moonlight as counter-terrorism experts. We knew that wasn't funny.

Some of us were in the city on 15 December when the siege took place. I was nursing morning sickness with ginger beer when I heard a faint wail from my desk. I leaned over my work and looked down through the window to try to see what was happening on the street, thirty-one floors below. Within a few minutes an email arrived from our Human Resources team telling staff that the building would be put into a lockdown because of a security issue somewhere nearby. I messaged Moey whose building was only a short walk from mine.

'Are you okay? Something happened, we're in lockdown.'

'We might be sent home early, I'll try and find out what's happening,' he replied.

'Okay, keep me posted. Love you xx'

*

Once I was safely through the first trimester of my pregnancy, I brought a tray of *baklawa* to work and shared the news with my colleagues. I notified Human Resources and carefully filled out my paperwork, estimating that I would start my maternity leave at the end of June.

'I'm due in August,' I told my colleagues as they bit into their sweets and congratulated me.

I wondered what they were thinking. Was I too young, too junior to be starting a family? Were they happy for me, or would my more competitive colleagues be glad to see me gone? Was I being too much of a work-mum by bringing a tray of desserts to work? I had read a comment on a forum by a lawyer who said she was planning to go back to work two weeks after the birth of her baby. I sometimes still wonder if she did it. Was it lazy that I had planned to take a year?

'I've worked so hard for so long, I deserve a change of pace,'

I said to one of the secretaries, naive to the challenges that mother-hood would bring.

'Oh, absolutely!' she affirmed.

Around the same time, I dove into the first two subjects of my Masters in Islamic Studies. 'It will give me something other than work to think about,' I told my friends when they asked why I'd chosen Islamic Studies when I could've chosen to specialise. 'Plus, I want to be able to answer my children's questions about religion and at this stage I don't feel like my parents gave me enough to work with.'

*

'The baby does not know the world while it is in the mother's womb.' My theology tutor spent the morning explaining the movement of the soul from one world to the next. 'When she is born, she cries because she is in a new place. Scholars suggest that death is analogous to birth; a transition into a new state. We fear that because we can only perceive what we have here, now.'

I felt breathless at the idea of billions of souls in a state of bliss somewhere in the universe, suspended above *sidrat al-muntaha*, a lote tree that grows in the uppermost strata of heaven. We'd been plucked out of that state and tossed into a warm womb, next to a heartbeat. In that dark fleshy capsule we had waited before being heaved, ejected into this world where there is so much to fear. Landing in the arms of a mother, she ushers us devotedly and imperfectly, into what she already knows will be a complicated and perhaps painful life.

Sunlight streamed into my little Mazda as I drove home after class, half my mind still far away with the spirits. The sun's rays bounced off small beads on my dress, throwing specks of light around the dashboard like a disco ball. The specks danced in my car, oblivious. I pictured my baby's spirit, like a ball of *noor*, an orb of light, about to be hurtled into this dimension. I sighed, '*Alhamdulillah.*' As I followed the bend on Rawson Road where a new mosque was being built, a cloud paused in front of the sun and swallowed my car into its shade. The little stars disappeared and, as though the shadow had reached right down my throat, I felt my stomach turn to stone. I ran my palms down the warm, smooth leather of the steering wheel, trying to ease the niggling dread. There was no reason to feel this way but a thought arrived like a whisper from the sky: *Everything is going so well, something bad is bound to happen.*

ELEVEN

I don't think Mum ever fully settled in at Valda. The atmosphere there was thick with resentment, and clutter had followed her from Four-One-Six; clothes remained stored in plastic containers, mirrors and pictures piled and not hung. Something would rub off on me and my husband when we went to visit, and we would find ourselves arguing the entire way home. Afterwards, I would wonder what ghoul had followed us down that long driveway.

I imagined a baby might bring some much-needed *baraka* to my parents' lives and shared news of my pregnancy with Mum one afternoon in late January. I lay on the soft suede couch at Valda conversing loudly across the room with Mum, who was pottering around the kitchen.

'I feel sick and nauseous,' I said, meaningfully.

'Could you be pregnant?' she asked.

I admitted I was.

'Aww!' She looked back towards me. The expression on her face was bittersweet. I felt a pang of disappointment that she was not more excited. I realised later that she saw what I did not yet see: the loneliness, the endless demands, the joy, heartbreak and

79

exhaustion. She knew her daughter had invested years into her education and career and was now making one of the riskiest decisions a woman can make in relation to both of those things.

She had raised four of us and longed for herself that entire time. Maybe she knew I would soon miss myself too. A few days later, I was back on that couch with Dad nearby and I asked, 'So Dad, did Mum tell you the news?'

He looked puzzled and I realised they must have not been talking.

'Amani's pregnant,' my husband offered, breaking the pause.

Looking uncomfortable, Dad got up, paused, and patted me awkwardly on the head. He said, 'That's good, *baba*,' before walking away.

*

When I was about thirteen, we had a house fire. Mum was entertaining her friend Hajji Fatima in the backyard and no one else was home. My siblings and I were at Arabic school and Dad was at work. Mum popped into the kitchen to warm some milk on the stove and darted back outside to serve biscuits. Within minutes she could smell something burning. She ran back inside to find the kitchen ablaze. She tried to put the fire out herself, but it was too wild. She tried a blanket, but the synthetic fibres didn't suffocate the fire and instead turned to a fine dust that filled the whole of Four-One-Six, even my bedroom, which was the furthest from the kitchen.

A clump of molten plastic flew into the air and scalded Mum's forearm, but she and Hajji Fatima got out of the house otherwise unharmed. Firefighters arrived and drenched the house. The next day it smelled like smoke and mouldy carpet but us kids were cheering because we could have Maccas and *farooj* and *manoosh* for a week now that the kitchen was out of order.

When Dad arrived at the scene, he didn't hug or comfort Mum. Instead, he rushed past her into the house to see the extent of the damage, even while she was being treated by paramedics for burns that would leave a big scar on her arm. Dad was embarrassed at all the emergency vehicles outside and annoyed by the insurance paperwork that would follow. He berated Mum for not knowing precisely how the fire had started; she suspected she'd accidentally lit the stove under a pot of oil or left a kitchen towel near the stove top. He hounded her with questions. Why wasn't she watching it? Why didn't she know how to put it out? Why was she so distracted? Mum was rattled at how quickly and violently the fire had spread but Dad never showed her any compassion.

For years, Dad laughed and teased that Hajji Fatima had been a distraction and a curse. 'Fatima *al-hara'a*' he called her. 'How's your friend Fatima the firebug?' he would sneer. 'I haven't seen Fatima the arsonist lately . . .' He'd encourage us kids to laugh along. Looking back, I am aghast now at how immature and cruel it was.

*

When I was fifteen, one of my older cousins got married. It was the first wedding within our immediate family and we were quite excited.

My mum bought me a purple outfit with sequins and lace and booked us to get our hair and makeup done at the bride's house. 'Not too much!' Mum instructed as the makeup artist, a lady named Siham who was also a hair stylist, applied purple eye shadow to my lids and teased my hair into a bigger mess of curls than it already was. After Mum's turn, I admired her clear skin and her eyes outlined in *kehleh* and gold. We went home feeling pretty and excited for the reception until Dad looked up at Mum from his place on the couch and said, 'What have you done to your face? Your eyes are too big like that.'

Mum was offended and they argued. She began to cry, and charcoal tears ran down her face, spoiling the morning's work. When she went to the bathroom to wash the makeup off, I followed, urging her to leave it, insisting it could be saved. She turned around and clutched me by the shoulders and said, 'See what I've had to live with? Now you've seen what he's like.'

I think that was the first time I really understood her. As a fifteen-year-old I couldn't imagine anything meaner than what he had said. I cried too, catching the tears with a tissue before they could run down my cheeks and spoil my face. We re-lined our eyes and went to the wedding reception that night, playing our parts as a happy family, with the gloom of the day hanging over us.

The fractures between my parents widened every day. My father reassured us, saying 'I love your mum' and 'every couple fights'. I believed those things as a child but, as a teenager and adult, I grew increasingly skeptical. I sensed that there was something smelly and sick in the air we breathed. I started to wish they would just get a divorce. 'Just do it and get it over and done with!' I shouted at them once and they both stared back stunned.

I pictured them living separately and it made me sad to imagine them alone because, as unhappy as they were, I didn't believe that a break-up could bring them happiness either. The idea that my parents could split and be happy seemed impossible. Good families don't have divorces, and we were a good family.

*

Back in 2010, while I was still living at home and working as a junior solicitor, Mum found some family lawyers on Google and approached me to go with her. 'I need your help,' she said. 'But don't tell your father.'

There had been twenty-three years of trying; what was left to try?

This was different to the other times she'd spoken about divorce. She did not yell that she wanted the sheikh to come immediately, she did not tell my father that it was over. I didn't understand why it needed to be a secret – wasn't it obvious they weren't happily married?

The lawyer we saw was a tall, balding, tanned man who talked more than he listened. He asked my mum about her assets and Dad's assets and the car and the house, writing a list as he went along. Mum kept taking deep breaths, her voice was shaky and her hands fluttered a little as she passed over the pieces of paper she had thought to bring with her.

I can't remember if the lawyer asked anything about violence or abuse. Mum listened quietly, nodding slowly, as the lawyer explained what she might be entitled to in terms of a property settlement. I can't remember if I spoke during the meeting.

Later, Mum came to me with a pile of original documents that were mostly in Arabic. She said, 'These are from your dad's suitcase, can you make photocopies for me without telling him?'

I told her that I felt bad being sneaky.

Her mouth was downturned, and her voice was low. She said, 'I need your help. I thought once I had a daughter your age, you'd help me.'

Reluctantly, I took the papers from her and copied them at work. She returned the originals to Dad's briefcase.

*

I remember my parents fighting all the time when I was young. At some point my mum said she wanted a divorce. I hadn't heard her use the word *talaq* before; I sensed that it was a shameful thing to say. It was *makrooh* – a thing that is permissible Islamically but said to be hated by God. People referred to it as 'a last resort', but they made it sound worse than death. Dad had contempt for the divorced women in our community and described them in harsh ways, the undertone being that they had not just done something immoral but that they embodied immorality. There were no respectable divorces, just scandals. Women never divorced for happiness or for health but snaked away from their husbands in pursuit of dark desires, to abandon their children or to rebel against their families.

Whenever Mum uttered the words, 'I want a divorce,' he called her requests nonsense and rubbish and *bala-taʼmi* – tasteless, nonsensical. By shaming the very concept of divorce, he made sure that Mum would be too embarrassed to voice it, let alone pursue it. It wasn't hard to do this because lots of people in our community shared the same attitudes, or at least Dad gave the impression that they did.

When I lived at home, I went to bed some nights hearing Mum shout and cry in the background, but I didn't understand her hurt or her desperation. One night I watched from the stairs as Dad rushed up to her. She was suddenly up against the wall and he had his arm raised – maybe in a fist, maybe open, maybe reaching out towards her neck. She wrangled him off her and he retreated. I did not know what to think. It didn't seem extraordinary or horrible. It was just an extension of the perpetual fight between my parents who deep down loved each other. I didn't think about it again for a very long time.

Even though their relationship was clearly irreparable, I didn't think that Mum was in danger living with Dad at Valda. My parents were unhappy, but I'd never seen my dad *hurt* my mum. At least, I never thought I had.

TWELVE

Moey and I went over to Valda for lasagne with my parents one afternoon. Four months pregnant and totally satisfied (it was one of Mum's best dishes), I sunk into my usual spot on the couch next to Moey while Mum and Dad remained at the dinner table. Dad was done, but Mum was still eating. As it often did, the conversation turned to the topic of wartime in south Lebanon.

Dad began to retell an old incident, from memory, in which a family had been killed in an explosion by Israeli agents in the village – there were so many stories like these, they sometimes blurred together. In this instance, the agents had dined at the victims' home, speaking Arabic fluently, pretending to be dislocated Palestinians. Then they came back to kill the villagers for expressing allegiance to Palestinians.

Mum grew visibly uncomfortable as the story became more graphic. I squirmed in my seat, hoping Dad would stop. I didn't say anything; I was embarrassed that all these years later, I was still struggling with anything that triggered memories of my grandmother's death.

The next few words Dad spoke were delivered matter-of-factly, in a tone of morbid fascination. They were not lamentations or expressions of sympathy. He could not have possibly been ignorant to the discomfort they would evoke, but he would not stop.

'They were blown up into so many pieces,' he detailed, 'parts of them were found in the roof gutters.'

Mum slammed her fork down into her plate with an explosive clang. She burst into tears and shouted across the table at him, 'DON'T YOU REMEMBER HOW MY MUM DIED?'

My dad shrank his shoulders, suddenly small and hunched. He looked across the room with a slight pout, an expression like *look at how unreasonable she is.*

'Dad, I don't understand why you just told us that story, you knew it would make us all uncomfortable.' I spoke carefully, doubting what I had just seen in him. It was dark yet juvenile.

I know now that this behaviour was designed to gaslight and discredit Mum. Emotional abusers use language to deeply hurt and provoke their victim. Often the tactics they use are hard for an outsider to the relationship to detect; they have the appearance of casual conversation, or are even framed as a joke, but are always intended to humiliate or hurt the victim. When she lashes out, he behaves as though she is overreacting.

The temptation to illicit this reaction from Mum, in front of my husband and me, must have been so overwhelming that Dad hadn't considered how Teta's death also affected me. Perhaps he never really had. After all, he didn't know I had combed through the media reports for details surrounding her death. That I had reconstructed the scene in my mind, and hovered over it, repeatedly, trying to visualise the horror, to reconnect with my grandmother's last moments. I was not yet eighteen when I read one report about how my grandmother's body had been violated, decimated in such a way that there was barely anything left to bury. Preferring not to believe some of what I'd read, I've never asked my surviving relatives if this report was true. Even though they were intended to hurt Mum, I felt the collateral hurt of Dad's words and something inside me was set off.

I had seen my dad. I had seen through him to the version only Mum knew.

Still, in my desire to calm the situation, my embarrassment at Mum's loud outburst, and the compulsion to appear impartial towards my parents, I asked Mum to calm down.

The only fair thing I could have done in that moment was to walk over and comfort her.

*

Dad received calls from his family saying that his forgetful and frail mother needed her children to visit, for some reason, perhaps she was unwell. He decided he would be going to Lebanon. We went over and exchanged quick goodbyes, handshakes, pecks on cheeks.

While he was away, I had a threatened miscarriage. I was attending a scheduled ultrasound at about nineteen weeks when the sonographer picked up on an abnormality. Moey and I were running late to the appointment, and when we got there the sonographer asked if I minded that she had a student present. I said I didn't. She said she would be talking the student through the scan. I knew something was wrong when the sonographer began pausing and umm-ing and ahh-ing. She asked if I'd felt anything that morning – I hadn't. She said my uterus was contracting and funnelling. The cervix, which hardens and closes during pregnancy to support the growing uterus, was pulling open. Where there ought to have been about four centimetres of closed cervix, there remained under a centimetre, and the baby's head was pushing down into that space as the cervix stretched and thinned. I didn't have any symptoms, or at least none I recognised. I had never been pregnant before and I thought it was normal to feel a bit of pressure as the baby grew. I had no pain or bleeding, and I'd been attending work as normal. But during that appointment, I was told that I was on the brink of a miscarriage and that I would need to be referred to the hospital emergency department.

Moey drove me to Bankstown-Lidcombe Hospital where I was diagnosed with 'cervical incompetence'. An offensive name for a condition I had no idea existed before that day. No one had ever talked to me about the intricacies of a pregnant body. The sonographer at my appointment had miraculously picked up on the 'incompetency' just in time, and my doctor later told me that other women in my circumstances would most likely have miscarried because the cervix isn't always checked at scans, unless there is a known problem or a history of miscarriage. The accident of being late to my appointment and having been allocated to a sonographer with a trainee may have saved my pregnancy.

The recommended procedure was a cervical cerclage. The doctors explained that this would involve a suture being placed around and through the cervix to prevent further effacement. A stitch. There were two main risks: a surgical tool could accidentally pierce the amniotic sac and create an increased risk of infection and/or miscarriage; or the procedure itself could induce early labour, triggering miscarriage. Suddenly my growing belly felt fragile, as though it had been blown from glass. I didn't feel like there were any other options but to go ahead with the procedure.

I spent that night wondering whether I should have bought private health insurance, and whether it would be scary to go into theatre. I chatted to a woman who was there for her third or fourth miscarriage. She said 'Alhamdulillah' – she'd also given birth to three healthy kids. What-ifs kept me up until I fell into a restless sleep.

Mum was on the way to work when I called her before the surgery the next morning.

'Mum, I'm going in for a little procedure to make sure I don't have a miscarriage. The baby and I are fine, though. I don't want anyone to be worried. I – I – just thought I'd let you know.'

'Should I come?'

'No, there's no need,' I said automatically. 'I'm going in now and will only be here for a short time. Might even be home by the evening.'

I had never had surgery before, and I was scared, but this is how we communicated. My mum had moved away from her mother when she was a shy eighteen-year-old – she did not know how to speak to me about sex or pregnancy or cervical incompetency, and I was used to that. I wonder now, however, how much of her inability to talk about these things – intimacy, life and death – had been learned from my dad, who had been so awkward about my pregnancy.

I was taken in, put under, and woken up before I could worry much more. Afterwards, I was given progesterone pessaries to stop the strong contractions.

'They remind your body that you're pregnant,' one midwife told me.

I wondered how a body could forget.

THIRTEEN

The last time I saw my mum alive, she was vibrant. She wore an abstract floral shirt and coral heels. She had started looking after herself and I could tell she was fitter and healthier. She was working full time as a drug and alcohol counsellor at St Vincent's Hospital, helping people quit addiction. She was enrolled in university, building on years of experience in social work. She had a sense of direction and purpose; she was a woman in growth.

We sat down in Abla's in Granville for coffee. I was scooping my delicious *mafrooki* and sipping froth off my cappuccino when the conversation turned from my pregnancy complications to my dad.

'He's being nice now, trying to get me to meet him in Lebanon,' Mum said.

I rolled my eyes. 'You shouldn't go if it's because you think you can change him – he won't ever become what you want him to be.'

'I think he wants me to go so that he can do something to me . . .' she trailed off, with an expression I couldn't read.

'Why would you think that?' I asked. By this point I was so used to minimising Mum's concerns, and perhaps my own, that I was more puzzled than alarmed.

She held a faint smile that belied the seriousness of what she had just said. As though she felt bad for vocalising such a sinister prospect about the father of her children. My father.

'You know, I made him pack all his things before he left, and he isn't happy about it. Now he's talking nice so that I will give him another chance.'

'Well, you can give him a thousand chances if you like, but don't expect him to change,' I repeated, irate that we had to talk about this, again. 'You either compromise and live with him unhappily, as he is, or you break it off once and for all and find your own way to be happy.' I wanted to say, 'You can't teach an old dog new tricks,' but I'd used that phrase before, and Mum had told me that it was rude to refer to my father as a dog. 'It's just a metaphor mum,' I had argued. 'It isn't meant to be offensive – only Arabs think dogs are offensive.'

As always, the conversation went in a more casual direction and we ignored the darkness she had alluded to. We didn't care that it loomed. That's how things had always been. We just left it there, unresolved, and we smiled away the rest of our meeting, talking about baby plans, baby names and baby furniture.

'If it's a girl, I'm going to name her Layla, like your mum,' I said.

Mum had given me a hint at the danger she sensed. It had been too hard, too incongruent for me. She had again revealed to me something dark and hollow about the inner workings of my father's mind – something only she could know.

And yet again I had said goodbye without doing anything to help her.

*

Today, I scroll down Mum's old Facebook page, examining it for clues of what was to come. I didn't pay much attention to what she did on Facebook before; and I am somewhat surprised to see how political she was. She shared articles about Tony Abbott's proposed burka ban, which she strongly opposed, along with snaps from her last trip to the village and a video from her sister's balcony, surrounded by potted geraniums, looking out over the town to the horizon.

She shared a post from the Asylum Seeker Resources Centre that read, 'If you're not careful, the newspapers will have you hating the people who are being oppressed and loving the people who are doing the oppressing – Malcom X', along with the 'Shut up your mouth, Obama' video that went viral in 2014.

In mid-November 2014 – just before the United Nation's sixteen days of activism against gender-based violence – Mum shared a White Ribbon Day post, an article about Stella Young and another about the death of Reza Berati on Manus. Then she followed the Martin Place siege and #illridewithyou. She posted about the Charlie Hebdo attack and Chapel Hill shooting, and the impending execution of Myuran Sukamaran in Bali.

She shared a meme that said, 'Kindness. It's free. It never gets old or used up or worn out. It is sometimes more important than all the other things, simply to be kind.' On 25 February 2015 she posted, 'Isn't it so frustrating when you are the only person who can see how evil and sneaky someone is and everyone else is blind to it.'

On 21 March she shared a post by journalist Jane Gilmore, famous for 'fixing' sexist headlines about gendered violence. Eerily, the post reads: 'Women, if you want to be safe, stay at home. Except that you are more likely to be killed at home by someone who claims they love you, so don't stay at home . . . Don't show too much skin or laugh too loud or dance too much but come on love give us a smile.' This was followed by an article titled, 'Don't call me oppressed because I am an Arab woman.

It denies me the right to my own experience' by Randa Kattan from Arab Council Australia, where Mum once worked as a settlement officer supporting refugees, and where, as a university student, I'd worked with youth from Arabic-speaking backgrounds.

On 28 March Mum worked late at her local election ballot centre, and again the next day. My mum, the victim, fought every day.

*

Mum's posts are buried under subsequent posts by people who knew and loved her, expressing grief and disbelief. On 31 March her colleague wrote, 'Farewell to a wonderful colleague and a warm, compassionate person.' Another shared, 'Salwa was a beautiful person and I loved knowing her both at St George Multicultural Resources Centre and Quitline. The world has lost someone truly special.'

Mum's brother Hussam wrote in Arabic, 'My sister, my heart burns, *Allah Yerhamik*.' Mum's sister in Germany wrote, 'You will remain immortal in the minds of those who know you until you rise to the highest levels of Paradise.'

FOURTEEN

I tried to take things easy after my near miscarriage but returned to work as soon as I could, a dull heavy sensation still sitting in my lower abdomen.

I was at my desk on 30 March 2015 when my phone lit up with a message.

It was Nour. 'Hey, Dad's home early, I woke up and found him here.'

'Oh, why is he back so soon?'

She answered, 'He said he didn't like the weather in Lebanon and got bored. Will you come tonight?' I knew that by 'weather', Nour meant atmosphere; the Arabic word for both being *jow*. We'd received news that Dad's frail mother hadn't recognised him and that his uncle had suddenly passed away. He must've grown tired of the misery, I thought.

I responded, 'Yes, I'll try.'

I got through an otherwise unremarkable workday.

By the time I got home that evening, I had almost completely dismissed the idea of visiting my parents. Moey was showering and I was changing into my pyjamas, preparing for *maghrib* prayer when I received a call from Khalto Jinan's daughter, Iman. Something pricked under my skin as I answered – we never spoke on the phone. *Why is she calling?*

Her voice was high-pitched and she spoke quickly, 'Amani, where are your sisters?'

My heart plunged into my belly. 'I don't know, I texted Nour this morning but –'

'My mum just ran out of the house screaming. Something about your dad. He turned up at Amo Khalil's house covered in blood.'

Warmth and feeling drained from my body. My arms felt like they'd turned to stone.

'Okay – okay, don't panic,' I urged calmly. 'I'll call my sisters and see what I can find out. We don't know anything yet. I – I'll figure out what's happening.'

I hung up and tapped on the bathroom door. 'Moey, something really bad has happened at my parents' house, we need to go.'

'Uh – okay, I'll be out in a second.'

As I was getting dressed, I tried to call my sisters. Neither of them answered. Then I tried to call my mum. I stared at the screen of my phone as her voicemail spoke. I didn't know what to think. My instincts told me not to call my dad.

'Where have they all gone? No one is answering . . .' I told my husband as we got into the car and headed for the M5.

As we were driving, my phone rang. It was Khalto. Overwhelmed and afraid of what I might hear on the other end, I passed it to my husband.

'Your aunt wants us to try to find Ola. She wants us to intercept her before she gets to Valda if we can,' he said after ending the call.

'Okay,' I replied. The pieces didn't fit, but I was too scared to ask questions. 'Let's start at her bus stop and then follow the route home and see if we can find her before she gets to the house.'

A few minutes later, Khalto called again and Moey answered.

'What did she say?' I asked when the call ended.

'She wants us to just go straight to the hospital,' he replied, flat-toned.

'I don't get it – what? What about Ola?' I asked.

'She said to just meet them at the hospital.' I couldn't tell if he was as puzzled as I was or protecting me from something.

'Okay, to the hospital then. But where the hell is Ola?'

*

I was still calm but confused by the time we arrived at St George Hospital. We parked and walked towards the main entrance, only to run into a big group of my cousins at the front. They were red-eyed and sorry-looking. A voice in my head begged, *Would someone tell me what the fuck is happening?* But ever the polite daughter of a respectable family, I greeted them with handshakes and niceties and asked, 'So, what's wrong?'

An older male cousin just shook his head. Someone ushered me inside.

Once in the white fluorescent glare of the hospital emergency entrance, I was met by two police officers, both women. Their eyes were red. Both had been crying.

'Are you Ola's sister?' one of them asked.

'Yes – I'm Amani – I don't get it. Is she here? Who is hurt?'

I couldn't understand why I was being asked about my sister when, in my tummy, I felt like something had happened to my mother. They refused to answer and led me to a room. Grey carpet, more glare. Khalto Jinan was with her friend and Amo Ali's wife, Hala.

'Can someone please just tell me what is happening? Is someone hurt? Where is Ola?' I think I was smiling. No feelings, just confusion. Someone handed me a small plastic cup of water. I took a sip. It was ice cold.

Hala was the first to speak. Her eyes were red but her tone was short. Almost snappy. 'Your mum is gone,' she said once I had settled into one of the chairs.

Time was warping and language had started to fail. The word 'gone' resounded in my head but I couldn't come up with a response. I did not break down. I did not wail or gasp or collapse. I made a mental note that I was now motherless, but it wouldn't stick. I felt suspended like I was in Ibn Sina's floating man experiment. I took another sip of water and wondered whether the death of a family member could bring on a miscarriage.

'Okay. Where is Ola?'

'She's in one of the rooms down the corridor.'

'Is she okay?'

'You will see her soon.'

I fell silent again. A cog was stuck somewhere, whirring.

'So, Mum's gone?' I asked one more time, as though there was a chance I had misunderstood.

For an hour I had been receiving all kinds of information and still I could not work out a storyline. An hour of nothing making sense. I listed the facts I had managed to gather so far. Dad was covered in blood; in the commotion I'd understood that he was in custody at the local police station. There had been a fight. Mum was gone. Nour was on her way. Ola was down the corridor . . . *Oh my God, my brother!* I turned to the police officer who was still standing in the door frame. 'I have a brother,' I said. 'He's in gaol – Long Bay. This is really important – someone needs to get to him before he hears this on the news. Can you please make sure you get to him as soon as possible. He's alone, he won't cope.' The officer assured me they would send someone.

*

I don't know how long I waited before my sister Nour arrived. My mouth kept drying up and I floated back and forth to the water cooler, refilling, as though the weight of that ice-cold water was the only thing keeping me from drifting off. Moey stayed close, asking if I was okay and if there was anything he could do, to which I replied, 'I'm okay, I'm so glad Ola's okay.' My eyes were still dry but Nour was already in tears when I met her in the corridor. *She's in shock,* I thought to myself. *Or am I in shock?* Nour kept repeating affirmations about how we would be fine, and we would get through this and have amazing lives. I didn't feel so sure.

There was nothing I could do for Nour, or my brother, or myself. Some of my amos were still lingering around. One of my cousins kept grabbing my hand, holding it in hers and telling me to 'let it out'. I withdrew gently because her palm felt like a dead fish. The most horrible thing, however, was that down the corridor, Ola was giving a recorded video statement to the police about the events of that evening. We couldn't see her just yet. We were told she had been at the house – the crime scene – at the time of the incident. She had been injured, she had called the ambulance. But what shattered me, made me want to disappear, was that she had not yet been told that our mum was dead.

She did not know she was gone.

*

A police officer came and said someone could see Ola now. I said to Nour matter-of-factly, 'Look, I don't mind telling her – but I think it might be better if you did.' Nour agreed. I didn't want her to know that I wouldn't be able to face it. I couldn't bring myself to do it. My avoidance of this task was selfish; perhaps a part of me felt guilty that I hadn't been spending enough time with them. Perhaps I wasn't ready to face the fact that I'd decided not to visit that evening.

Of all the difficult things that I would go on to do that night and over the next few years, nothing hurt more than that moment: the dread of Nour walking into the room where my baby sister sat bleeding, and telling her that everything she had done had been futile. Witnessing Ola's face fall as she learned that it had not been enough.

*

We were asked to attend Kogarah Police Station to give statements. As we entered, we ran into the officer who had visited Mum at the eye hospital. When my face met hers, she said, 'I remember you,' and I said, 'I think I remember you too.' Two years had passed since the police officer's premonition and no system or law or mechanism had stepped in to stop it. The law saw Mum as the victim of an individual person in an isolated incident: not as the victim of an entire society geared against her. There was nothing the law could do about the husband who hadn't said anything worth remembering about the injury to her eye. There was nothing the law could do to challenge Mum's belief that it was her job to continue holding the family together, no matter the risk. The system had followed the men in our family from one crime to the next, but it hadn't saved us from them.

I sat across from a police officer at Kogarah Police Station with my tummy in my lap. My insides swirled with baby, hormones and too much cold water. A headache had started to build as my brain contorted itself around the events of the evening, trying to place them in order. The pressure of too much information, too many people and too many bright lights ballooned against my skull. The room I was in wasn't as formal or official as I imagined a police station would be. Dad had been arrested. Was he in a cell under the building? I didn't know what I was allowed to ask. The police officer told me that I would be providing a statement. I nodded. Her blue shirt was crisp and sharp, but her face was blurred and far away.

It made no sense. My words and movements played out in front of me like a film. My father had never bashed my mum. How had he killed her? I couldn't join the dots between what had happened and the person who existed in my mind as 'Dad'. I had no reason to believe that he was insane, but could he be? I tried to remember what we had learned at law school about rare cases where people did things without knowing what they were doing, in a state of dissociation or sleepwalking. Could this explain what he'd done? The alternative was too new, too horrible to consider. Did his mind break on the way home from Lebanon?

'We'll be getting a statement from you and anyone else who might know what's happened,' explained the police officer.

Something stopped me from asking, *Where is my dad right now? Is he okay?*

'Sure, I'm, um, happy to help.' I smiled the way you do when you want to show someone you're not the enemy. Was she already judging us? What assumptions had they already made about my family?

Ola was still at the hospital. Nour and Moey were in other rooms waiting to give their statements. I needed to be with them, keep them safe, but I understood we'd been separated to prevent us from talking. From the perspective of the police, we could each have vital information. For all they knew, someone could have been an accessory. I tried not to be offended by the suspicion I sensed as I was being questioned. I tried to focus on what the police officer was saying but I started to feel restless, and my mind kept scurrying to other things. I thought of my brother who was probably asleep in his cell. We were all fragmented. *How do I put this back together?* I felt protective, closed. *What am I allowed to say? What will happen tomorrow?* I had more questions than answers. I felt useless.

Mum and Dad always said not to tell people outside the house our personal business, but I was sitting in front of a stranger and she was raking through my parents' relationship. It seemed important to be open but neutral. I answered truthfully but cautiously, not saying any more or less than what her questions directly required. 'Yes, they fought a lot, but it was mostly over normal things, the same stuff all couples fight about,' I told her. They fought about my brother being in prison, but they fought before that too. No, Dad wasn't violent. I didn't associate him with violence, and no violent memories came to my mind at that moment.

I told her he was supposed to be in Lebanon but he'd returned unexpectedly. No, I didn't know of an affair. Mum's quite a conservative person. No one had said anything about an affair until just then. Were they together? They were sort of separated but still married. They had sold the family home, split the money, but ended up living together.

Dad had been stressed. He was quite traditional about relationships and divorce. I thought his new job teaching English as a second language had made him happier than he had been driving a taxi. His mum had Alzheimer's and didn't recognise him anymore. His uncle had died while he was overseas and they'd held a funeral for him. *Can these things make you kill someone?*

She tapped at her keyboard while I spoke. When she was done she handed me the pages she had typed up and said to sign them. I hesitated and said I was really tired and couldn't properly check the whole document. I skimmed over the pages and the words danced and morphed in front of me. Nothing I had said seemed useful or of *forensic value* to use lawyer speak. I asked if I could add to my statement or change it if I thought of anything later. She said I could. Unable to think anymore, I signed the document and slid it back across the desk to her.

*

After our police interviews Moey and I collected Ola from the hospital. I don't remember what we talked about or if we even talked at all. Nour stayed behind at the police station to finish giving her statement. An officer promised to bring her home when she was done. It was about 2 am when Moey, Ola and I got home. We trudged up to my front porch, my belly drooping, teeth chattering and head throbbing. I was anxious that we'd been split up. At least Ola could finally get some rest.

Ola was still covered in blood and we were both weary. Her hand had been injured at Valda and was wrapped from elbow to fingertip. Following doctors' instructions, I waterproofed her arm with plastic bags and sent her in to shower. Once she was out of sight, I busied myself pulling pyjamas, spare pillows and blankets from my cupboards. I then buzzed around the kitchen, scanning for sharp objects. I'd watched lots of crime shows. I knew enough about trauma to understand that these household objects were likely to be triggering. Barely wanting to touch them myself, I shoved the scissors out of sight and put the knife block Mum had bought me as a wedding gift at the back of a cabinet. As I hid these horcruxes, my heart raced, and images of soft, bare skin flashed through my mind until I felt mushy and vulnerable. *We are literally surrounded by weapons.*

I couldn't stop my imagination from conjuring the crime scene, a frenzy of blood and metal and screams in an ordinary villa at the end of a long driveway. Every gory thing I'd seen in movies and television shows unravelled like film reel in my mind. *Where was God in all this mess?*

I wondered where Mum's spirit was, trying not to think about how her body was cold in the morgue at the Coroner's Court by now. I looked to see if I'd left any knives in the sink and made mental notes of things I'd need to take care of over the coming days and weeks: get my sisters' beds and belongings moved into the spare room, sort out paperwork, check on my brother, look for Mum's valuables. *This is going to be so hard.*

Ola re-emerged and I helped her to get settled on the couch. We chatted, like it was the most normal thing in the world, about what would happen now that Dad had been charged. She asked questions about whether there was any chance he'd be released, and I explained that he would go to trial for murder or manslaughter, depending on the evidence about the *mens rea*, his intent.

'If an accused person says they were mentally impaired at the time, they get sent to psychiatrists who conduct an assessment and give an opinion. If he pleads not guilty to murder, there will probably have to be a trial . . .' The police had suggested we didn't discuss the contents of our statements and I couldn't cope with any of the emotions yet. Talking about procedure felt safe.

As I spoke, Ola's eyes were wide with horror and I felt like I was missing something. The police had issued an AVO stipulating that Dad couldn't come near or contact her in any way, but she explained that she was still terrified at the thought she might have to see him again someday.

'He cut her face, Amani; she had a big gash in her cheek,' she said.

I flinched, imagining the panic, the blood everywhere. Mum's beautiful face. I felt weird worrying about a facial wound now that she was dead.

'I screamed and begged him to stop, but he just told me to be quiet.' Ola's big brown eyes awaited my response. I looked at her hand, where she'd been injured trying to defend our mum.

Had Mum bled to death, wondering whether her eighteen-year-old daughter, who had stayed to save her, was hurt or in danger?

'I called the police and he just left. He just turned around and left. I thought I had done enough, I thought she was going to be okay.'

I wished I'd been there instead.

My thoughts were still robotic. I wasn't ready for anger yet, but Ola's recount had lit a tiny spark. *How could he do this? What was he thinking?*

The hospital had given Ola some Valium for the pain and instructions on how to position her arm to keep the blood flowing to her injured finger. She would be examined and operated on the next morning at Sydney Hospital. I insisted that the only thing we could do was get some rest. I could tell she was in shock and broken and I had no idea what else to say so I filled the air with plans for the next morning. I couldn't tell her how relieved I was to have her there after the ordeal of the evening, searching for her, wondering what had happened. She was okay. *One of them is okay.*

She was settled in and I needed a shower. I went into the bathroom and shut the door. I looked into the mirror, checking to see if I was still the same person. Meeting my own eyes, I clasped my hands to my mouth, catching a scream that wouldn't come. The blue-grey light made my skin look blotchy. I felt dirty. *I'm still here, I'm intact.* I put a hand to my belly and tuned in to see if baby was squirming, waiting for the familiar jiggle or jolt of confirmation. *Baby is okay.*

Water ran over my head and terror scurried like insects through my body. Something internal threatened to give way so I recited silently, *Subhanallah, Alhamdulillah, la illaha illa Allah. You have a baby in your belly and siblings to take care of. You can't afford to lose it.*

FIFTEEN

Nour was dropped off at my house at around 3 am by a police officer. Ola slept on one couch and Nour settled in on the other. It was 4 am by the time I got to my bedroom where my husband, who had been giving my sisters and me some privacy, was preparing to sleep. Surrendering to the sheets, I buried my face and allowed a guttural cry-scream straight into the mattress. I looked up at my husband. 'This is so hard.'

Moey stared at me, clearly at a loss as to what he should say.

'I don't get it,' I mused tucking myself in and struggling to settle with my big belly in the way. 'I don't understand any of it. Ola was daddy's little girl – how could he do this to her?' *I can't think about Mum.*

We chatted in exhausted murmurs until we fell into a sickly sleep cut short by shrill alarms telling us that it was almost time to drive into the city for Ola's appointment. My morning sickness had completely subsided a few weeks prior, but when I waddled into the bathroom to brush my teeth, the events of the previous night came crashing back and I threw up into the vanity. Visions of knives and flesh filled my mind and my chest ached as I heaved.

'Are you okay, babe?' Moey's voice came through the door.

'I'm okay,' I reassured him, but my arms tingled, my chest burned, and I felt unsafe. The numbness was seeping away only to be replaced with flashbacks to a scene I had not even witnessed. I was hovering over Ola's version of events as though I had been there myself. *If only I'd been there.*

The tightening and burning sensation in my chest made me queasy with every breath. I wondered whether my heart was broken and willed my baby to stay put. *Just a few more months.* Struggling with both heartbreak and heartburn, I got dressed. There was a grizzly task ahead of us, and it wasn't the trip to the hospital. Someone would need to formally identify Mum's body. I imagined her cold and blue in a metallic drawer in the morgue with that big gash in her cheek. I was trying to be strong and had already agreed to do the ID, but it was too much. I wasn't ready to see death.

'I can't do it, I'm so sorry,' I blurted to Moey, as we got ready to leave home, immediately feeling guilty because that meant it would have to be him.

*

Heavy traffic and moist autumn air triggered fresh waves of nausea as we travelled along Parramatta Road into the city. We decided that Moey would stop at the Coroner's Court to ID Mum and we'd get a taxi the rest of the way to Sydney Hospital, where Ola would be receiving attention for her hand and where Khalto had promised to meet us. I kept drinking water, but the fire in my chest was intensifying. When we got to the Coroner's Court, Moey went in to do what my sisters and I could not. Another pang of guilt hit me as I wondered whether my mum would be offended that I didn't come down to see her. I was scared, repulsed, weak.

I could hear her voice saying, 'You didn't even bother coming in to see me.' Upset, the way she had been when Dad didn't visit her after her eye surgery.

My sisters and I hailed a taxi. I suffocated in the front seat of the hot, leathery car while my sisters sobbed in the back. The Bangles' 'Eternal Flame' played on the radio, reminding me of Mum humming along to Mix 106.5 as she chauffeured us to and from school. In unison, my sisters and I asked the driver to turn off the radio just as the song reached its crescendo.

He must have been so confused, but he didn't ask any questions. Mum loved that song.

I cried for the first time when we arrived at the hospital. It was a brief, stifled cry. A disciplined cry. We hugged Khalto and our family friend Rania in the hospital courtyard as humidity rose from the cobbled brick pavement. My husband and I had once stolen quiet moments in this place. After work, on the wooden benches surrounding the Robert Brough fountain, we'd looked up at the moon and planned a life together. Today I wanted to collapse there, evaporate, turn into mist.

The cafe across the courtyard called me in with green awnings and the buzz-bang-swish of baristas at work. I decided to get some coffee to wake me up and banana bread to settle my stomach. My chest was still tight, the fire spreading into my shoulders. We walked into Courtyard Cafe Da Capo in a defensive huddle. *Your mum is gone.* My aunt Hala's resolute proclamation sounded in my head.

But she wasn't gone. Mum beamed up at me from the front page of a newspaper laying on the closest table. Instinctively, worried that Ola would see, I flipped the paper over, face down, and again as I walked past another one.

There is a lag between a life-altering event and all that we already know about the world and how to behave in it. For a second, when I saw Mum on those papers, I wanted to call her and say, 'Mum! This is the most random thing, but you're on the front of today's paper.' I had to teach myself now that I couldn't call, I couldn't tell her that. She was in a place where the front pages of newspapers didn't matter at all.

I turned to Khalto and we managed a sad joke – that Mum would have been pleased with the photo they chose.

'She would have liked that.' Khalto smiled but her eyes were still and black.

All around us, people munched breakfast and sipped coffee over Australia's most recent murder, with no idea that we were right there with them.

*

We found the ward Ola needed.

'And what are you here for today?' the nurse asked dutifully.

'My sister has a bad cut to her finger, and we were referred to this hospital last night,' I answered on Ola's behalf.

'Okay, and how was the injury caused?' she asked.

I knew the answer but had no idea how to respond. Do people talk about murder in regular conversation?

'Oh, um, it was caused by a knife,' I explained, keeping it simple.

'Got to be careful with knives!' she joked.

Ola and I glanced at each other, unable to articulate the enormous truth. I felt like I had committed an injustice by omitting the details, but the question had left no room for our new reality.

Ola was admitted. Assured that she'd be okay without me, I decided to break away.

'Khalto, can you stay with her? I feel really unwell, I'm going to go down to emergency.'

Khalto looked concerned.

'I'm fine – I – I just need to check that everything is okay. I had surgery two weeks ago, for the baby.'

'Of course, do whatever you need to do to look after yourself.' She smiled another distant smile.

*

At the main entrance to the hospital, I stood calmly at the emergency window and tried to put into words why I was there.

'Hi, um, I'm five months pregnant –' I said as I pulled my Medicare card out of my bag along with the yellow pregnancy card that Bankstown Hospital had given me to track my appointments. 'I had a cervical suture placed two weeks ago. My dad, um, killed my mum last night and I am having really bad chest pain and it might be heartburn, but I thought I'd come here in case, and can you check on my baby?' I blurted it all out like I was spitting out lumps of coal. *Will I ever get used to saying this?*

The triage nurse looked concerned. In a steady voice she explained that the usual procedure for all chest pain is to be admitted and monitored. As she prepared my paperwork, I looked up at a notice board hanging to my right. It had a black frame with a glass front and it was filled with posters and fliers. For the second time that morning, I saw a ghost.

There, on a glossy government health promotion poster, was a picture of my mum at work. She was leaning over a table in a dark hijab, engaged in what looked like a staged conversation with a client or colleague. I blinked a few times to make sure it was real. First at the cafe, now here! Forgetting again, I had another urge to call her and say, 'Mum, you won't believe this!'

She hovered above me and I smiled to myself, feeling immensely proud to be her daughter, sad that my mum could no longer do the things she loved. The triage nurse interrupted my thoughts and I couldn't be bothered telling her that my mum was on her notice board. She swept me to the first available bed and strapped me with gadgets and monitors. When she closed the curtains, I was glad to be alone.

I can't remember if I called Kim from HR or if she called me, but my temporary solitude was quickly interrupted.

'I can't come to work today . . .' I was in tears before the sentence was out.

She said she'd seen it on the news but wasn't sure if it was my family. She asked if we were okay. 'We're okay,' I sniffed in return. She'd get back to me later about work arrangements, but for now I should take the time I needed. I ended the call and stared at the ceiling, relieved I didn't need to have any more macabre conversations, cringing at the thought of being the subject of today's workplace gossip.

I'm not sure how long I was there, or if I fell asleep waiting, but a doctor later came back and told me that the baby and I were fine, to keep an eye out for bleeding, and to take antacids for the heartburn. Ola and I were both discharged later that morning; her injured hand was in a cast and in the other hand she carried an A4 sheet of paper setting out the aftercare and her next appointment. A tendon in her finger was damaged, and she would need therapy to regain movement. The scar would need regular massaging so that it wouldn't heal too stiff.

We drove back to Bexley and pulled up in front of Amo Ali's house where all four of Dad's Australian brothers were a blubbering mess. I comforted the grown men with reassurances. 'We're okay. Things will be okay.' They looked at me like I was supposed to say something else. Something felt off but I didn't know what was normal for when your mum's been killed by your own dad.

We spent the day there as visitors came and went telling us how sorry they were. Muslims will typically hold three days of grieving to allow for visitors to pay their condolences and comfort the family of the deceased. I didn't feel ready to see anyone and I didn't feel ready to grieve, but I went along with it. A couple of my friends dropped by – I was grateful to see them. One older lady said, 'I'll be your mum now,' and I just patted her on the shoulder because she probably meant well. She smelled like the perfume people bring back from Hajj. Some people stared like they were there for a sticky-beak rather than to comfort us. *Look at those poor girls. Their mum is dead and their dad is in prison. How will they cope?* Lined faces, soggy cheeks; I greeted guests one by one, trying to act normal so they wouldn't have to be too sad. They offered vague condolences. *Inshallah b-teslami* – may you find peace.

*

When we were kids, Mum would take us to the local parks where we'd play and eat Unica bars and suck the salt off pumpkin seeds until our lips chafed. The playgrounds around Bardwell Valley were our favourite. Mum's friends – women from our local community – would bring their children and we'd know that we were going to roam until sunset. 'Watch your sisters, keep your hats on and don't go too far!' Mum would shout at our backs as we shot down the hill at Silver Jubilee Park. One year, a local Lebanese politician turned the hill into an olive grove and from then on, we'd have to dodge the young trees as we tumbled.

You can see the city from Silver Jubilee and our amos and cousins would sometimes meet us there on New Year's Eve. We'd watch the official fireworks sparking from the Harbour Bridge on the horizon and the dodgy fireworks sparking from the slippery-dip right in front of us. I loved the promise of a new year and I'd go to bed afterwards, heart thumping like the skies above, believing that this could be the start of happiness. Today the same sky was a dull grey, shutting in overhead like a lid.

I don't know where the rest of our first day of mourning went. One of my closest friends, Miriam, says we drove to the park up the road – one of the parks we used to visit with Mum. I have no memory of this. Nour remembers but Ola is not sure. Miriam tells me we left Amo's house for a break because the atmosphere was tense and uncomfortable. She reminds me that Amo's place didn't feel like a safe place to grieve because it was unclear which grief it was meant to accommodate; the grief that our mother was dead or the grief that our father was the culprit. As soon as we got out of Miriam's car, Nour and I began to break down. We sat there crying in the fresh air until I straightened up, wiped my tears and said it was time to return to the guests.

'You felt like you had to swallow it back up again, get in the car and go back to that house,' Miriam recalls.

That memory is gone, just like those days at the park are gone, just like Mum is gone.

SIXTEEN

The second day of mourning was held at Khalto's place, which felt more like home than Amo Ali's place had. Emotions started to arrive in throbbing waves, stronger and longer. I felt sorry for myself and Mum and for all these uncomfortable, awkward people who didn't know what to say.

Towards Dad I felt a strange mixture of pity and disgust. I'd seen him briefly in the news, handcuffed, escorted, dressed in something that looked like blue tarp, presumably to preserve the evidence on his body. People said things like, 'You poor girls, you lost both your parents at once,' which didn't quite capture how I was feeling. I was baffled by Dad's actions. Whatever relationship we'd had already seemed far away and pretend. Everything we'd ever shared was twitching, writhing, contorting, like a spider dying in front of me. I did not feel like I was grieving him. I felt like I was escaping him. He was at once pathetic and terrifying to me.

During a lull in visitors, I went to the backyard where the men were to find Amo Abbas. He had been in Lebanon with my dad.

'What was he like when he left?' I asked when I got his attention.

'He just said he was bored and restless and that he wanted to get back to Australia,' Amo answered.

'Was he behaving normally?' I pressed.

'He was upset and kept making comments about how miserable he was after our mother didn't recognise him.'

I tasted bile. Dad was losing his mother when he decided to hurt mine.

'Have you seen him since the other night?' I asked.

He said he might be seeing Dad later.

I was cordial and told him to pass on my *salaams*, but the words were bitter in my mouth.

The little spark of anger from two nights before was now a small flame dancing on a candlewick. I went inside to get away.

*

The news had already reached Lebanon, Germany and Canada, where Mum's family lived. Someone at the ABC had linked the reports of the stabbing of forty-five-year-old Salwa Haydar in Bexley to a nine-year-old news story about my grandmother's death. The headline brought me to a pause as I hid in Khalto's bedroom, scrolling through Facebook. Visitors were slumped in the lounge room and my phone was buzzing with questions and condolences. I was too tired and overwhelmed to sit with people or answer calls.

'Tragedy hits family again as war victim's daughter, Salwa Haydar, stabbed to death at Bexley.'

All the moments in my mother's life had been overwritten by those words. The present and the future had caved into the past. Two mothers, two wounds, two black holes. A wound within a wound. My baby jolted inside me. *We're like a set of Russian dolls.*

The photo accompanying the article was of Mum grieving. It was so different to the smiling front cover in the cafe at the hospital. She wore a black one-piece hijab and held a framed picture of her mother, my teta. The wall behind her was blue, because Mum liked to decorate. Each room at Four-One-Six had a colour scheme. The sunroom was sky blue, and there was a matching blue lamp on the side table. Seeing that photo dragged me back to that same blue room in July 2006. It was a day or two after Teta's death. We'd been crying. My hair was tied back in a ponytail, a halo of frizz at the hairline. I would be turning eighteen the following month, and I hated the way I looked. I tried to smooth the fly-aways behind my ears before the news crew arrived to watch us grieve. Mum was still kind of in shock. She wouldn't stop smacking the palm of her hand into her left thigh. Every now and then, she suddenly clasped her hands together and dropped her bottom lip as though she realised something. I waited for her to speak but she didn't say anything.

Khalto had just been discharged from hospital. She had taken the news really badly. She wouldn't talk or eat or cry. One of our visitors, an older lady, told me to mix sugar into a glass of milk and offer it to Khalto through a straw. Khalto refused to unlock her jaw. Her shoulders tightened like one was trying to reach the other, folded up like she was cold. I was in way over my head.

Guests kept coming. I was the eldest daughter, but I did not know yet how to make coffee in a *raqweh*. Other Lebanese girls could already cook *kusa* and *kebbe b-laban,* but Mum didn't like me in the kitchen because I was messy and she believed girls my age should be studying. Relatives walked in and addressed me in Arabic, and I couldn't remember the proper response or which of the men I was not supposed to shake hands with. Everyone knew I was in my last year of school, so they ask me about my upcoming exams and what I planned to do after graduation.

I stuttered disjointed answers. I couldn't hold a conversation in Arabic and I'd been too sad and distracted to study. They all had high expectations because I'd got into a selective school while their kids didn't.

When the news people arrived, a journalist asked if we had any photos of my grandmother. I went to the massive black TV-unit with fancy gold details and pulled out a small stack of photos I'd taken on a disposable camera when I was in Aitaroun just months previously. The first photo was Teta in a red velvet *abaya* with a broom in her hand. I heard the tshhhht-tshhhht-tshhhht of her sweeping, sweeping, sweeping. I felt like I was back there in her garden. She was bothering me because she said that I needed to respect and serve my brother. 'Lay out his blankets and bring him what he needs,' she said.

I told her my brother is nobody and I do what I like. Plus, I'm older. '*Ana akbar meno!*' I reminded my grandmother.

I could be cheeky with her because I felt safe in the knowledge that she would love me no matter what. I spent all my time trying to show her how clever I was, even though my Arabic was broken and my jokes didn't come across well. Or at all. I put my foot in it so many times that my parents said I shouldn't talk so much, that people would like me better if I was calm and mature. *All the young Aussie girls get marriage proposals when they visit Lebanon*, I'd been told, but no one asked for my hand. Maybe because I was talkative and clumsy and I would rather play foosball with my cousins than sit with the adults and listen to their politics. Maybe because the news reports said that people were rioting on the beaches in Sydney and the Lebs weren't welcome there anymore.

I never liked the beach. I told myself that I was a village girl from the Holy Lands, and that I didn't care if we never went back to Sydney. I was so excited to know Teta, and for her to

116

get to know me. I mopped her tiles and watered her plants. She gave me a pine cone to shell. It felt like the most important job in the world. I banged it with a hammer until the nuts fell out.

*

In the blue room, the journalist instructed Mum to look through the photos for the camera. Mum did as she was asked, and I felt frustrated because the war was still happening and these journalists – who could say whatever they wanted and make a difference – were not offering to help. They wanted to talk about my grandmother being a mother of nine. They wanted to hear how happy Mum's childhood was. Mum told them that there was war in her childhood too.

It didn't feel like Teta was dead because she was far away and I couldn't see her anyway. I wouldn't believe she was gone until I went back to that garden and checked for myself. I began to worry about how damaged her house might have been, whether her kitchen was in ruins. I had an urge to go there immediately and salvage something; her sewing machine maybe, her brass pot, the old crochet blanket.

After the news people left, I wanted to lay on the floor and thrash and scream like a toddler. I couldn't watch any more news because I felt like all the dead people in all the wars were related to me. I did not watch news again for a very long time.

*

Almost ten years later, hiding in Khalto's bedroom, I scrolled through the news and everything was about Mum. My mum. Muslims in my feed shared articles with the words 'Inna lillah wa

inna illayhi raji'oon' (We belong to God and to Him we return).
Xenophobic and racist strangers commented gleefully on public
posts: 'Another victim of the religion of pieces!' and 'Looks like
an honour killing!'

My amos hadn't shared any articles. A journalist was in my
private messages saying that they were sorry and would like to
talk. I couldn't distinguish the sympathy from the voyeurism.
I kept scrolling.

'Counting Dead Women' and a couple of other sources reported
my mother's death as an act of domestic violence. This somehow
surprised me. I never thought of my dad as an abuser. He'd let
Mum study and work. Men who hurt their wives were drunkards,
gamblers, poorly educated people.

This isn't like that . . .

In the quiet of Khalto's room, my mind began to work like
it was trained to, shuffling through evidence, joining dots. *How
is this different?* I pushed past the stereotypes and biases. Hadn't
I read something about emotional abuse being just as traumatic
and dangerous? The news reports said Mum texted a colleague to
say she was feeling vulnerable.

What was that thing she said about being afraid, the last time
I saw her at the cafe? What about the time she made a secret
appointment with lawyers in the city? Hadn't she said he was
'controlling' and 'gaslighting' her? For so many years, all she
wanted was for him to treat her right or leave her alone . . .

Over the next few days, silenced and almost-erased memories
came in like tides, lapping at my consciousness. I thought back
to things Mum had told me when I was younger. I thought about
how bad the fights had been. Hadn't he lifted his fist? Hadn't she
screamed? Hadn't I heard him use terrible words about divorced
women?

Hadn't she told me an awful story on the way to school one morning?

*

When my sisters and I got home that evening we all agreed; even though people had come and gone all day, no one had said or done anything that could help.

About to graduate from her degree in journalism, Nour's instinct was that we should organise a visit to see Dad and interrogate him.

'I feel like I need to ask him questions,' she announced.

Ola shook her head at the suggestion. 'Nour, he knew what he was doing, he kept telling me to be quiet.'

I nodded. I had a lot of questions too, but they were all for Mum: *Where are you now? What do I do with your daughters and my baby?*

'I don't think there's any point, Nour. His lawyers will already have advised him not to speak to anyone and there's no way he can give you the answers you need. We'll just have to wait for the trial. You never know – maybe he'll plead guilty and we won't have to go through that.'

We slept with all the lights on that week.

SEVENTEEN

Muslims normally bury their dead within a day, but we waited three days for the coroner to conduct an autopsy and prepare a report before they released Mum's body to the mosque. Before an Islamic burial, *janaza* prayers are held at a *masjid*. Islamic funerals can be very informal but there are strict obligations that need to be met. It is the whole community's responsibility to make sure that every dead person's *ruh* has people to recite prayers for it.

My tummy quivered as my baby rolled over inside. I had no idea what to expect; I had never been to a *janaza* before Mum's. I felt anxious and impatient as I got dressed that morning.

Khalto's house was just around the corner from Al-Zahra Mosque so we walked there in a small group. As we arrived at the gates I saw that people had already begun to gather out the front. Some were chatting, some were crying, and there were people I didn't recognise at all. The crowd grew. The women who knew Mum became more and more upset. Hala, who had been very close to Mum, had a stroke while waiting for the *janaza* to begin and an ambulance had to be called. Her daughter, my cousin, ran through the driveway screaming for help. During the *janaza*, I rubbed aunties and cousins on the back and begged them to be calm; I brought them plastic chairs and bottles of water. I turned my palms to the sky and recited whatever words came to my lips. Moey, Khalto and my sisters stood beside me and I sensed their tension and frustration at the surrounding chaos; the sirens, the screams and the commotion surrounding Hala. *This should be about Mum.* I didn't feel like I could cry in the midst of so much activity. My brother, who was released for the day on compassionate grounds after we'd helped him lodge an urgent request, waited near the entry of the mosque grounds, accompanied by two guards. He wore black dress pants and a white button shirt; the ones I'd bought him for my wedding. A clunky metal chain shackled one of his ankles to the other, scraping against the concrete as he walked.

Before the *janaza* prayers, we were given an opportunity to see Mum. A roller door went up and the mosque mortician, a smiley *hajji* with a tight black hijab and dark eyes, led us into the room where she washed and prepared bodies for burial.

I stood straight and tall, for Ola and Nour. I hadn't admitted it to anyone but I was terrified of seeing a dead person, even if it was my own mother. I needed to be calm and in control, but I had no idea how seeing her would make me feel. I imagined that she would be pale and blue like the dead girls on *CSI*. I didn't think I could live with that image in my heart for the rest of my life.

I hesitated as we stepped into the cold room. It was the size of a garage but clean and bright. She was right there, resting, on a long silver bed. I felt slightly relieved as I moved towards her; I couldn't see my mother's wounds. Her cheeks were as pink as ever and her eyelashes were daintily shut over them. *Like a porcelain doll.* Her body was wrapped in layers of white cloth and the *kafan* came right up over her chin and around her head. She glowed.

I recited prayer after prayer, carefully gifting every word to my mother.

I'm okay, I can do this.

When I leaned close to say goodbye, I noticed that her skin was smooth and cold. I flinched. Suddenly, my goodbyes felt futile. I took a small step back. *She isn't here.* I thought of Mum, whose body I'd once inhabited. The woman I saw a couple of weeks before had blood rippling through her, she was talking, laughing, eating. This body was not my mum. I looked around the room to see if anyone else was bothered by the emptiness. My siblings, Khalto and her daughters were busy with their own sadness. Everyone had their heads down in prayer except for the mortician. Her black eyes met mine and, as if she'd read my mind, she said, 'Don't worry *habibti*, your mum is in *jannah* now.'

*

Many people turned up to the burial at Rookwood that afternoon; my relatives, my husband's relatives and Mum's colleagues. *This will be over soon.* We listened to the sheikh recite *duas* for Mum and watched the damp earth close over her white garments. Then we covered the bare soil with roses and wreaths. It was a warm afternoon but a cool breeze drifted over the cemetery as we prepared to leave. I hugged my brother goodbye, promising I'd visit him soon. Two guards led him to a white van with tiny windows that would deliver him back to Long Bay. I looked back at the rows of tombstones. I'd expected the cemetery to be creepy but this place was not creepy at all – it was profoundly serene.

I shut my eyes as we drove away. Both Mum and Teta were gone from the *dunya*, but I had to be here. I thought back to what my grandmother had said in her dewy south Lebanese accent.

'*Kel shi byeblash sgiir w ba'den bysiir kbiir . . .*'

Everything starts out small and grows bigger over time.

'*Ella el-mawt! El-mawt byeblash kbiir w ba'den bysiir sgiir . . .*'

Except death. Death starts out huge but it gets smaller. Grief shrinks over time.

EIGHTEEN

I had another pregnancy scare the morning after Mum's funeral. I didn't feel anything, but I woke up early, bleeding. Before the sun had come up, Moey and I were speeding down the Hume Highway to Bankstown-Lidcombe Hospital where I was rushed straight into the maternity ward.

When I told the midwife everything that had happened, she grabbed me, pulled me against her soft breasts and said, 'Oh! Your poor mother! I am so sorry.' She said she would look after me. It felt nice to be comforted like this, to be a child for a moment.

Despite the gigantic trauma I'd been through, my bleeding was deemed inexplicable. Baby was fine. I was told to stay hydrated and rest.

'You had surgery about two weeks ago,' a doctor explained, 'and your body is still healing. You can stay here for the night for observation.'

My sisters and a couple of friends came to check on me. Miriam brought me *mjadara* made by her mum. My appetite came back. I had never eaten *mjadara* that good.

My guests went home and I settled in to spend the night. It felt good to be away from people, to be alone with my thoughts for the first time in days. I was sitting in my hospital bed that evening, chatting to the pear-sized child in my uterus and eating Ferrero Rochers and strawberries, when one of my dad's overseas sisters called.

'Allo?' I answered.

'Allo, Amani. Ana Amto.' I recognised Dad's sister's deep, oily voice.

She asked me how I was. I didn't feel like talking about Mum. Nor did I have the proficiency required to get into the details of cervical incompetence in Arabic, so I simply replied, '*Alhamdulillah.*'

Amto began to sob and wail and sniff. 'Your mum is gone' – sob – '*Allah yerhama*' – sniff – 'but we need to help your dad.'

My gut churned like the baby was trying to swim out of me again. *Help him?* Why was she demanding this? Who was going to help us? Who had helped Mum?

I calmly repeated that I was okay and thanked her for calling but my mouth was dry when I hung up. I forced myself to forgive her for her words.

She's just upset and confused, I told myself.

*

I lost count of the unbelievably cruel and insensitive responses my grief received. They made the grief bigger, impenetrable.

However, I also witnessed acts of empathy and kindness, and I collected those small gestures as evidence that there was still some love in the world.

A student who was enrolled in the same course as Mum at Western Sydney University started a fundraiser for us. Some of my husband's relatives donated money to the building of a water well in a developing country on Mum's behalf. Girls I went to high school with and hadn't seen since sent flowers to my home.

A teacher from my Islamic Studies course came to visit my husband and me. He took his shoes off at the door, as Turkish people always do, and when he sat on my couch, he asked whether he could recite Quran for my mother's *ruh*. I said, 'Of course,' a little taken aback that he was seeking permission. He recited softly, entirely by heart, and the words filled my house.

I will never forget those kind deeds, and I whisper a *dua* for each of those people whenever I think of them.

My dad's brothers and their families, on the other hand, moped around visit after tedious visit, sat on my couch, perplexed. They complained about everything from arthritis to property prices to the fact that the family reputation was now ruined – anything but the black hole at the centre of my world. '*Rahat El-sem'a*,' one of them lamented. His son, a banker, thumped my coffee table with his palm to get our attention. He said, 'I'm not justifying it, but she must have done something to make him do this!'

My sisters and I fell silent. It was becoming apparent that Dad's family were more upset about Dad being in gaol than the fact that Mum, who they had known for twenty-eight years, was murdered by him. Amo Khalil said that in Islam it was his duty to be like a father to us and that we should ask him if we needed anything, but he didn't make me feel like I could ask him for anything at all. As they were leaving, my cousin apologised to my husband for banging the coffee table. Within a few weeks, I learned that he was instructing the lawyers for my dad's defence and had visited my father in gaol. I imagined this cousin's palm, which had slammed my coffee table, resting between Dad's thick brown fingers. The same fingers that gripped the knife. The ones that had been covered in my mother's blood. I felt nervous and nauseous around Dad's family from then on. How could they shake his hand one day and drink tea from my mugs the next?

*

Unless they are well trained or have lived through it themselves, people are terrible at responding to trauma. And if individuals are careless and uninformed (or, indeed, malicious), then the institutions we rely on when we're vulnerable are an exponent of that carelessness, ignorance and malice.

About a week or two after Mum's death, I went into the Centrelink at Bankstown with my sister. I was still very jumpy and felt bare being out in public. We stood in the loathed line. I resented the building and everyone in it, but I tried not to show it. It is impossible to be happy or optimistic in a Centrelink queue, but I had to pretend so that it wouldn't be too depressing for Ola. A friend had suggested we ask to see the social worker. Ola was an unemployed, full-time student studying design and architecture at university and living at home before the murder; she had been dependent on Mum.

Ola would have to take a break from study and live with me while I was on unpaid leave, waiting to have a baby. When I got my first job at a law firm, I had thanked God I no longer needed to stand in a Centrelink line. Thanks to Dad, I was lining up again, missing my little grey office and the omelettes at the Dymocks cafe on George Street.

I don't belong here.

It was overcrowded. Angry bodies wrapped right around the section where people sit and apply for jobs on old computers. Arab women hushed their babies, 'Shh shh, *ya mama*,' and bogans muttered under their breaths, 'Fuck this.' I was sweating around my hairline and my hips were aching under the weight of my belly when we finally got to the front.

A smiling woman with a big blow-dry and a loud raspy voice greeted us with an iPad in her hand. She said, 'So why are you here today?'

'Hi, I'd like to be referred to your social worker urgently, please,' I said quietly.

She waited for me to continue but I didn't want to say anything else. Her finger hovered stubbornly over the iPad. There were boxes on the screen.

'What is it about?' she asked, itching to tick a box.

I begged with my eyes that she wouldn't make me say it out loud, in that long miserable line, in front of all those people. In front of Ola.

'We need to know why you're here, darl,' she insisted.

I'll have to get used to saying it.

I put on my best neutral face and you-asked-for-it tone.

'My dad stabbed my mum to death last week and we need help sorting out our living situation.' *There is no box for that, is there?*

The smile dropped right off her face, joining the squiggly patterns on the carpet. She looked down at her iPad, her manicure still hesitant above the screen. I waited for a response as her eyes flicked from myself to Ola to her iPad, like maybe I was making a bad joke. Like people ever go to Centrelink with good news.

'Oh, I'm sorry to hear that,' she said after a second. Tap-tap, tap-tap. 'Please take a seat and wait to be called.'

When we were finally called, I took a deep breath and told the woman behind the desk what happened. *I just want to go home.* We sorted out the things Ola needed, and I asked her if there was anything I needed to do given that I would be having a baby and claiming Parental Leave Pay in a few months. She said I could simply lodge the claim online using the same reference number I had used as a university student. *Like a lifetime membership.* I had time; I didn't have to do anything right away. For now, I could focus on getting my sisters sorted. She handed me a stack of flyers and brochures. None of them were about domestic violence.

*

I try to watch TV but everything is fleshy and violent.

I develop a habit of eating whenever I feel stressed or bored. When I eat too much, the heartburn returns, and I have to stop. I eat so many cheese and tomato toasties, Nour says I will probably give birth to one.

I try to distract myself by being silly and funny with my sisters, but I feel guilty for laughing. There's a video of me somewhere dancing to 'Apple Bottom Jeans' in my lounge room. I'm wearing a stripy pink onesie. My tummy is up to my mouth at this point (to use one of my grandmother's phrases). It bobs up and down in front of me while my sisters giggle in the background, begging me to stop moving so fast.

I laugh, 'The baby is sutured in, it can't fall out anyway!'

When the fun ends, I am thrust back into reality, unable to escape a heightened sense of my own mortality, and the mortality of those around me. When I rest my eyes, scenes of blood and gore paint themselves against my eyelids.

Everything is a near and imminent threat. When I feel a kick or contraction, I see myself going into premature labour and not making it to the hospital in time for the cervical suture to be removed. When I wash the dishes, I see the knife slipping from my grip and plunging into my arm. When I drive, my anxiety is so bad I confine myself to a tight and familiar radius. I see my car crumpled up against a pole or crushed between two trucks.

As I run errands, I keep my eyes down, careful not to offend anyone or cut them off. What if they're violent? What if they keep a knife or bat or gun in the glove box? I imagine the news reporting my freak death. A trifecta of inexplicable horrors. A big goofy picture of my face on the front of the paper. I'd die again of embarrassment.

I climb into bed knowing that my husband, who is kinder to me than anyone, who I love down to my bones, is statistically the most likely person to harm me. I stare at the ceiling, wondering whether Dad could have been insane. What restraint must he have exercised all those years in order to disguise the dangerous side of himself from us? How unwell could he have been?

Did he feel guilty?

It was hard to believe that the people under my roof could be so hateful or damaged that they might think to hurt me. Dad had already brought this within the realm of possibility.

Couldn't any of us just snap then?

Are we all narcissists who simply haven't chosen violence yet?

My sisters lay in their beds asking themselves the same questions.

*

In shows like *Law & Order*, the victim of crime is pitied but not empowered. She is gripped by a mental illness, damaged by guilt or addicted to drugs. She does not know how things got so bad. A detective or a lawyer comes along, puts a hand on her shoulder, tells her, 'You're okay, it's going to be okay.' They capture the bad guy, and in the final scene we see him spitting and ranting in the witness box, caught in a web of his own lies. Someone tall and blonde turns around, pleased. She rests her case. Scene ends, credits roll.

In the weeks after the murder, I fought with that image of the victim of crime – weak and unable to cope. I didn't have the option of not coping. In a few months I was going to be a mother, plus I had siblings to take care of and a trial to prepare for. I had to keep going. How had Mum done it in the days after Teta was killed? She'd been cranky but proactive. She had spoken to the news, sent us back to school and organised Teta's *arba'een* – a ceremony that takes place exactly forty days after burial.

I flicked through a stack of pamphlets about grief and counselling that had been given to me at the hospital the night everything happened. We were calling it 'the night everything happened' because everything else felt too literal. It would have made sense to call it 'murder', but the lawyer in me felt wrong saying that without 'alleged', even though Mum was dead and Ola had seen the whole thing with her own eyes. We couldn't call it 'the night Mum died' because she didn't just drop dead. All of the available words betrayed reality.

Someone named Jann had called from the Homicide Victims Support Group (HVSG) and left me a message in the days after everything happened. I decided to call her back and see if my sisters and I could go to a meeting. If I was going to deliver a baby into the world, I would need to start working on my trauma. No one else could do that for me. Mum talked a lot about mental health. She would be disappointed if I didn't accept help.

The HVSG provides counselling and support to homicide victims throughout New South Wales and lobbies for their rights. The Group was set up by the parents of Anita Cobby and Ebony Simpson in 1993. Anita was walking home from Blacktown Station on 2 February 1986 when she was brutally sexually assaulted and murdered by five men with the surnames Travers, Murdoch and Murphy. One of the men is now dead, while the others serve their sentences across New South Wales. Ebony Simpson was only nine. I pause when I read this, skin prickling. She was murdered by Andrew Peter Garforth when she was walking home from the bus stop after school on 19 August 1992, in Bargo. Her murderer confessed and pleaded guilty. His papers were marked 'never to be released'. He tried to claim victim's compensation after he was allegedly assaulted by other prisoners. His claim was rejected after public uproar.

My sisters came with me for our first visit. The HVSG office is in Parramatta, so it was convenient to get to. It's a short walk from Criniti's on Church Street, the restaurant where we had our last Mothers' Day lunch with Mum. Convenience was important because even the lightest tasks, at this stage, felt insurmountable. My sisters and I went up the lift silently.

I wanted to start counselling right away, to get away from this sick and lonely feeling as soon as possible, but this afternoon was just an information session. In the HVSG offices, we met three or four friendly staff, including Jann who was tall with short grey hair and funky earrings. We sat in a circle and the support workers told us about their programs and retreats. Jann explained that they would help us organise paperwork and access counselling, and would later accompany us to court. They didn't expect anything in return and could even come to our home if we needed them to.

We came home from the meeting with a bunch of forms so that we could lodge a claim with Victims Services. In New South Wales, the family members and dependents of a homicide victim are able to receive a 'recognition payment', designed to acknowledge the trauma and the upheaval it is likely to have caused. This wouldn't depend on what charges had been laid, and we wouldn't have to wait for a verdict. It was a small sum but validating.

I took an extra form for my brother who was still at Long Bay. He'd called a couple of times after the funeral, emotional, asking for updates. I'd tried to fill him in, help him process some of what happened. The frustrating six-minute cap on prison calls made it difficult to understand what supports were available to inmates aggrieved by homicide, but the impression I got was that they wouldn't be any good. In any case, there would likely be stigmas around seeking them. The prison system scarcely differentiates between the worst offenders and those who are younger, more vulnerable, or still in custody on remand. Even though I had given explicit instructions to police that my brother would need to be notified of everything that had happened in a sensitive way, he'd still found out about the murder from the television before they got the news to him. I worried about him. He was a homicide victim sharing facilities with people accused of homicides. Mum would have wanted me to help him in any way I could.

Jann reassured me that we would be able to lodge a claim on his behalf and provide him with other support if he wanted it. She also reassured us that Victims Services would cover any lost or damaged property and funeral expenses. In the fog of the days immediately after the murder, I hadn't asked who had paid for Mum's funeral, but I was grateful it had been taken care of. A few months later, one of my uncles sent me the receipt and asked me to transfer the funeral costs back to him. I put in a claim and reimbursed him. Why should he have to pay for Dad's actions? I didn't anticipate that, two years later, that same uncle would turn up to the trial in solidarity with Dad.

Jann had made it easy to ask for help.

'I'm going to make a proper appointment to start counselling,' I told my sisters as we walked back to the car. 'And I'm going to write a speech for Mum's *arba'een*.'

NINETEEN

The microphone felt cold and heavy in my hand as I took my place at the lectern. The congregants attending Mum's *arba'een* at Masjid Arrahman in Kingsgrove were waiting for me to speak. The women sat to my right in a tiled and sterile space. A large projector screen behind me told me this part of the mosque was usually used for classes. Today, the women were packed into rows of plastic chairs. They were all familiar to me. I had grown up around them; some were family, some were Mum's friends or acquaintances. They were all dressed in black, as is expected for a Shia mourning congregation or *majlis aza*, clutching soggy tissues and watching me through red eyes. Ola held her iPhone up above the crowd, ready to record my speech. Nour and Khalto sat quietly beside her.

To my left were twice as many men. We were segregated by a glass partition, but they could see me at the lectern, and I could see them. They would be able to hear me too. Most of the men sat close together, cross-legged on the floor of the mosque. Gold and red carpet flashed through the gaps between their bodies. Older men sat along the walls in wooden armchairs with maroon upholstery. The white walls were inscribed with silver calligraphy, which glowed in the light of the large crystal chandelier hanging from the centre of the ceiling. The men looked back with saggy brown cheeks and dark stubble. I spotted my uncles and their sons. I wanted to look them in the eye.

Murmurs across the two rooms softened into whispers and I spoke.

'*Assalamu alayakum.*'

My audience responded with a sombre, '*Wa alaykum assalam,*' extending all the vowels so that it sounded more like a hymn than a greeting.

'My name is Amani Haydar and I am the eldest daughter of *al-marhoomi* Salwa Haydar.'

My chest tightened and I felt a hot flush ripple through my skin. I'd never been to one of these things without my mum. I took a breath and forced the next sentence of my speech out of my lungs.

'My mother's tragic death has caused me to reflect deeply on the contributions she made to her children's lives and to her community. After dedicating most of her life to raising and educating her four children, Mum began to pursue an education and career of her own. But even the career path she chose was not a selfish one . . .'

I'm so proud and so angry.

'During her relatively short career, my mum assisted many underprivileged people. She was a counsellor and a mental health advocate. She helped struggling women, children, refugees, people with disabilities and people with mental and physical illnesses without judging or blaming them for their problems.'

She's being judged and blamed now.

'Very few of us can say that we've helped as many people as she had. As part of her dedication to mental health, she had recently commenced a degree in social work. She had also completed two months of training with Gorman House at St Vincent's Hospital, which specialises in assisting people who are drug and alcohol dependent, many of whom also have mental illnesses or are also homeless . . .'

Dad's going to say he was mentally ill. They're going to believe him. They want to believe him.

'Inside and outside of her work, my mum lived the spirit of the Quranic expression *Inna ma'al 'usri yusra,* verily along with every hardship comes ease . . .'

People sniffed. Some women hid their faces in their hijabs and sobbed. Some just stared at me; their cheeks were wet but I sensed there was more curiosity in their eyes than compassion.

'Despite the hardships she faced inside and outside the home, my mum rose energetically every day and worked very, very hard to better herself, her family and her community. Despite the loss of our grandmother in 2006, my mum still knew how to laugh and maintain friendships.'

I recognised Khalto's heightened cries in the crowd.

'Mum taught me and my siblings to be fiercely independent. To face life's challenges head on. To speak up about our wants and needs. To pursue happiness. To be kind and respectful but courageous in our dealings with others.'

I paused, took a breath and glanced up at the men's side. I made eye-contact with my eldest uncle who was seated towards the back of the men's section. *Listen to me!* His face was sunken with self-pity. There were no smiles of encouragement or nods of agreement.

I felt a sense of urgency, a burden to say something before the moment could be snatched away. The whole world had ended, but Allah had put this microphone in my hand. Maybe this is what the men felt when giving the *khutba* at the pulpit on Fridays.

'*InshaAllah* because of mothers like Salwa Haydar, our community will grow into one in which a woman's voice is not just heard but listened to and understood. *InshaAllah*, our sons will learn to value a woman's contributions to the home and to society at large. *InshaAllah* every man here tonight will honour my mother's memory by reflecting on how he might be a better husband.'

I paused again. *For now, you are all complicit.*

'I am confident that Salwa Haydar has been reunited with her own mother, *al-shahida* Layla Shaikh Hussain Haidar and the others from our community who have died, defenceless at the hands of an oppressor . . .'

The sobs grew louder as my allusion to war picked at old scars.

'I am faithful that Salwa Haydar is now enjoying the fruits of the many, many good deeds she sowed in this world. May Allah make each one of us as energetic and dedicated as she was. *Al-Fatiha*.'

Heads dropped and the air hummed with the soft whisper of prayer. I adjusted the grey silk and lace *mandeel* I'd wrapped around my head as a makeshift hijab. It had belonged to my mum. Waddling back to my chair, I noticed that mine were the only dry eyes in the women's section.

Were they judging me? Did they feel sorry for me? Did they think I was broken?

I was pregnant. I was numb. I had to keep it together.

There was still so much left to do.

TWENTY

23 MAY 2015

I had my first appointment with the Homicide Victims Support Group this week. I like Jann. It was a good session and came at a good time. I'm finding it harder to keep my anger and frustration in check. I'm also finding it harder to hold back tears when I miss my mum. I've been crying almost every morning.

I'm frustrated at my uncles who are supporting my father. Using my own initiative yesterday, I found out that my father's lawyer intends to make a bail application this week, which is absolutely ludicrous! Also, my uncle has not checked on me since my speech at the mosque – good riddance!

Nour and Ola are living with me and we get along well. The baby seems to be doing well too and we are all looking forward to meeting him/her. Jann says that childbirth will probably give way to a very emotional time. The hospital also flagged that I am at an increased chance of post-natal depression. I have to keep an eye on these things, and I will be seeing Jann and the psychologist at the hospital in order to receive the necessary support.

My husband has been an absolute blessing and I constantly thank God for him. Tonight, on a whim, we drove to a cafe in Cabramatta called 'What the Fudge' and had deep-fried Gaytimes with my sisters. We laughed and talked and there was no one around who knew or could recognise us. It was nice to do something spontaneous and light-hearted.

I'm back at uni and my theology studies are helping me cope with these otherwise unbearable circumstances. Exams are coming up.

There are so many positive things going on, but it is still impossible not to be heartbroken. I hope that one day I will come to terms with this loss and develop a deeper, more solid sense of acceptance. I hope also that this will eventually be an event I can leave in the past and that the pain will slowly be replaced with fresh hope and excitement for the future.

Jann said that sometimes situations like this require us to use our heart and express our emotions – as opposed to using only our mind to reason through the pain without ever express-ing sadness. She can probably tell that I find it hard to be sad around other people.

*

As recommended by Jann, I continue journalling between appointments. I document my nightmares, which start to follow a formula.

I am sitting in the grey lounge room at Four-One-Six. My mother is in the kitchen. I cannot see her well, but her silhouette moves between doorways in the labyrinthine background. The news is on loud. Al-Jazeera or some station like that. Just sirens and explosions. I look at Dad and he is sitting on the couch, watching the TV like a normal man. I feel angry in a way that makes my insides hot. I want to shout but I cannot immediately remember why I am so angry at him.

Then I feel grief like ice in my stomach and I salivate with all the words that I am unable to scream at him when I am awake.

I decide to confront him. 'Do you know what you've done?'

Dad turns to face me. He is annoyed because I'm talking over the news. His attention is always over there.

In real life, Dad has hazel eyes. In Arabic, hazel eyes are called *'assali*, which means honey-like. When I confront him in the nightmare, Dad turns to look at me and his eyes are yellow; not golden-yellow like honey, but an acidic yellow. Like sulphur.

I shout, 'How could you do something like this? I will never forgive you! You are disgusting. YOU ARE PATHETIC . . .'

I can't stop. The words spill out of me like blood from a fresh wound. I search his acid eyes for remorse, shame, empathy, but they just sizzle back at me. He doesn't say anything. I am unable to get through to him. I don't think he still feels.

The nightmare ends a different way each time.

Sometimes he snaps back at me with, '*KHALAS!* DON'T SPEAK TO YOUR FATHER THAT WAY!' Sometimes he rolls his acid eyes sarcastically like I am being unreasonable. Other times he laughs at me through gritted teeth. Sometimes he is absent, and I am shouting at one of the many members of his family who are trying to protect him.

I wake up breathless. I can't wait to forget.

6 JUNE 2015

There's a huge hole in me now that I'll never be able to mend. Some days I'm too busy to notice it. Other days it is gaping, wide and hollow. It makes me flimsy. Should a gust of wind blow too hard, I'd probably topple over. Too many feelings stretch it wider and wider, hollowing me out even more.

I argue with Nour and Ola about the housework and about their routine. They don't help often, and when they do, it's like pulling teeth. They'll do half the job (and not well). They guilt me about their circumstances; not having a car, not having a routine, not having parents. I am not sure what I can do to help.

No one seems to appreciate how hard this is on me. I am the eldest; I have shared a lifetime of Mum's suffering. I am pregnant and motherless. Recently motherless. I've inherited a household of problems. I'm doing papers for the estate, making heartbreaking phone calls, lonely trips to the hospital, devastating baby-shopping experiences. Awkward conversations almost every single day.

I'm thirty-one weeks pregnant today. Nour is planning a baby shower that I only slightly want. I feel like manufacturing excitement will just make my big hollow worse. The more I ignore it the louder it screams. I am so far from everyone. I worry that my friends and relatives will never understand me again.

19 JUNE 2015

I had this dream last night.

She was sitting beside me, quietly, on my bed. She was dressed in grey with her legs curled up and her hair tied back, soft wisps around her forehead. I reached out and touched her glowing face. I spoke but did not recognise my voice. The words, 'I love you, Mummy,' come out of me in a child's voice.

Her face was pale and her eyes looked into the distance. I stood up and she suddenly seemed farther away. The room tilted out of focus. She said she wanted to tell me two things. I felt a sense of duty. I listened as hard as I could, but I couldn't retain what she was trying to say. She slipped away and I do not know what she said or what the two things were or what she needed me to do.

I've found it very hard to forget that dream.

*

Grief refused to shrink but trauma does an incredible job of re-focusing the mind. In the months after everything happened, I struggled to care about anything other than the discovery and articulation of truths about Mum's life. Some days, I saw my dad so clearly, it was like Mum's soul had stepped into my body. As if I was peering at him through her eyes. I couldn't mute the things she had said about how controlling he was, how harsh and inconsiderate he had been, how we, his children, would never know him the way she knew him.

Repressed and untold truths that had struggled to articu-late themselves immediately after the murder began to find a language. One memory in particular kept resurfacing. It was old but it was vivid and undeniable, and I couldn't understand why its relevance hadn't stood out to me sooner. Perhaps in trying so hard to understand the incomprehensible facts directly surrounding the murder, I had neglected pieces of information I'd collected years earlier, failing to recognise their relevance. I was so focused on my father's state of mind, angry at him for his betrayal, and protective of my family, that I had forgotten clear and important clues that Mum had given me.

Mum knew Dad had it in him. She hinted it enough times for me to feel mad at myself now, writing this, for not doing more. It was there in the days and weeks leading up to the murder. It was there each time they fought and every time he made her cry.

It was there in his disdainful glances and in his sarcastic, mocking tone. It was low level but persistent. It was there all along.

Having had time to re-read my childhood, I could see it. I pulled out my laptop one afternoon and started typing up the *little things*. Anything I could remember. I would need to give another statement to the police, and it would include this one particular *thing* from about fifteen years earlier. It was important enough at the time to have made me nauseous and nervous and unable to think all day at school.

It might not prove anything about my father's guilt or state of mind at the time of the murder. It might not even make it into evidence. But this memory demanded, at least, to make it onto the page.

TWENTY-ONE

As my due date crept up, the room I'd planned to use as a nursery remained a dusty storage space – until it became a dusty storage space with a cot in the corner. People had stopped calling, the flowers had dried up and my mind and home were crowded and dim. Clothes and junk accumulated in mounds around me. I wrote lists and ignored them. I bought things for the baby but simply stacked the shopping bags into a hollow bassinet until I had forgotten what was in them. I bought piles of grey (or, as I called it at the time, 'neutral') baby clothes. There was a white onesie with grey raindrops on it and a grey wrap covered in clouds.

I slowly felt more and more estranged from my father's family. They didn't contact me as often after my speech at the *arba'een*: I felt their support ended where my need for accountability began. That they didn't want me to talk about what had happened. That they didn't want me to write about it. That I wasn't supposed to get angry at my father or judge them for empathising with him. That I was expected to receive them as guests and behave as though nothing had happened.

'Please, wait until after the trial,' one amo begged over the phone.

'You're a lawyer, you're supposed to listen to the whole trial and be objective,' one amto wrote in a message. Her profile picture was a photo of Dad in his graduation robes.

In the meantime, I heard that some people were victim-blaming, that some had even sent 'proof' of an affair overseas – as though anything could justify my father's actions. Did they not know that he had been cruel and abusive to Mum before the murder? As though the murder wasn't enough evidence of that cruelty and abuse. The very document that had been sent overseas stated that there had, in fact, been no affair, and the police had already come to the same conclusion.

My amos and amtos were embarrassed about their brother being in prison awaiting trial. *I* was accused of being insensitive and hasty. Up until the *arba'een*, I'd never had conflict with my aunts and uncles, and had been raised to speak to them with courtesy. I didn't know how to express my distrust and frustration to them. When I confronted people about their defamation and victim-blaming, they gave conflicting explanations of who said and did what, or responded with flat-out denial. The fear that I would hurt someone or attract more hate by speaking up eventually silenced me. I was growing tired of fighting. I barricaded my anger and locked it up with my grief. I would not let it consume me, for the sake of my baby.

August drew closer and I did not attend a single birthing class. I didn't walk, I didn't stretch, and I didn't mop floors or wash towels. I wore Mum's old clothes as they were loose enough for my growing body. I distracted myself with food and television.

When people were around, I flicked my hair and laughed to prove I was fine. I didn't want to talk about Mum or the murder because people often said the wrong thing, like 'maybe this was meant to be' or 'forgive and you will feel better'. A thing can be true and still be the wrong thing to say to someone experiencing a unique and profound trauma. When no one was there, I returned to bingeing on fried food and sweets. Mood swings came in waves of outrage and loneliness, terror and hope. I dragged myself to the necessary hospital appointments and tracked the baby's growth with an app that uses fruit analogies until the baby's birth.

*

I spent my first night as a mother in hospital, alone. Visitors aren't allowed to stay overnight so when the nurse began checking the ward and dimming the lights, Moey went home and I spent the evening studying my baby. The first thing that surprised me about my newborn was the way she held eye contact; she was the small helpless thing, but here she was making me feel so vulnerable. The second night she surprised me with the way she could wail; she was the small helpless thing, but she would make her needs known. I practised breastfeeding her until the discomfort was no longer tolerable. I saw shadows in her eyes, another realm. I don't know where I got the idea, but by that second night I had convinced myself that my daughter had met my mother on her way into the world. I didn't dare say this out loud.

I had told the midwives about the murder so, through some mysterious process, the hospital organised a social worker to visit me in my bed. I played with my baby while she asked me questions about whether I had support and how I was feeling. Without looking at her, I told her that I was 'lucky' because I had a counsellor at the Homicide Victims Support Group, two sisters, a husband and good in-laws.

I didn't tell the social worker that my daughter had a portal to another world in her pupils. That she could read my mind.

I didn't tell her that I was part of a secret code. I knew something about the universe that she could not know.

*

My physical needs had been met as a child. Mum was attentive to how I looked, what I was learning, how I walked and how I sat. She wasn't always paying attention to my feelings, but she paid attention to everything else. Sometimes Mum was hyper-aware of my movements and appearance. She was especially strict with me out of fear of Dad's reprimands and finger-pointing. 'If something bad happens to you, if something goes wrong – I'll be blamed,' she said when I cried that I wasn't allowed to do this thing or that with my friends. 'Ask your father, I can't cope with the responsibility,' she would say.

Perhaps because all my tangible needs had been met, I hadn't given much thought to the practical and physical labour of motherhood until my daughter arrived. Instead, I had conceptualised motherhood as an intellectual endeavour; I would instil the right values, teach my child to read and write, to play, to love. They could be artists! I imagined my children as beautiful, passive things that I could cuddle and dress. I wanted five of them!

The first night we spent at home, the baby woke me with a suspected wet nappy. Within minutes she was red-faced and flailing with rage. Overwhelmed, I passed her to Moey who changed her as though he had done it a million times before. I watched, mystified.

*

Moey and I spent about three hours preparing for our first doctor's visit. My newborn seemed too small, clean and fragile for the world. I filled my carry-bag with way too many nappies. I'd never even changed a nappy before I had my own baby. I had no idea how many nappies to take.

In the mirror, my reflection was all straight lines and dark patches, now that the round was gone. I grabbed a coral scarf to wear around my neck but wrapped it around my head instead. It made me look grown-up, womanly. My reflection now reminded me of Mum. That was my first day of hijab. The doctor's rooms were in Auburn. Nobody looked twice.

Putting the baby to sleep, feeding her, dressing her: it was all tinged with pain and exhaustion. The baby wouldn't breastfeed properly. I read every single breastfeeding article I could find, tried every position and even hired a private lactation consultant who gave me a clear silicone nipple shield. I didn't like wedging this flying-saucer thing between myself and baby and it did nothing for the pain. One day a rim of fresh blood emerged in the nipple shield and I realised I wanted to quit breastfeeding.

I didn't know how long I'd been breastfed. This question triggered an obsessive curiosity about my own infancy. Had breastfeeding been a positive experience for *my* mum? I faintly remembered her saying it wasn't. My daughter was diagnosed with a tongue-tie. Did I have a tongue-tie? Had anyone checked? I stood in front of the mirror examining my mouth, wondering.

For all the ups and downs I was having, my daughter was a calm baby who seemed to love the repetition as much as I resented it. Her dark hair was already longer than her fingers. She sucked her dummy in a rhythm – suck-suck-suck-suck, pause, suck-suck-suck-suck, pause – like she was thinking hard. She stared at me all day and night with wide walnut-brown eyes and raised her eyebrows like she knew something I didn't know. There were a hundred flecks of light in her irises. If I watched her for too long, my throat would get tense and sore and I would have to look away.

Every night, I held my gorgeous bundle in my arms. She gazed into my eyes and I searched hers for clues about what kind of mother – and daughter – I needed to be. Had my mum looked at me that way? She, too, had given birth far from her mother. We argued and said mean things to each other when I was a teenager, but had our relationship once been as easy and unspoken as this? Would things have been different if she didn't have to deal with Dad? If she'd had her own parents around?

Apart from the compulsory trips to the doctor, I stayed home for a whole two months, surrounded by dirty laundry and dishes.

Every milestone in my daughter's life left questions about my own unanswered.

*

The feminism I'd been carving out for myself in the months before Mum's murder had begun to crystallise. The violence was so extreme and undeniable, and the response to it so dismal, that it had reframed everything for me. I found myself reflecting more and more on the messages I absorbed when I was younger. The feminism I absorbed as a teenager was fraught and inconsistent. At my selective all-girls high school we learned about women's rights and equality in the past tense, as though we had already achieved all there was to achieve. We were required to wear our skirts to the knee. Mum approved of that. Candy-striped tie, socks visible, no dangly earrings. Our textbooks showed black and white pictures of suffragettes in old-fashioned clothes and we applied a feminist reading to each of the classics (Discuss: Is a text feminist simply because it sympathises with women?). Tess of the D'Urbervilles told Angel that she wasn't a virgin. Sarah from *The French Lieutenant's Woman* pretended she wasn't a virgin even though she was. All this worry about chastity and reputation reminded me of things I'd overheard older women discussing over tea. They'd always lower their voices when they realised unmarried girls were listening.

A brown girl wore shorts and got with the white coach in *Bend It Like Beckham*. We watched it at school camp, cheering as the protagonist broke from tradition as though a teenager ending up with her soccer coach is any kind of break from patriarchy. I related to the film on some level, even though it didn't seem realistic how quickly Jesminder's parents got over things. My friends and I swooned, munching red frog lollies and braiding each other's hair. As we got into bed that night, the most blue-eyed white-haired girl in the grade (and one of my closest friends at the time) casually informed me I was going to hell if I didn't embrace Jesus. She was on the bunk above mine. I looked up at the bottom of her mattress, trying to think of a response that wouldn't make Muslims look bad – or worse, rather. 'I let you have the top bunk, dude' was all I could manage. We stayed friends throughout school even though, on another occasion, she told me she feared Lebs. That she feared me.

As seniors we learned to check for breast lumps, how to count standard drinks, the merits of a range of birth control options, and the side effects of various illegal drugs. No one talked about the damage caused by abuse or the different forms it could take or the side effects of living in the fumes of it. I don't remember anyone asking whether we could identify abuse, or whether we had witnessed it.

No one talked about barriers. At assembly, inspiring speakers told us, 'You are this country's future leaders,' and I had no doubt in my mind that one day everything was going to turn out fine because we were lucky young women living in a modern time. We weren't in Lebanon or Pakistan or Egypt. Even *I* could be Prime Minister.

I wonder how many of my classmates went on to accept poor treatment and infringements on our freedoms on the basis that, in another time or place, some other woman has it worse? How many of us accepted that this was as good as it would get? How many explained away injustice or unfairness through a series of at-leasts? *At least he doesn't mind you working, at least you get to finish your education, at least he doesn't hit you, at least he doesn't drink or gamble.* I raise my hand on all counts. I hadn't said enough to allow Mum to believe that she deserved better and that better was attainable. That's how low the standards were – and perhaps still are.

These poor standards were echoed in the questions and reactions I got from people.

When I said I was '*bint* Haydar Haydar', they said, 'Isn't he the one who killed his wife?' Like I was related to him and not her.

When I said, 'No, Mum isn't around to help with the baby, my dad killed her', they said, 'Do you know *why* he did it? Surely, he has an explanation.' Like there could be a good enough reason.

If I said, 'He's awaiting trial for murder', they asked, 'Do you visit him often?' Like there was any reason to visit him at all.

I tried to engage with these assumptions graciously. However, when the same attitudes were echoed on a national level by commentators who expressed shameless contempt for victims of violence, blaming feminism, 'welfare incentives' and women for 'having children to a string of feckless men' it was hard to be nice about it.

I tried to articulate my disgust on Twitter, drawing attention to the fact that these assumptions were harmful to people who had been impacted by abuse the way I had.

Within minutes someone had responded that they had lost their brother to violence by a Muslim 'gang', implying that I was, by extension, responsible for that violence.

I had only recently changed my Twitter profile picture to one of me in a hijab and had never mentioned my trauma there before. I'd forgotten that my appearance would affect my right to participate in conversations on gender-based violence. How could I have forgotten? People were so accustomed to correlating Muslims with violence that I wasn't allowed the compassion that might be extended to other victims. I wasn't even allowed an opinion about my own mother's death.

*

A few months after my daughter's birth, I found myself stuck in a fight with Centrelink. Apparently, I was ineligible for Parental Leave Pay because I had taken too much time off work after Mum's funeral. They had never warned of this risk or advised me to return to work to avoid prejudicing my claim, even though I had reported the violence to them within weeks of it taking place. After submitting my final paperwork, I was informed that my application fell five days outside of their 'work test', which requires the applicant to have worked for ten of thirteen months before their baby is born. There are exemptions for premature births and 'pregnancy-related illness' but there is no exemption for women who take extended time off because of bereavement or to deal with the consequences of domestic violence. I took a deep breath before calling them to challenge the decision. A polite woman was responding to my queries.

'So, you're telling me I would have received my benefits if my mum had been murdered five days later?' I snapped down the phone. My daughter was struggling to free her arm from her swaddle.

'Well, um, or if your baby had been born earlier.'

'So I'm being punished for things that are completely outside of my control!'

The woman explained the exemptions again.

'I'm a lawyer,' I said. 'I can read the legislation. The legislation *is* the problem. Look, this isn't your fault, but can I please speak to someone more senior?'

'I'm really sorry, there is no one else,' the woman replied. 'You can lodge a request for a review but there is no exemption for your circumstances.'

'This is – ugh – okay. Thank you,' I replied quietly.

I hung up.

Surely I wasn't the first pregnant person to have a domestic abuse–related reason for taking extra time off work? How many other women had been turned away in situations like mine?

I used my baby's blanket to rub tears from my face, took a deep breath, and texted Moey. 'No luck with CL. Bullshit. Gonna write a letter to someone.'

Suck-suck-suck-suck, pause – my daughter looked up at me from her rocker, both arms free now, stretching towards me. It was time to feed her again. I lifted her from her cradle, 'Hello, mama! Time to have some lunch.' I faked a cheerful tone. The hurt caused by the conversations I was having with people and institutions was physical. A whole-body tightness, a tingle in the palms of my hands, and a flush of heat through my forehead. Was I transmitting it to my daughter? It felt wrong to allow a baby to be so close to me when I was on fire.

At the same time, I was learning from these interactions. They were radicalising something in me. Women in my life had been killed, babies born, possibilities abandoned. I couldn't imagine returning to work. I had no parents, no extended family, limited community networks and, now that I wasn't working, no independent income. I couldn't relate to the past or get excited about the future. *It is as if he slayed all of humanity.*

I held my baby's bottle with one hand and scrolled through Facebook with another. Some days, the only conversations I had any tolerance for were the ones being had by women online. Women were talking about their feelings and experiences on pages and in articles in a way that made me whisper, 'Yes!' under my breath. The more I read, the more my anger started to find words, the more urgent it all seemed.

I was still following 'Counting Dead Women'. By the end of 2015, eighty-one women had been killed by a current or former partner in Australia, and Dad hating Mum enough to kill her didn't seem as unlikely as it once did.

TWENTY-TWO

'One on the outside and one on the inside!'

I laughed when I caught people looking at me with concern during my second pregnancy, which began before I'd recovered from the first. Somehow another baby didn't seem like a big drama in the existing chaos. I told myself that being mind-numbingly busy with a baby was better than vacuous depression, ignoring the fact I already had both. *Maybe this is how I'm meant to get through this.* I wasn't thriving as a mother, but my daughter still seemed as delighted with me as I was with her. Plus, there was something cute and novel about the idea of two-under-two. How much harder could it be?

I did what I could to prepare myself for the arrival of baby number two. I committed to my counselling with Jann at the HVSG, often taking baby number one with me. She'd crawl around and poo during my appointments. I talked about practical things because I didn't want to end up crying around my child. Through counselling and reading, I started to understand what was happening inside my body each time I was triggered.

I cut back time on social media and delegated any communications with Dad's side of the family to my husband.

I slept better and spent more time journalling. I didn't do these things because they brought me joy; I did them because they made my everyday responsibilities bearable. Somehow, by the time I was in my final trimester with my second baby, I had established a routine that allowed me to draw, paint and even knock over the 'Methodology of Islamic Jurisprudence' subject in my masters course.

Art was something I'd always loved but, in a family in which success was viewed through a traditional framework, it hadn't been valued as anything more than a hobby. In fact, it had been actively discouraged. I was regularly cautioned not to 'waste time' on art but I couldn't stop. Over the years, dots of paint accumulated on the shaggy beige carpet of my bedroom at Four-One-Six. And on my desk. And on my school uniform. I'd learned to entertain myself this way whenever I was stuck at home or fighting with my family. It was a coping mechanism that I'd relied on after losing Teta. And it resurfaced after my daughter's birth.

While one baby slept and the other grew in my belly, I sat like Humpty Dumpty on a cushion and spread my art supplies out on the floor. I drew women with yellow foreheads and pink cheeks. One image after another, their eyes became more exaggerated and oval-shaped, sometimes wide open, other times closed. Always sombre. I added tears that dripped down the page and sprayed beyond the margins. Sometimes I dressed my crying ladies in paisley-patterned hijabs, using one of my own as a reference.

Researchers have long recognised the role of creativity in processing traumatic events, especially when putting things into words proves disappointing or dangerous. Emotions associated with trauma are experienced in the right hemisphere of the brain. The left hemisphere, which is responsible for putting experiences into words, 'may struggle to make logic of the incoherence and attempt to form a logical story with words to describe the trauma'. Creativity, which occurs through the right hemisphere, 'provides alternative channels for communication that might have otherwise remained unprocessed'. For this reason, professionals have reported that 'creative arts therapies allow for repressed memories and feelings to surface and be processed in a way that is less threatening and at the client's own pace'.

I wasn't conscious that I was treating and healing myself through creativity or that, in doing this work, I was reclaiming my agency and my childhood. I simply enjoyed not needing to take instructions or gain permission or approval from anyone. These moments were all mine. All the complicated, banned, wordless emotions could come out to play as pictures without fear of repercussion. Creating made my arms feel loose and free. My traumatised, post-natal muscles relaxed. Fingers returned from numbness as they gripped brushes, slid over wet paint and rubbed charcoal into paper, which warmed in response. Thoughts slowed to a more manageable pace. Imagination, which seemed to have stopped at the time of the murder, came back during these creative moments. I could think *forward* again. Plan my next mark, control the outcome, master the process.

Between feeds and nappy changes, creative time was hard to come by. I maximised opportunities by making sure my supplies were always ready to go. I made my creative time non-negotiable; no number of dishes or mounds of unfolded laundry could encroach. I bought a trolley to store my supplies and set up a makeshift studio in my dining area. I made everything portable so that I could cart things around the house and hide them away when the baby was up. I kept a journal and took photos of inspiring patterns and objects. I started researching artists, techniques, styles and opportunities. There are so many people making beautiful things. I wanted to be a part of this.

I began sharing my work through an Instagram account, keeping quiet about Mum, Dad and the impending trial. This was an online safe space where I could enjoy the work of painters, poets and storytellers without being seen or talked about.

*

My Parental Leave Pay was eventually approved, but only after I had exhausted all avenues. I wrote to the relevant minister and sought the intervention of my local member of parliament. They didn't fix the legislative exemptions. They found a way to bend my story to fit one of their boxes.

What if I had not had the skills, knowledge or resources to pursue the matter further? What if I could not read or understand the rules or write to the appropriate people? What if I had been too tired to keep revisiting my trauma when I was already over-whelmed by the needs of my newborn?

To this day, pregnancy-related illness or premature birth are the only two available exemptions from the 'work test', and it wasn't until late 2018 that the government introduced five days (per year) of unpaid family and domestic violence leave as part of the national employment standards. So, a pregnant woman who has taken extra unpaid time off work due to abuse, separation from an abusive partner, or the loss of a loved one to domestic violence, risks losing her entitlement to paid parental leave.

We know that pregnancy is a risk factor for domestic abuse. We know that financial uncertainty is one of the reasons women may be reluctant to leave an abusive situation. This is a clear example of how policies fail to respond to known risk factors.

This was one of several examples where I was let down by the system. I'm sure I'm not the only one.

*

Nour sat on the end of the couch, holding a mug of tea in one hand and the television remote with the other. There was a pile of laundry between us. 'Hey, do you remember that Bankstown case? It happened like a year before Mum.'

'You're going to have to remind me,' I said, folding a towel into a square and placing it on the coffee table. Working full time in a newsroom, Nour was always up-to-date.

'Well, the guy – his name was George Tannous – killed his wife, and was found not guilty today.'

'Why not guilty?' I asked.

Nour pulled out her phone and after a few taps read out, '"NSW Supreme Court judge Jane Mathews found Tannous not guilty of murder by reason of mental illness following a judge-alone trial." It says he kept accusing his wife of cheating on him . . . she asked for a divorce, he killed her in the house and then went and handed himself in to police.'

'Shit.'

'The defence and the prosecution agreed with the psychiatrist who diagnosed him with a "major psychotic disorder he referred to as delusional jealousy or morbid jealousy",' Nour continued, still reading from her phone.

'What! I can't believe that someone can be diagnosed with that,' I said. 'How does the prosecution just agree?' I picked up a second towel.

'They're going to detain him indefinitely in a mental health facility. Apparently the woman's family aren't happy –' Nour added.

'Who would be? It's actually insulting.'

' – and his kids believe he's faking the disorder.'

We fell silent for a few minutes, both of us assessing the proximity of the facts of this case to the details of ours.

'What's the bet that so-called "morbid jealousy" is way more common in men,' I said, slamming the second folded towel on top of the first.

*

One week after my daughter's first birthday, I gave birth to my son in what the midwife at Bankstown Hospital called a 'textbook' delivery: dim lights, lots of at-any-other-time-ridiculous hip wiggling. I munched dates and chatted to Moey and Khalto between contractions. Khalto hadn't been there for my first labour but I made sure to invite her to this one. I drifted in a warm bath and imagined the baby floating out of me. I said no to morphine this time and didn't want an epidural either. The gas did nothing, so I sucked it hard and fast until it gave me head-spins. I hallucinated that Mum and Teta were living in a yellow tent on a green field. They were standing out the front of the tent and Teta had her palms facing the sky like she was making *dua* for me.

When it was time to push, I tossed the gas pipe aside and screamed through shifting bone and cut flesh. I reached down and touched my son's head, which was damp and fuzzy like a kiwi fruit, before letting out a few more screams. I didn't care if all of Bankstown could hear me. Maybe pain should be heard.

After a full twenty-four hours of labour my son was born. I was in awe of my plump baby who frowned up at me like he was a little surprised to be there. I was in awe of my body; that it had travelled right to the edge and returned intact, again. *Alhamdulillah*. I felt stronger, more focused than I was with my first. Khalto patted me on the back, then Moey took the newborn from me and I rested. The small steps I had taken to look after myself were paying off. More importantly, however, I had stopped appeasing Dad's family. This baby had very few visitors and a calmer, more confident mother.

I welcomed the quiet.

*

In late 2016, I started thinking about the trial again. It was set down for hearing in early 2017. The feeling of doom crept back. I had worked so hard to lift myself out of the horror. Why wouldn't Dad just plead guilty and let us get on with our lives?

The Crown kept us loosely updated about progress in the case. There had been a series of mentions and my father was seen by two psychologists; one instructed by his lawyers and another instructed by the Crown. The psychologists opined that he had 'mild to moderate depression'. I rolled my eyes as a solicitor told me this over the phone.

'Depression doesn't turn people into killers,' I told her. 'I think he was capable of this all along.'

'Whether he can make out a defence of substantial impairment will be a matter for the jury,' she said.

If established successfully in court, the defence would reduce the charge of murder to one of manslaughter and that, in turn, could result in a lesser sentence. Even though this information was no surprise to me, the conversation triggered the usual numb arms, heavy legs and all-consuming thoughts. These physical symptoms were occurring whenever my still-healing psychological wound was aggravated by stress, new developments or reminders of *that day*. I wanted to drive fast to the cemetery, but there were babies to care for and dinners to be made.

The supplementary statement I drafted months earlier sat unprinted, unsigned and deliberately forgotten on my computer. It contained this crucial *thing*, this memory, this Big Secret. It felt wrong, traitorous even, that I hadn't thought to mention this thing in my first statement – no matter how valid my reasons were at the time. With the trial so close, it seemed vital that this *thing* make it into the proceedings. It was my duty as my mum's eldest child, as an officer of the Court, as a woman of faith, to make sure it did. It might help the Court appreciate what Mum had gone through.

Yet, I hesitated. I wasn't sure I was brave enough to speak explicitly about abuse. I was still getting used to calling it *abuse*. Could I really sit in a courtroom with my father present and talk about it to his face?

Growing up, I assumed that everyone was faced with similar loyalties and taboos around family, relationships and divorce. Gradually, it became clear that the environment I had lived in was not normal. My friends' families – including those who shared my religious identity and culture – didn't seem as fragile and tumultuous as mine. My own partner loved me without making me feel like I needed to watch my words or tip-toe around his reactions. Ultimately, the accumulating crimes of my male family members tore away any remaining delusion that they were simply *overprotective* because they cared about me. Why did their care have to be painful? Why did it have to be isolating? In my first statement, I had told the police that my parents were 'incompatible'. But clearly what existed in our household was more than incompatibility between partners, more than stress, more than marital conflict. It was – and even as I type these words my heart jumps like I am misbehaving – a subtle but persistent level of coercion and control. The things I wanted to share in my second statement had taken place over a long period and felt normal at the time.

They were examples of how volatile Dad could be. They were examples of why I believed Mum was fearful of leaving him.

I understood now that the control came from my father and was reinforced by the pressures of living in a close-knit community; *What will people say?* It manifested as irrational and inconsistent rules about what was right and wrong. There was only ever a blade's width between praise and condemnation. Mum tried hard to pre-empt Dad's shifting disapprovals and even internalised his expectations. Worrying constantly that one day I would make some kind of life-destroying mistake, I, too, worked hard to maintain my family's praise and approval. Had controlling behaviours and implicit violent threats not been so normalised – even romanticised – by the world around me, these memories might have come to mind while I was giving my first statement. Had I known the prevalence of homicides by men without a history of physical violence, I might have made the connections sooner. Had they not been so taboo, so hush-and-move-on, I would have known that what Mum had told me and what I had observed were abuse. Abuse. Abuse. Abuse.

I needed to get the *thing* off my chest. It was a part of Mum's story, a source of fear and vulnerability. It couldn't have been the only thing. How many things had she kept to herself? How many other things had he said and done that she was too ashamed or embarrassed to tell anyone? How many red flags had seemed too minor or silly to mention, like the wedding celebrations she forfeited? How many things were too *'ayb*, too heavy, too disturbing, too mind-boggling to say out loud?

*

As the trial date drew closer, we were informed by the Crown that my dad was offering to plead guilty to manslaughter. If the Crown agreed, the matter would go straight to sentencing without the need for a trial. If not, the trial would run and Dad would have to prove his 'substantial impairment' defence in order for the charge of murder to be reduced to manslaughter.

My sisters and I were called into the Prosecutor's office for a meeting. The fact that the Crown was considering the plea with any level of seriousness gave me palpitations and hot flushes. We'd been careful not to discuss the details of our respective statements, but we were all convinced, in our own ways, that our father had acted deliberately and that the matter should proceed to trial.

'Do you think they'll accept the plea?' Ola asked.

'I'm not sure,' I answered.

'Does it even matter what we say?' Nour tested with an eyebrow raised.

'I think they have to hear us out, but the final decision is theirs to make. Let's just see what happens at this meeting.'

When we arrived at the Office of the Director of Public Prosecutions (ODPP), we were introduced to Janine, a friendly witness assistance officer with short curly hair. We also met the Crown Prosecutor Mr Michael Barr, and his assisting solicitor Arnold.

We sat in a circle in a cluttered office. Mr Barr informed us that the Crown consults with victims and family members before accepting a plea.

'The Crown is not bound by what victims want but is required to take it into consideration,' he explained.

I reiterated what I had told the Crown solicitors previously. 'We don't believe this was manslaughter. We're not convinced that our dad killed our mum because he was depressed. Depression doesn't cause people to commit murder. Honestly, we're all depressed!' I drew circles in the air to indicate I meant everyone in the room. 'He just didn't accept that Mum was leaving him.'

If he'd had no self-control, why did he attack Mum and not Ola? If he truly couldn't think straight, how on Earth did he read a ticket, find a gate, board a plane, change over in Dubai, board another plane, make his way home to Valda Street where he had waited for Mum? If he had never given it any thought, then why had he said and done things in the past that made Mum afraid?

I had already flagged with the ODPP – just as I had said to Jann and the police at different points in time – that I wanted the opportunity to provide more information. No one had expressed a sense of urgency about it. I, too, had put it off. Now I could see we were running out of time, and the *thing* felt more important than ever.

'Mr Barr, I've already started writing a supplementary statement – can I still provide it?'

He agreed and said he'd organise for it to be collected by the police.

*

As a commercial litigator I was trained to meticulously review statements and affidavits. It was my job to make sure they were abundantly clear, ask questions about inconsistencies and seek supporting documents or other corroborating information. If there was uncertainty about the admissibility of a piece of information, it was part of my job to look into the steps needed to overcome that or even find alternative ways to put important information before the court. However, in adversarial legal systems, victims and their families are not a party to the proceedings and don't have their own lawyers. A criminal matter is prosecuted on behalf of the public, out of the public pocket, within guidelines and limited resources. Where possible, police take statements on the spot on the basis that facts are fresh in the witness's mind and to prevent people from preparing or changing their version of events. This method is valid in a range of crimes; however, in the aftermath of a domestic homicide, are witness accounts really as reliable as they could be? When the accused murderer is a familiar person, a loved one, can a witness really be expected to immediately provide the most frank and relevant evidence to a stranger in a uniform?

At home, I read over my supplementary statement, straining my memory to make sure the details and observations were clear. Would this information help my father's family understand the situation better, or would it make them more hostile? Would it be worth all the fear and conflict if it didn't actually make any difference in the proceedings? Would this late statement cast doubt on the credibility of my first? Would my father just deny it all? I knew that there was no way to capture Mum's experiences in a document like this. Nor was it my job as a victim and witness to worry about the admissibility of my own evidence. Still, I fussed over my fragmented memories. Why hadn't I asked Mum more questions at the time? Why hadn't I paid more attention? I punched some final edits into my keyboard with my right hand, picking and biting furiously at my left thumb.

When I finally handed my statement to the detective on my front porch at the end of 2016, I was aware that it didn't comply with all of the rules of evidence. It included observations about how Mum was feeling at certain points in time and references to my father's attitudes and tendencies that couldn't really be used to prove his intention at the time of the murder. The part about the *thing* was technically hearsay, since Mum wasn't available to tell it to the Court herself. But I had paid enough attention in law school to know that this didn't necessarily make it inadmissible. The Crown would have to serve a hearsay notice and follow certain rules and procedures in order to rely on my evidence.

I trusted that the Prosecutor would see the significance of this statement, which I had agonised over for months, and know what to do with it.

*

One of my new year's resolutions for 2017 was to make more art. I wrote down the due date for the next Archibald Prize. I didn't paint anyone and eventually missed the deadline. I wrote down the due date for every upcoming local art prize and missed all of them.

TWENTY-THREE

January was hot and Mum's Valda Street villa sat vacant and full of stuff. There was no running water and the garden was overgrown. We weren't legally able to do anything with her estate until the criminal proceedings were complete. The last thing I wanted to do with two babies in the middle of a sticky summer was rummage through Mum's old belongings, but Khalto and Nour convinced me that it was time we finished the clean-up. 'It's only going to get dustier,' they pleaded.

It wasn't a bad idea. My brother had been released from prison, having served his sentence, and was keen to sell the property. My sisters were eager to move out of my place, and I was beginning to feel the stress of living on a single income with nappies and formula to buy every other day. We could all use a little cash. So, in anticipation that we would have a trial and a judgment soon, I instructed some lawyers to begin the paperwork. I also found myself at Valda Street sorting Mum's old clothes into 'keep' and 'donate' piles. Some items still had tags attached. I gathered her boots, a fluffy red bathrobe and the last outfit I had seen her in alive and piled them into my car. I looked around the kitchen with my hands on my hips and swore I'd never accumulate as much junk as she had. And yet I still hauled half of it home with me, because it reminded me of freshly cut lemons and Mum chopping *tabbouleh* in the summer.

Dad had packed and moved his things out of Valda before the murder and before leaving for Lebanon, but I found two tubs of old books – bilingual dictionaries and translation guides that had belonged to him. 'All these books and all that reading, for what?' I hissed under my breath as I moved the boxes into the rubbish pile. I changed my mind and moved them to the donation pile, then to my car. Cockroaches must have travelled to my place with the salvaged books, and within a few weeks we were dealing with an infestation. It had to be a bad omen.

*

I prepared for the trial by calling Mum's family members and giving them an update. I let my khaltos and khalos in Lebanon, Germany and Canada know that they could come to the trial if they wanted. But it was too hard for Mum's siblings to get here. They had families and problems of their own.

There was a series of interlocutory hearings in the weeks leading up to the trial. There had been some debate about my second statement, whether it was admissible, and for what purpose it would be used. I didn't know what that meant in terms of the trial, and I was growing tired of mentally problem-solving the case. I wasn't attending the proceedings, but I gathered my second statement had upset my father's family. My dad denied the claims in my statement. I heard that some family members thought I was selfish for wanting my dad to face trial, that my father had always 'fulfilled his duties as a father', that he was 'a victim too'.

The Crown informed us that Dad had applied for a judge-alone order to have the trial heard without a jury. Within this application he had contested the 'relationship evidence' in my supplementary statement, arguing that it was not admissible and was likely to prejudice a jury against him. I wasn't sure what his objections would mean in terms of my second statement and the *thing*. Tired of trying to pre-empt and mentally problem-solve the case, I remind myself that it was up to the Crown to establish the case against Dad, and I was just a witness. This did nothing to relieve the burden I felt as a daughter.

*

The judge-alone application was unsuccessful. Justice Garling, who was presiding over the matter, had acknowledged the significance of some of the concerns raised, but concluded that it was in the interests of justice that the matter proceed to a jury trial. This would allow the Court to consider the 'role and place of domestic violence in our society' and the 'role and place of cultural views with respect to the relationships between people born into cultures different to our own'.

I couldn't help but feel frustrated and nervous as a result of developments like these in the lead-up to the trial. As a lawyer, I believe unequivocally in the right to a fair trial. Even for my father. It's a cornerstone of both Islamic and Western legal traditions that even those accused of the most serious offences be given access to good legal representation, tried by their peers, and afforded the right to speak or be silent. However, on a moral level I was disgusted that this killer, who had never offered a proper apology, could be so arrogant as to claim every delay and indulgence that the (already biased against women) system could offer. As a daughter, I felt certain that these tactics were an extension of the abuse he had carried out against Mum and, in turn, an act of abuse against us.

Even as I acknowledged all this, a fragment of me remained connected to my father. This part of me held on to the little things; a whistling firecracker Dad brought home on my sixteenth birthday, the sour mulberries we picked together on our walks through Bexley gully, laughing at some silly joke until there were tears in the corners of Dad's eyes and we both couldn't breathe, the rose I pinned to his lapel on my wedding day. This part of me believed that Dad was just biding his time, working on something behind the scenes. He would sweep in at the last minute and turn it all around. He could still say sorry. He could still plead guilty and make this huge scary thing smaller.

Baba could do that for us if he loved us.

TWENTY-FOUR

The trial commenced on Monday 20 February 2017.

It was a muggy morning and I had the jitters right down to my bones. I dressed myself, trying not to scream at how ludicrous it felt to apply makeup and pin my hijab on a day like today; the beginning of the end.

I carefully gathered my children's things into their bags, but by the time we dropped them off at my in-laws I felt like I was forgetting something. Moey and I caught the train from Granville into the city, holding hands but barely talking. The next thing I remember is emerging from the ground at St James Station into the bustle and sticky air of Queen's Square. I focused on my feet as we made our way over to the sandstone courthouse on King Street. Leaves had started to turn brown and fall to the grey pebble ground. Cameras swivelled to face us as we approached the front of the court, preparing to get a shot of the sad people who were turning up to play their part in the macabre production that was about to unfold. My hijab felt tighter and heavier than usual. *Just keep walking. Stay calm and keep walking.*

I had spent a lot of time around Queen's Square as a solicitor, scuttling between my office and the courts, filing documents at the registries and conferencing with barristers in their nearby chambers. Now, standing in front of the Supreme Court, waiting for my dad's trial to start, I felt like a different person. An outsider. Looking up at the Law Courts Building, I counted twenty-four levels to the floor where I observed an appeal to the High Court just a few years prior, oblivious to the crime that was hurtling towards me. That matter felt incredibly important at the time but today it seemed petty. For that appeal, we had briefed one of Australia's most renowned barristers, Bret Walker AO SC. His chambers (also a short walk from where I now stood) were filled with art, books and a collection of vessels and vases – big, small, glass, ceramic – all sitting on shelves along both sides of the room. *I'll have an office like this someday*, I had thought to myself as I stared around at the artefacts.

I can't pinpoint when I lost touch with that image of myself, but it was gone by the time we arrived at the Supreme Court. How had I been so confident? Back then I believed that I could accumulate knowledge and experience and status and wealth and reputation. Today I was a footnote in my father's cataclysmic offence. In *Eggshell Skull*, Bri Lee talks about looking down from the Brisbane Law Courts at the constellation of crimes that were spread over the city beneath her. Sheltering by the brick and sandstone arches of the courthouse, I imagined my past self gazing down at the scared girl I had become. A tiny speck in the constellation. Unrepresented, a non-party, a mere witness in these proceedings.

There was a long wait ahead, Mr Barr explained as we huddled around him under the brick arches. He and his instructing solicitor had a friendly and casual way of talking about the case, which irritated me.

'They've probably done a hundred of these,' I whispered to Ola and she nodded. Nour stood next to her with her arms crossed.

Mr Barr explained what we should expect over the coming days. Detective Taylor and Detective O'Riley, the detectives who had been investigating the case, stood nearby. They seemed a little more sensitive than the lawyers, maybe because they see the everyday stuff and not just a file. They talked to us and gave us updates about what was happening behind the closed doors of Courtroom 2. Khalto, a couple of Mum's cousins and some close friends stood with my sisters, Moey and me. I appreciated their presence and Mum would have too. We were joined by Janine, our witness assistance officer, and Jann, who had come out of retirement for the proceedings.

I was always happy to see Jann. As we sat, waiting for the trial to begin, she asked me how I was feeling.

'I'm not sure,' I answered. 'I guess I still have a tiny bit of hope he'll just plead guilty, at least to save my sisters and me from having to go through all this. Maybe he still loves us just enough to do that.'

Jann looked at me with a downturned mouth and said, 'Now, I love you for believing that could be possible. But I want you to know that, in all the years that I've been doing this work, that has never happened. The people who are capable of a homicide, the people who get to this stage, have nothing left to lose.'

I sighed. She was right. What did Dad have left to lose? I had told myself that some great self-sacrificial gesture would make it possible for me to forgive him. It was a desperate hope. One that was born out of my fear of the trial and all the ways it would be painful and triggering, rather than any genuine faith in my father.

At the other end of the courthouse's long gusty veranda gathered Dad's family – who were supposed to be our family too.

They paced and chatted, occasionally glancing in our direction. We did not know they would all be here. We had not asked them to come. Even my female cousins were there, though it was clear that they were not there for us.

We were advised to wait outside while the proceedings commenced. Witnesses aren't supposed to sit in on the proceedings until they've given their evidence. It was a tedious wait. I scrolled through my phone, walked up and down King Street. Had a coffee. Scrolled some more. At around lunch time, Mr Barr emerged from the front doors of the court, robes ballooning. We gathered around him. He explained that a jury had already been empanelled but had to be discharged because of an issue with one of the jurors. I groaned as Mr Barr explained that there would be more waiting. No one would give their evidence today. Everyone was to go home and come back the following morning to start all over again.

*

That afternoon, the news reported that a decomposed body had been found in bushland at the base of Mount Macedon in Victoria. There was speculation that this could be the body of Karen Ristevski, who had been missing since 29 June 2016. Her husband was being interviewed by police.

*

A new jury was empanelled the next day. Again we waited outside, expecting Ola to be called in to give evidence first; again we shot dirties across the veranda; and again the Prosecutor swept over to where we stood to tell us that the jury had been discharged.

'I have never seen two juries dismissed in two days, my whole career!' Mr Barr said. 'Your father's lawyers have indicated they will re-open their application for a judge-only trial.'

Then he added, 'We're thinking that it might be appropriate to proceed judge-alone.'

'Okay, well, if it's such a rare occurrence, I think I'm prepared to accept it as some kind of sign,' I said slowly, turning to my sisters. Nour frowned, hands on hips. Ola slouched her shoulders and dropped her head to one side. We'd already spent two days captive on the steps of the court.

After hearing submissions from the parties that afternoon, Justice Garling accepted that, at this point, it would be appropriate for the trial to proceed without a jury. I accepted that there could be some divine wisdom in this. We didn't have the power to contest it anyway.

At the time, my understanding was that, during His Honour's opening remarks, some members of the jury appeared distracted and disinterested. Another had flagged that they wouldn't be able to bring an impartial mind to the proceedings.

I did not read, until recently, the material pertaining to that decision. When I did, I discovered that there was also a concern that the trial would be too distressing for some jurors because of 'particularly graphic photographs of the post-mortem examination'. I also discovered the distressing contents of the emergency call Ola made as Mum lay beside her. The details are publicly available, so to recount them all here would be both painful and gratuitous. But I want the world to know that Haydar Haydar left Salwa Haydar – his wife of twenty-eight years, the once seventeen-year-old girl he had chosen from a family who shared his surname and hometown, and the mother of his four children – on the floor of her home, bleeding from thirty stab wounds, begging that help would come quick. Know that he walked away and left his injured eighteen-year-old daughter to salvage whatever life was left in that little villa. Know that even his own lawyers argued that it was unlikely any jury would be able to see the disturbing photos or sit through Ola's panicked triple-O call and Mum's final gasps.

*

In granting the judge-alone order, Justice Garling pointed to the 'disharmony which arises in some cases between the norms of traditional practicing Muslims and the norms of the majority non-Muslims in the community'. His Honour's words seemed to reflect Dad's argument – which construed Muslim attitudes as *other* – rather than challenge them.

In re-opening his application for a judge-alone trial, Dad had argued that a jury might be prejudiced against him as a 'traditional Lebanese Muslim'. He argued that, because Mum was younger and no longer wearing a hijab, the jury would use this information to make assumptions against him. The 'good Muslim woman / bad Muslim woman' dichotomy that Dad and his lawyers presented in support of this application was reductive and exploitative. Reductive in that the argument implied that my mum was less Muslim than my father, often referring to her decision not to wear a hijab as evidence of this. Exploitative because my father was seeking to benefit from a stereotype that he previously disassociated himself from; pretending he was Greek and Orthodox when asked by a stranger, making fun of his brothers whose English had remained poor while he became a linguist, refusing to come to Islamic talks with us when Mum invited him.

Of course, Arab and Muslim men in Australia have experienced prejudice within the legal system. I have witnessed the effects of their criminalisation firsthand – in my own family, through study, and in my work with young people. Men born in Lebanon are one of the most over-represented groups in the Australian prison population. I've talked to women who have had their homes raided, mums and sisters who advise their boys to always speak politely to the officers lest they be taken away, women who have had to work extra hard to keep a family afloat after the breadwinner has been imprisoned. Arab and Muslim women have turned up for Arab and Muslim men and have been vocal for them, even though they haven't done the same for us. We have sacrificed time, autonomy and big dreams for them. Arab and Muslim women should be able to critique the system for the harm it has done and still be able to access it in a crisis. We deserve to take a dignified stand when it comes to our victimisation. There should be room for us to acknowledge the injustices that men of colour have faced and still seek justice for ourselves. Dad was a well-read, articulate person who was neither young nor vulnerable in terms of the prison population. His judge-only application irked me because I knew he was as interested in defaming Mum as avoiding prison. Dad was wielding harmful stereotypes as a shield against the law and a sword against Mum.

And what guarantee was there that a jury would desire justice for Mum when people she'd known her whole life had stayed silent? Why would the jury's biases stop at Dad? A jury might be prejudiced against Arab and Muslim men, but that doesn't mean they'll care about a dead Muslim woman. We are seen to have subscribed to our own oppression; not entitled to victimhood because we aren't allowed to claim innocence in the first place. Maybe this had informed Mum's decision to cease wearing a hijab after the assault to her eye. Maybe she got tired of having her complaints being understood only as a Muslim problem rather than a gender problem.

While Dad's case had a cultural flavour, it was essentially no different to what many men of diverse backgrounds had claimed before him: I was substantially impaired, I believed she was having an affair, I lost control. There is nothing culturally unique about this reasoning.

Our laws have allowed this victim-blaming to take place in murder trials. Until it was abolished in some Australian jurisdictions and redefined in others, the partial defence of provocation gave formal weight to these narratives. Vicki Cleary and Manpreet Kaur were both killed by men who would go on to allege infidelity and successfully rely on the partial defence of provocation to evade murder charges. Their killers secured short sentences with Peter Keogh serving only three years and eleven months for the murder of Vicki Cleary in 1987. In 2012 Chamanjot Singh argued that his wife's decision to leave him 'caused him to lose self-control' and received a six-year sentence for killing Manpreet Kaur, whose family expressed disbelief: 'How can you say this is manslaughter?'

The Singh case triggered an inquiry in New South Wales, and the law was amended in 2014 to restrict the provocation defence and prevent it from being used by 'people who kill their partners out of jealous rage'. I read about this change shortly after Dad's arrest. It was a small blessing to know that this defence was no longer available in cases like ours.

TWENTY-FIVE

The veranda of the courthouse is a limbo between lives that have been brought to a stop by violence and the busy streets of the city where lives rattle on. This was the fourth morning I'd spent hanging around the front of the court, journalling, rolling my eyes at my relatives and writing bad poetry.

She.

She is alive in us.

They say I have her laugh.

Her breath is in my lungs.

From time to time, the Prosecutor or someone else from our 'side' would emerge with an update about what was happening in the courtroom. This morning, Nour was inside giving her evidence. Between Dad's family waiting around the courthouse and media still lined up at the front, I was starting to feel caged.

Ola was off somewhere, having given lengthy testimony the day before, the full details of which I would not know until I skimmed the transcripts years later, while writing this book.

Ola's narration of the events of 30 March 2015 started with a familiar sequence: Dad had been spending some nights on the couch; Mum told him to pack his things from Valda before leaving for Lebanon to see his mother; Ola saw him packing his books from the bookcase. They were the books I'd found in boxes at Valda. The only compensation I'd ever get from Dad and the suspected source of my cockroach infestation.

I pushed myself further into Ola's evidence. Mum had told Dad to leave the keys to Valda behind, but when she checked she didn't find them. This detail was new to me. Dad let himself back in on the morning of the thirtieth, and to Ola he seemed 'just off'. A photo of the beige couch in Mum's lounge room was tendered into evidence, and the transcript told me that Ola was upset by the image. His Honour asked if she'd like a break. Ola sipped some water and continued. Sitting on that crime-scene couch, Dad had started telling Ola that he'd never been unfaithful. He swore he'd never been unfaithful. She described him as 'frantic'. Ola then headed off to university for the day and, although she'd normally make her own way home, Mum picked her up in the evening. Mum knew Dad was back but hadn't seen him yet. When they got home, Dad was still there, on the couch, when he should have been in Lebanon or at his own place. Ola observed that he seemed tired. Mum had been at work all day and immediately started to prepare dinner. She asked Dad to get the oil, which was stored in the garage. She was annoyed and her tone was 'sharp'. She expressed frustration. Why had he returned to her house? Why didn't he leave the keys like she'd instructed? Dad yelled back in Arabic, 'I'm not sleeping here tonight. I'm not sleeping here tonight.' The tone didn't come across in the transcript, but when I hear the phrase in my head, the words sound like a threat, not a fact. *He knows he's going to gaol. He doesn't care.*

Ola continued, 'I don't remember what I was doing, but I heard my mum scream. That's the next thing I can remember . . .

I remember thinking, *I think he hit her* and then I ran . . . to the kitchen. My mum was backed up in a corner and he'd stabbed her in her back.' Ola saw the knife and it was unfamiliar. Ola tried to fight him off and, when she tried to grab the knife blade-side, it sliced through her finger, causing damage to the ligament.

Ola became entangled in Dad's violence. 'I tried to get in the middle of it . . . to pull him away from her.' The scuffle moved into the living room where Ola started yelling, 'You need to stop, what are you doing? You are going to kill her – screaming, screaming for help.' At one point, Dad called Mum the Arabic word for a slut while she denied his accusations. 'Haydar, I didn't do anything. I didn't do anything.'

Undone by these details, I turned away from the page. *He had no right. He had absolutely no right.*

Feeling helpless against the attack, Ola went to the telephone, but this didn't deter Dad. He didn't stop attacking Mum, even after pausing several times. Finally, he picked up a briefcase and left while Ola was still on the phone.

There was no need for Ola to go into the details of her triple-O call. Justice Garling, and several people in the courtroom, had already heard it.

*

In cross-examination, Ola was asked whether there were other 'physical altercations' between our parents. She told the Court that Dad 'may have tried to push her once . . . I am not even sure'. Ola was asked whether she had seen 'bruises or marks'. She hadn't. *Nor have I.*

As I read through the rest of the cross-examination, I noticed a frustrating focus on the absence of evidence of past physical abuse. There were no questions about any other kinds of abuse – and even if there were, they would not be corroborated by police records or hospital records, because coercive control is not a crime in any Australian jurisdiction, nor does it constitute a medical emergency, nor had anyone seen a threat in Dad's behaviour over the years even as it slowly chipped away at Mum's emotional wellbeing. Mum was not there to correct the record or to tell us exactly how injured she was by Dad's words. Her story was buried with her, and whatever clues she left us with were hearsay, objectionable, nearly impossible to resurrect.

*

Waiting for Nour, I paced the veranda, knowing I was next. I thought about my former self, taking photos at my admission ceremony, a few years prior, across Queen's Square with two beaming parents. I remembered my young colleagues and I listening with pride and idealism as Chief Justice Thomas Bathurst gave a speech about our roles and responsibilities as officers of the Court. I don't remember his exact words, but I know it was everything I wanted to hear. Justice. Justice. Justice.

At about quarter-to-eleven, cameras lining the footpath in front of the court pivoted to the doorway. Nour stepped out. She walked quickly like always but her eyes were red and her head was down, curtained by her slick black bob. Before I could ask Nour anything, Detective O'Riley said, 'Amani, you've been called.' I took a deep breath.

Ola gave me a quick hug and said, 'Good luck.' Nour patted me on the shoulder and whispered, 'You'll be fine.' Khalto stroked my forearm and smiled with her head tilted. Jann must have been with me and a court officer must have escorted us but, in my memory, I am alone as my boots clip-clop over the chessboard tiles of the dim courthouse foyer towards Courtroom 2. *Bismillah, bismillah, bismillah.* The words gave me a rope to hold on to, something to pull myself forward with. I wore my favourite maroon hijab with a black-and-white polka-dot dress that belonged to Mum. I thought about the way Mum used to walk: swift strides, head held high. I felt big and clumsy but also reassured wrapped in Mum's garment, confident that this was the most important thing I could do for her, my sisters and myself.

Finally, I pushed through the creaky wooden doors. *Bismillah, bismillah, bismillah.* Conscious of every step and shaking on the inside, I paused, bowed, and continued towards the bench. His Honour Justice Garling sat before me in festive red robes and a white wig. Behind him were tall glass windows, which threw light into the room, making the space cathedral-like; more ceremonial than the sleek courts I'd practised in across the Square. I passed rows of elevated pews intended to be used by the public. Today, the public were my own family. Eyes burned into my back as I stepped up into the witness box. My stomach jolted like the carriage at the top of a Ferris wheel.

Standing in the witness box, I noticed the gated section to His Honour's left where *the accused* – my dad – sat. I made eye contact with him. Square-jawed and yellow-eyed, he was wearing his best suit. *Is that the one he wore to my wedding?* It was stone-coloured. Pumice. His hair was full and silver against his taxi-driver tan, which had persisted through his time on remand. He sat upright, shoulders broad and straight. He was far from the sick, scrawny, old man he was rumoured to have become. He was fine. *A real-life murderer looks just like a normal man.* Maybe it was all the *Macbeth* and *King Lear* we'd studied in school, but in the two years I'd waited to see my dad, I often imagined a man weak with regret and floundering for forgiveness. Ola said he'd cried throughout her evidence and I expected that our reunion would be emotional too. However, I felt nothing. He was groomed and composed. He seemed annoyed. A slight frown, lips sealed, eyes shifting side to side. *What is that expression?* I looked straight at him and asked telepathically, *How could you?* He didn't flinch. His gaze made my hijab feel tight and my legs warm with adrenaline. My confidence was slipping away. *You're a mother now, a grown woman. The worst has already happened, you're just here to talk about it.*

From the witness box I could see the faces of uncles, cousins and more cousins. I'd spotted my brother earlier but couldn't see him now. I saw Amo's moustache twitching and, next to him, his son frowning so hard I could see his upper teeth. Dad's nieces sat in a row towards the front, their legs crossed, handbags in their laps and red lips pulled into tight sideways smiles. I felt stung; we were friends, shared the same house, cried over the same war, ate Mum's food together.

In front of His Honour's bench was a long wooden bar table where Mr Barr and Dad's barrister, Mr John Stratton SC, shuffled through files. They were draped in black and had their wigs on. At the back of the room was a mezzanine level. I guessed from the notebooks and laptops that the people up there included journalists and law students. I remembered one of my last university assessments where we'd been assigned the task of observing court proceedings. Moey and I had taken the opportunity to meet at Burwood Court where we watched lawyers argue their cases, wrote some notes, then drove to Drummoyne to get seafood at a shop that professes to have 'the best fish and chips in the universe'. I couldn't believe how complicated our lives had become since then.

I had seen people swear oaths in court many times and had even done it myself once before, when I gave a character reference in my brother's case. Still, I was so distracted by the competing threats in the room that I was startled when the court officer held a book up to me. She handed it to me on a piece of dark silk and asked me to confirm that it was a true copy of the Quran. I lifted the front cover and fanned out a few pages, witnessing flashes of black calligraphy. They, witnessing me.

I put my hand on the cool cover of The Book and, as I took my oath, I remembered the verse, *O you who have believed, be persistently standing firm in justice, witnesses for Allah, even if it be against yourselves or parents and relatives . . .*

*

'Thank you, Madam. Please replace the book into the cover and return it to the Court Officer, and have a seat when you're ready,' His Honour said as I lifted my hand from The Book.

As I sat down something beautiful sat with me, in my body. Mum's spirit perhaps.

I felt a little lighter, shielded from the gaze of my disapproving family members. *They're here for a murderer, you're here for justice.*

I turned to Mr Barr who would be leading me through my evidence in chief. He started by confirming my name, age, and the fact that I was the daughter of the accused. Then he handed up a copy of my statement from the night of the murder.

I placed it on the wooden desk in front of me and looked back to Mr Barr for guidance. When he got to paragraph four of my statement, he said, 'You say that growing up you would not describe Mum and Dad as compatible?' I confirmed with a 'yes'.

'You say they were never physically violent towards each other but there was always a lot of resentment?'

'Yes.'

'You thought your mum and dad had a large age gap of about 13 years, and that made it hard for them to get along?'

'Yes.'

Mr Barr went on through the facts at the beginning of my statement: the fact that I thought Mum was too young when she first got married. The fact that I thought my parents 'were just completely different in personalities' and my assumptions that 'there was no specific point or incident that made the relationship bad' and 'they just didn't get along'. That was how I had interpreted my parents' relationship until the night of the murder, and it was what I had said as I gave my statement to the cop across the desk, who stared at my face while I answered her questions. My mother was gone, and my father was already in the belly of the police building. The language of abuse was still foreign to me. The language of family, loyalty, privacy was all I knew.

'We do not talk with people about family problems,' Mum had warned.

'We fight a lot, but I do love your Mum,' Dad had insisted.

Mr Barr then asked, 'Apart from your brother who gave your Mum and Dad a hard time growing up, you were good children?'

I looked from the pews to the mezzanine, but I still couldn't see my brother in the audience. As children, he and I would play tackle footy on the grass, karate in the school hall, cops and robbers in the park. As adults, we couldn't agree on a single thing. Our relationship had deteriorated over questions about family, loyalty, privacy, in the lead up to the trial.

Mum was the bond between us. She was the womb, the tie, the thing we had in common. I didn't destroy that. I answered with a flat 'yes'.

Next, I was asked about the nature of my relationship with my parents. Again, I confirmed what I'd told the police: that we'd get into arguments over wanting to do things that my parents didn't want me to do and that my childhood had been no different to what I'd expect in any parent–child relationship.

But had my childhood really been ordinary? I'd had persistent, violent nightmares. Wet the bed until I was thirteen. Kept secrets to avoid being confronted. Sustained a quiet pre-occupation with the details of my grandmother's death. Picked at my skin. Worried constantly that something bad would happen. Something bad was always about to happen.

Mr Barr's questions edged closer to the present day, asking about when I had married and moved out and my brother's subsequent arrest.

It stung to think about my wedding day. All those photos that I couldn't look at anymore. The video we never collected. My wedding day was our last day as a family unit. The next minute, I was trudging up the driveway of Long Bay Correctional Complex, pregnant and drenched in rain. I stopped at the little window where a corrections officer looked at my hijab, then my face, then my tummy. I told him that I would like to drop off clothes and socks for my brother. Because he called and asked for them. Because that's what Mum would have done.

Mr Barr asked about my parents' decision to sell the family home: 'Somehow mum and dad came to an agreement to sell the house?' I confirmed, 'Yes.'

Somehow. I helped them work it out, played mediator. So much energy lost trying to cultivate peace, please everyone. I couldn't take sides, I didn't want to hurt their feelings. I believed Mum deserved an equal share. She got less than that, but no one wanted to go to court. It was enough for a fresh start . . . Mum then bought the villa and Dad had convinced her to give him another chance.

Mum let Dad come to Valda, but all she wanted was for him to leave her alone. He benefited from the split, having gained an investment property and no debt. He'd continued receiving an income from his tenants until my brother, after his release from gaol, took ownership of the apartment and sold it. I'd found the rent receipts in Mum's mailbox at Valda and added them to a pile of bills and fines and letters all addressed 'URGENT' and 'LATE' to Haydar Haydar. I put them in a lime green file labelled 'IMPORTANT' then hid the file in the pantry so I didn't have to see it. I had no idea what to do with that stuff. *Why doesn't the tax office know he's in gaol? Why doesn't the tax office know Mum's dead?*

Mr Barr pressed ahead with more questions about the period after my marriage. He read from my statement: 'When I would visit home, sometimes mum and dad would fight if something had come up, but other times they would just move on so they would enjoy our company'. *What about the time he made her cry with that story about the body parts in the gutters? What do I do with that memory?* This was followed by a series of questions about the nature of my parents' relationship:

'As far as you were aware, they were sleeping in the same bed together?'

'Whenever your mum was particularly upset about something, she would talk about separating from your father?'

'And she would think about it out loud and go back and forward about whether she should give him another chance or not?'

I responded 'yes' to each statement as the words were put back to me.

All. The. Time.

'Your father had never spoken to you to suggest that your mother was having an affair?' Mr Barr asked.

'No,' I replied.

This was never about an affair. Mum wanted to leave him after the house fire that happened when I was in my first year of high school, and again when I was fifteen, and again when we saw the lawyers in 2010. She was afraid and ashamed. Always waiting, always compromising.

Mr Barr moved on to the last time I saw my father. 'You don't remember anything remarkable about that night. You sat and had snacks and at the end of the evening you gave your father a hug and a kiss goodbye and you said you would see him in a few weeks when he got back?'

I remembered Dad's stubble grazing my cheek like sandpaper as we said goodbye. He was so bloody awkward with goodbyes. 'Yes,' I answered.

The Prosecutor continued to lead me through my first statement and I provided my banal responses. From Dad's departure to Lebanon, to a weird text he sent while he was away telling me to 'look after' Mum, to Dad's early and unexpected return, to the frantic call I received from Iman on the evening of 30 March 2015.

'And then it was at that stage you became aware that something had happened to your mother and your sister?'

'Yes,' I responded, 'she said her mum ran out of the house screaming and saying that my father had arrived at my uncle's house covered in blood. I said to her, "I will try to find out what is going on. Stay calm."'

The muscles in my neck tensed as I remembered those moments. The cold dread of not knowing what had happened as I hung up. Numb arms. A horrible empty feeling in my stomach. Getting up from the tiles where I'd sat to take the call. Numb legs. A moth spinning around the light in my hallway. My hand stroking my round belly in slow circles. My knuckles knocking on the bathroom door. My voice trembling, 'Moey, something really bad has happened at my parents' house . . .' Getting dressed. Not knowing where we were going or who to contact. Calling Nour. Calling Ola. Neither of them answering. Calling Mum. Reaching her voicemail. Hearing her voice. Not knowing.

'I won't take you through the details of what happened after that?' said Mr Barr.

'All right, thank you.'

I let out a breath and drank from my cup. The water quivered as I raised the glass to my mouth.

Mr Barr then moved on to my second statement. 'You added some further material to what was not included in the first statement?'

'Yes.'

'In particular, in relation to your second statement in relation to your parents' arguments, they were generally restricted to everyday matters?'

I checked the document in front of me. I had been handed a copy of my first statement, but I hadn't been handed a copy of the supplementary one. I was confused. I wanted to talk about *the thing*. I wondered how Dad would react when I told the room what Mum had once told me.

'Sorry do you want me to have a copy of that statement now?' I asked, wondering why it wasn't being handed up as the first statement had been.

'I will just ask you questions for now, if that's all right?'

'Sure.' But I wasn't sure. Why couldn't we go through my second statement like we did with the first?

The first few paragraphs had been about the frequency of my parents' fights and my dad's general disgust towards divorce. Mr Barr asked, 'There were discussions about divorce between your parents?' I confirmed, 'Yes.' There had been *hundreds*.

'And your mother said to your father words to the effect that, "I want a divorce" and your father replied with words to the effect, "What you are saying is disgusting. You are disgusting for mentioning divorce. Do you know what kind of women seek divorce?"'

I flinched hearing the words put back to me. They were so stark and naked in this room full of strangers. In the corner of my eye, I saw Dad straighten up and open his mouth slightly.

He's denying this? In that moment, I couldn't find the words, the stories to paint the picture around my 'yes'. He compared a divorced female relative to a gob of phlegm. He told me not to associate with an older student at uni because she was 'dirty', because she had children by 'like five' different fathers. He called one of my friends a 'pig' over a rumour she had kissed a boy at Bexley Oval when we were teenagers. I'd set out examples like these in my statement but all I could manage in the witness box was 'yes'.

'After that conversation do you remember going to bed and hearing your parents fighting very loudly?'

'Yes.' *Sometimes I'd get up and ask them to be quiet because I couldn't sleep.*

'In particular, in relation to one argument that took place between your parents, do you remember an occasion when your father threatened your mother at any stage?'

'Yes.'

'Do you remember a particular time when he threatened her?' It didn't occur to me that this question might be an opportunity to talk about the *thing*. I was waiting to be asked about it directly. But, I see it now as I read and re-read these moments: a gravity train that I could have used if I'd been better prepared, more focused, less afraid. Understanding the question literally in the moment, I responded, 'I remember a few different occasions.'

I gave examples of my father's gesticulations in Arabic, which is how I'd witnessed them all those years ago: '*Wallah bethbahik! Bekhne-ik! Hajik tehkay!*' Coming from my own mouth, the syllables were strange, disjointed. I'd always thought of these words as opinions about divorce, reactions to a difficult topic. I suddenly realised they were threats; so much more serious now that they were orphaned from their context and uttered out loud among strangers. So much more violent with the benefit of hindsight. The court reporter paused and looked up. People in the pews stirred and whispered. Dad's nieces turned coal-coloured eyes to one another. I was confused by these reactions. *Why is Dad shaking his head? Why is he looking at me like that?*

Justice Garling interjected to ask for the meaning of the Arabic words I'd used in my statement. I turned to the judge. 'That means, one of the meanings is, "I will slaughter you" or "I will choke you". I have bad memories of that happening during arguments when they got very heated. And another memory of him approaching her in an aggressive stance and I have another memory of him pushing her up against the wall. But, as I said, the arguments were generally verbal rather than physical. I have those images in my mind.'

His Honour wrote something down. Dad wiped a hand from his forehead to his chin before returning it to his lap. The tick-tick-tick of the court reporter's keys resumed. The whispers settled. *We're at a murder trial, why is anyone surprised that words like that had been thrown around our house? We are here because he did exactly what those words mean.*

Mr Barr moved on to other incidents from my supplementary statement. He asked about the time I'd watched from the stairs as my parents fought. The time my father had raised his hand in a fist. The time he'd pushed Mum against a wall by the neck. The time I'd asked Dad why he wouldn't just divorce Mum, and he'd said it was because it would be inappropriate to get divorced while my sisters remained unmarried. That it could ruin their chances. He didn't love Mum, he just wanted her on hold, indefinitely.

The Prosecutor did not ask about some of the things that I thought were vital; like the time I went to see the lawyers with Mum, or the way my father's family had behaved over the course of the two years that had passed, or the *thing* Mum told me in the car when I was fifteen. My mouth grew dry and sticky with evidence, and still the Prosecutor did not ask me about that *thing*.

'After your father had left to visit Lebanon, you had a discussion with your mother and she told you that your father had recently messaged her and invited her to join him back in Lebanon?'

I answered, 'Yes', but I felt bamboozled by our sudden turn into later events. *Why is he skipping ahead to this?*

'And you say that she said to you that he started speaking to her nicely and was trying to make amends?'

'Yes.'

I thought of Mum. She looked so pretty the last time I saw her, so fresh. We talked about cots and prams for the baby. She was afraid to join Dad in Lebanon. *He won't change, Mum!* She was clinging to this hope that he might. I thought of her shadow appearing in my nightmares; she's back at home, living with him, giving him another chance. She's in the kitchen, moving slowly. He's on the lounge. I'm outraged. I yell, I fuss, I try to kick him out. I can't save her.

Again, I waited to be asked about the *thing* in my supplementary statement but, again, a different question came; we'd arrived in the present.

'Yesterday or the day before my instructing solicitor showed you a knife?' asked Mr Barr.

'Yes.'

It had been pulled out for identification with barely any warning. Not that anything could have prepared us for the blood-stained blade. The knife had upset Ola and left Nour and me in a fury. I complained to the detectives, and to Jann and Janine. 'I understand he didn't want to give anything away, but there must be a more appropriate way to do it,' I said. Sometimes the only thing you can do is complain.

'Had you ever seen that knife before?'

'No.'

'Was it a knife that matched any of the knives or cutlery at your house?'

'No.'

'Did you ever see your mother carry a knife or knives in her handbag?'

'She carried the small type of knife occasionally, it had a plastic lid over it, the kind that comes with a lunch box and you take to work to cut an apple with it. I have the same one at home. She would never have carried a knife like that in her bag,' I said, in reference to the stained knife. 'She kept her things in nice condition. It would be very weird for her to carry a large knife loosely in her bag. She had nice bags, nice items. I can't imagine that at all . . .'

I shook my head, frowning. *Where is this going?*

None of these questions had anything to do with my supplementary statement. What was the relevance of the handbag? The suggestion that Mum might have carried a knife like that in her handbag, sharp, loose and naked, was bizarre. I looked over at Dad. He scratched his neck stubble.

My father was alleging that he had found the knife in Mum's handbag – the one she'd taken to work that day. His argument being that his crime was unplanned and spontaneous, that he'd simply stumbled upon a murder weapon in the moments before the attack.

All I'd wanted was for the Court to know how life had been for Mum, but the further we'd delved into my evidence, the further we'd drifted from her. The moment for the secret Mum had shared with me when I was a teenager was lost.

*

Mr Barr stepped back to the bar table. I thought about how his name matched his job as I took a sip of water. Mr Stratton, Dad's barrister, stood up to cross-examine me, holding a single piece of paper. Small brown eyes peeked out from under his horse-hair curls. His glasses sat on the tip of his nose. He circled back to the fighting I witnessed as a child.

'Ms Haydar you say that there was an occasion when your father pushed your mother against a wall by the neck?'

'Yes.'

'Who was present when that happened?'

'I don't remember.'

'Is that something you actually saw or heard about?'

'No, I have a distinct image in my mind –'

– It's evening. I'm crouched, peering down from the staircase. I feel the shaggy carpet under my toes. There is a clock on the wall above Mum's head. Her limbs become tangled with his and she's wearing a cotton nightgown –

'– My mother was in a pink night gown. That is what I have in my head.'

I understood that he was trying to cast doubt over my recollection. I felt myself getting defensive, straining between questions to think of how I could better contextualise this memory. Prove it somehow.

'Are you able to say if any of your siblings were present?'

'They ought to have been, as I remember it being in the late evening and going to bed shortly afterwards. I don't remember my siblings being present. I have, as I said, a distinct image in my mind of that moment.'

'When do you say that happened?'

'I was young, it would have been when I was a high school student, maybe Year 9. Yes, around the same time as when their arguments escalated in about 2003.'

'Would that have been about 15 years ago?'

Has it really been so long?

'Yes.'

196

'I put it to you that that incident never happened. Am I right or wrong?'

Mr Stratton looked at me over the frames of his glasses. Did *he* really believe what he'd just put to me? Was it so far-fetched that his client, who had already confessed to attacking Mum with a knife, might have also pushed her against a wall during a fight fifteen years ago?

I held Mr Stratton's gaze as I gave my answer.

'Wrong.'

Mr Stratton stepped away.

There would be no further questions, no re-examination. I turned to His Honour, waiting for him to say something. I wanted to know that I'd been helpful, that Mum and the Court would be pleased with me, even if all the poisonous people in the pews were not.

Through impenetrable blue eyes, Justice Garling said, 'That concludes your evidence. You are excused from further attendance. You are free to come, go, stay or leave as you wish.'

I'd already decided to leave. I had seen all I needed to see. I needed to get away from this place and be as far away from my father as possible. I needed to hug my children and ask them to forgive me for my absence.

I was shaking and rambling when my husband and I boarded the train for Granville that afternoon.

'You should have seen him! He just sat there shaking his head! He knew he was tormenting me. After everything that's happened . . . everything he's done . . .' I let my head drop onto Moey's shoulder. 'I'll go back to hear the verdict and to give my victim impact statement. Apart from that, I'm never giving him an audience again.' I felt sick. Like a part of me had remained trapped in that witness box, fighting to find a way to say more, trying to tell them what Mum had told me.

TWENTY-SIX

Giving evidence was like walking on broken glass. In just half an hour, we'd trodden over a lifetime of traumatic, fragmented memories, pausing occasionally to pick up a shard and examine it as it cut back into my skin.

My brain was still pulsing and spinning when we got home. Moey put his arms around me. His hands warmed my shoulders.

I was glad to have him there and to be back in our house, but I couldn't be still.

'I need to take a shower or something before we pick up the babies.'

'Take your time, we'll get the kids when you're ready,' he said.

I felt as disoriented and disgusted as I did on 30 March 2015. My head was too heavy for my neck. I quickly unpinned my hijab, flung it aside and gathered some fresh clothes. I hurried to wash the yuck away. Mum had entrusted me with something and I had let her down. Every time I blinked I saw Dad's face, Amo Khalil's moustache, my cousins' smirks and Mr Stratton's glasses. I didn't want to infect my house or my family with this feeling.

I flicked the handle, full blast. I needed to start forgetting again. Water rushed down my temples. *She's gone. Gone. Gone.*

*

The wound was wide and fresh, but now I was more angry and frightened than sad. The next morning, I stared at my phone screen until I got pins and needles in my hand. Maybe I shouldn't have looked. I saw my words as big black headlines and our photos on websites and Facebook feeds. The girl in her mother's polka-dot dress was a stranger. I read the comments. Seeing myself from the outside made me dizzy.

I wanted to erase the memory of my time in the witness box. It had disappointed and horrified me in so many ways. I was awake but the experience sat on my chest like a *kaboos*, like the incubus in Henry Fuseli's painting, *The Nightmare*. My body was rigid and numb again, like when you try to run from the bad guy in your sleep. I reminded myself that giving evidence was important and right, even though it was scary and confront-ing. Even though it felt so incomplete. I would go on with my life having answered the questions put to me to the best of my ability, reconstructing as much as I could remember and articu-lating it no matter how vague, fractured or ugly it was. This was a source of comfort.

True to my word, I did not attend the rest of the trial. I stayed home with my babies instead. I tried to forget the witness box and the sensational headlines, which had turned a really shit day – an experience completely out of my control – into clickbait. I logged off and got busy stirring pots, changing nappies and cycling anxious energy off on the exercise bike. I misplaced my son's dummy. My coffee went cold. The Wiggles sang 'Do The Propeller!' I found the dummy, misplaced it again, ripped a new dummy from its packet.

Once or twice, I peeked out the window to the street, checking to see if anyone had come to kill me too.

My sisters and husband returned to their usual occupations and my days dribbled on in this way, the trial continuing in our absence for the next couple of weeks.

*

A lot had to happen before I could articulate why giving evidence wounded me this way. It had something to do with being accused of lying in a space I considered sacred. It hurt that my attempt to disclose a complicated but more complete version of the truth was not met with sympathy or support. Speaking my accusations against my father in front of him was terrifying. He had reacted with his body and face like I was betraying him, through a secret language of subtle frowns and bared teeth. The abrupt and public denuding of details about my family, which I had thought of as private for a long time, stung like the exposed pink flesh around my thumbnail.

It was also guilt, because at the end of all that talking, I felt like I still had not done enough for Mum.

*

The *thing* that Mum told me when I was a schoolgirl, that had bothered and confused me, that I'd seen as a smoking gun in the trial against Dad, remains uninterrogated and unproven. There's nothing I can do about that. I do not care that it is inadmissible or hearsay. I do not care that my father denies it. I believed Mum when she said it, even though it puzzled and sickened me. I wrote it in my supplementary statement in the hope that the Court would hear it and I would have helped. I didn't get to share it then, but I can share it now.

EXCERPT FROM SUPPLEMENTARY STATEMENT

My mum drove me to school, as was our usual routine. However, that day she had very puffy eyes and seemed extremely distraught. After dropping my siblings off at their respective schools, she started to speak to me about the argument which had occurred the previous evening.

She said, 'I am sorry it has gotten so difficult, but your father does not know how to make me happy. I want to get a divorce but I am afraid that he won't let me. He thinks divorce is shameful and whenever I suggest it he gets very angry. I am afraid that he will do something to me if I try to leave him. I haven't told this to anyone else but I once found a suicide note in his bedside drawer which was written by him but purported to be written by me. I knew when I read it that he had thought about killing me and making it appear as though I had killed myself. It frightened me when I read it, but don't mention this to anyone.'

I recall that I teared up and felt angry when my mum told me this story, however, I did not ask any questions. I recall that this conversation took place as we were driving along Harrow Road towards my high school. I recall that I was sitting in the back of the car but my mother was making eye contact with me in the rear view mirror. I recall that towards the end of this conversation, we passed the roundabout near Hogben Park in Kogarah. I clearly recall that conversation, including the fact that a Robbie Williams song was playing on the radio and the Jacaranda trees in the park were in bloom.

I recall that I was extremely troubled and disturbed by the story my mum had told me. I did not ask any questions. I was only about fifteen years old at the time and the conversation had made me extremely uncomfortable. Only about a minute later we pulled up at my high school. As I got out of the car, my mum said words to the effect of, 'Please try to forget what we just spoke about, your priority should be to concentrate in school'. I remember feeling tearful and insecure for the remainder of that day, but I did my best to put that conversation out of my mind, and managed to do so for quite a long time.

The courtroom is a man-made space, governed by rules that strive to capture a truth. My faith in that system, my training as a lawyer and my expectations as a victim, set me up for disappointment. Focused on what that space could offer and hoping to find meaning and closure there, I had momentarily forgotten that truths also exist outside courtrooms and judgments.

Some of these truths cannot be documented or captured. They shift and morph like gems in a kaleidoscope when we try to put them into words.

Other truths are passed on to us through our mother's DNA – like my curls, my laugh, and the way I eat and eat when I'm sad.

There are truths that are firm and tangible, like Teta's thick gold bangle, which I keep in a small velvet box when it should be on her wrist – a reminder of the injustices that live on without prosecution or resolution.

Some truths are secrets told to us when we are girls so that when we grow up, we know who to trust and what to believe. They exist unspoken and inviolable within us.

TWENTY-SEVEN

Nour sat opposite me with her knees pulled up to her chin and socks pulled up to her knees. We were watching *Gossip Girl*. 'There's no amount of evidence that could convince me that Dad killed Mum because he was depressed,' she spat.

Ola was slouched beside her. She looked up from her phone. 'Honestly, I don't even want to think about it.'

Ola, Nour and I didn't attend the rest of the hearing. It continued in our absence. We knew that evidence as to Dad's state of mind had been presented, with each psychiatrist taking a turn to opine about how much of an impairment he'd suffered and the extent to which it was evident in his actions at the time of the murder.

I was glad I hadn't sat through it.

'You know what really bugs me is that we had matters at work where people jumped through hoops to prove that PTSD or depression affected their work and lifestyle. Employers and insurers would go to town to discredit them. Yet killers can argue that the same conditions have caused them to get up and murder someone, and *they* get the benefit of the doubt.' I took a sip of coffee.

'Speaking of which – how'd you go with uni and your payments, Olz?'

'I have to be enrolled full-time if I want support, otherwise I have to be working or looking for work. They don't see PTSD as an excuse for anything, even if you literally can't get out of bed.'

'Well, there you go. Institutions find it easy to believe that mental illness makes people violent and dangerous but find it hard to believe that violence and danger makes a lot of people mentally ill.'

'Pretty convenient, eh?'

*

The trial wrapped up on 20 March 2017 with each party summarising its case in closing submissions. I wasn't present for the submissions but later read an outline of the case as presented by each party. The facts of what had happened on 30 March were largely agreed upon between the parties. The questions that remained were where the knife had come from, what had motivated Dad to attack Mum, and the extent to which his 'depressive illness' contributed to this.

CROWN CASE – IN OUTLINE

The Crown case is that the accused, in the context of and against a background of a volatile marital relationship with his wife, Salwa Haydar ("the deceased"), returned home from a two week visit to his family in Lebanon. By that time, he had formed the intention of living apart from his wife in separate residential accommodation.

On the day he arrived in Sydney, the accused was present at the deceased's house ("the Bexley townhouse") when she returned in the evening, having been at work. Their 18 year old daughter, Ola, was also present because her mother had collected her from university where she was studying.

Shortly after the return of the deceased and Ola to their home, the deceased entered the kitchen and started preparing dinner. She asked the accused to fetch some cooking oil from the garage. He declined. Thereafter an argument developed between them about the manner in which the deceased contributed to the domestic life of the family.

On the Crown case, the deceased [sic] picked up a knife which he had brought to the premises, and entered the kitchen. There the argument between the accused and the deceased continued, and the accused stabbed the deceased. Upon hearing the argument and attack, Ola entered the kitchen and by placing herself between the accused and the deceased, attempted to stop him from attacking her mother. In the course of that interference, and whilst he was wielding the knife at the deceased, the accused stabbed Ola and caused significant injuries to her right hand.

The violent scuffle between the deceased and the accused then moved into the lounge room where the accused continued to stab the deceased in a frenzied attack. The accused stabbed [the] deceased over 30 times, to her front, her back, her face and other parts of her body.

Ola, who was present in the lounge room and witnessing the attack, called upon the accused to stop attacking the deceased. When he did not, she telephoned 000. The accused attempted to discourage that call whilst he continued attacking the deceased.

When the accused could not persuade Ola to cease calling for help, he took the knife and the deceased's handbag and left the premises in his car. He drove to his brother's house and left his car there. The police later found the blood-stained knife in the accused's car. There were blood stains in the car as well.

The accused's brother drove him to Kogarah Police Station where the accused informed the police that he had stabbed his wife.

The Crown accepted that it is open to the Court to find that at the time the stabbing occurred, the accused was substantially impaired in his capacity to control himself because he was suffering from an abnormality of mind due to an underlying depressive illness. However, the Crown contended that the Court would find the accused guilty of murder because the accused was motivated to kill the deceased, and carried through that motivation in an attack for which the moral culpability is at a very high level, and the impairment of the accused was not sufficient to justify anything other than a verdict of murder.

CASE FOR THE ACCUSED – IN OUTLINE

The accused accepted that he attacked his wife with a knife and killed her. He accepts that at the time he did so, he had an intention to cause her grievous bodily harm. He does not accept that he intended to kill her. However, the accused says that the Court would be persuaded that he had a long-standing depressive illness which had subsisted for over two years.

The accused submitted that it was clear that, at the time of the killing of his wife, he was suffering from a deep depression relating to his marital relationship and family events in Lebanon. He further submits that when confronted in a domestic context with an argument provoked by his perception that his wife was unfaithful, he completely lost his self-control, took a knife which he had found by chance in his wife's handbag, and in an impromptu reaction to his wife's comments, attacked her.

His case is that the Court would find that he was substantially impaired by reason of his depressive illness in controlling himself, and that that substantial impairment caused his inability to control himself such that he killed his wife. He submitted that the impairment was so substantial, and his moral culpability so diminished, that the Court would reduce his offence to one of manslaughter, consistent with his plea.

The accused did not advance any case, or make any submission contrary to a finding of guilt on the second count of the Indictment. He accepted, by his plea of guilty to the third count on the Indictment, that he wounded his daughter Ola. He accepted by his plea of guilty to manslaughter on the first count that he intended to cause grievous bodily harm to the deceased. Notwithstanding these facts, he simply does not accept that the Crown has discharged its onus with respect to each of the elements on the second count.

*

When the trial ended, the Prosecutor's office let us know that we would be waiting until the end of March for the verdict. Trying to pre-empt what would happen, I had developed a habit of reading about similar cases. It was strange to be watching conversations about domestic violence on my screen without ever really being involved in them.

On 17 December 2015, the man who murdered Nikita Chawla, in what the judge deemed an 'extreme case of domestic violence', was sentenced to a minimum term of seventeen years in gaol. He had claimed he couldn't control himself and was taken over by anxiety.

On 25 August 2016, the man who murdered Leila Alavi was sentenced to a minimum term of fifteen years and nine months in prison. Justice Hulme said the offender's thinking was 'chaotic in the weeks and months leading up' to the day he killed his former partner in a carpark, and his 'intention to kill had crystallised' that morning.

'[He had a] breathtakingly arrogant and misogynistic attitude towards the rights of his wife to choose her own destiny,' Justice Hulme said, according to an article in the *Sydney Morning Herald*.

There were similarities between these cases and ours, including some of the social and cultural context. The way in which the offenders seemed to think that their actions were somehow proportionate to those of their partners. The ghastly, unrestrained stabbing. The complete disregard for the independence of the victim.

It was reassuring to read that these men had been found guilty of murder. Not so reassuring was the fact that a minimum sentence of fifteen to seventeen years seemed to be the standard for crimes like this.

Leila's sister had expressed her pain in an article for the ABC:

'My sister and I left Iran for a better life away from violence,' she said. 'Leila was everything to me, she was the only family I had for many years and only family I had in Australia.'

How could this loss be quantified? How would the offenders make up for the murder if they felt no sorrow over it? Would any amount of gaol-time make them feel anything? What should we do with this category of person?

As I read the facts of each case, I tried to weigh up where Dad's actions fell on this scale of cruelty.

On one hand, the verdict was more important to me than the sentence, because it had the power to affirm Mum's truth. But sentencing mattered too. The thought of running into my father in a few years' time terrified me. Why should he ever be free to contact me or my children? Who would protect us from that intrusion?

*

I had a lecturer in law school who ended every lecture with a slide that said, 'Don't confuse justice with the law.' I reminded myself of this as we waited for the verdict.

In order to successfully argue the defence of substantial impairment, the law says Dad would have had to establish three elements. First, that 'he was suffering from an abnormality of the mind arising from an underlying condition' at the time of the murder. This would have to be deemed an existing mental condition rather than a transitory one. Second, that 'his capacity to control himself was substantially impaired' by the stated abnormality. And finally, 'that the extent of the impairment was so substantial as to warrant the liability for murder being reduced to manslaughter' in order to reflect his reduced 'moral culpability'.

I knew what I *felt* was true; that Dad had been capable of this for a long time. He had contemplated it on at least one occasion that I knew of. Still, I thought of some of the cases I'd worked on where a judge or assessor's decision had turned out differently to my own assessment of the facts. Sometimes it had been a matter of interpretation or a matter of emphasis. Sometimes the whole thing hinged on one seemingly minor detail. I had no experience with criminal trials involving violence; I wondered what facts would stand out most to the judge. I thought about the confidence with which opposing lawyers had argued their client's version of the truth and the strength with which I'd been trained to resist. I wondered about the grey areas. I wondered whether I'd missed something. I wondered whether I *was* too emotional; then I wondered whether I'd been gaslit into wondering about this. I could feel my mind tying itself into knots. It was terrifying to surrender to the fact that the verdict always was and always would be in the realm of things I couldn't control.

I decided to concentrate on what I could do: remember Mum. I began organising a memorial for the two-year anniversary of her death and set up a fundraiser with the Cancer Council in her memory – she'd done some work with them in the past and was passionate about health. I could have done one with a domestic violence organisation instead, but I needed a break from the themes in the trial. Plus, I wanted this to be about how Mum lived, rather than how she died.

TWENTY-EIGHT

The Prophet said that heaven lies at the feet of our mothers.

Some brothers will use this line to tell me that *real Muslims* can't be sexist because we all know this hadith by heart. They argue that this is intended as a message of gender equality. However, to me it reads as an acknowledgement of the thankless labour of motherhood. Either way, platitudes are useless if they do not manifest as compassionate action in a crisis. By the end of my father's trial, I felt abandoned by all the men I grew up around, even though my mother could have been any one of their mothers. Did they believe what I had to say about my parents' marriage? Did they find it easier to believe that my father had randomly and impulsively killed my mother in an act of momentary insanity, demonic possession or 'maybe even love' (as one cousin put it), than to acknowledge that he had always had an array of concerning attitudes when it came to Mum exercising her right to leave the relationship? Perhaps it was easier to avoid me and the questions I posed than to admit that they might themselves harbour such attitudes.

The day before the judgment was due to be handed down, I sat alone at my mother's feet, in between the rows at Rookwood Cemetery. It was an overcast day and drizzle had cleared the area of visitors. I didn't care about the damp. I unwrapped my roses and carefully placed them around Mum's headstone and made *dua*, asking Allah to give my sisters and me an outcome that could heal us. I didn't know whether Mum had access to any special privileges, but I implored her to intercede if she could. 'This probably doesn't matter much wherever you are, but it means everything to us, here,' I said into the air. The rain intensified, making the gum trees droop and muddying the gravel around the graves.

I don't know how long I was there. The concrete under me was hard and my hijab and sneakers were soaked, but I wanted to stay there at the cemetery with its quiet inhabitants so that tomorrow wouldn't come. There were droplets on my lips as I whispered, 'Please let it be better not worse. Please help us heal.' People say that Allah does not deny a prayer invoked during rainfall, but Mum might have thought I was ridiculous, letting myself get so wet. She would have said, '*Yallah, bala bekah*! C'mon, enough crying! You're going to catch a cold!' I thought of her and Teta, sitting in a field of lush greenery, sipping milk and honey from goblets. For a moment, I felt calm, imagining their spirits together. Then I felt mad that they could be enjoying each other's company while I was on this side, miserable. Then I felt guilty for envying them and angry at my father; it was his fault that I was here and Mum was there.

Eventually I ran out of ways to pray for justice. There were two possible outcomes. I believed in my soul that Dad was guilty of murder, but if the Court found that it was manslaughter, I would live with that. He would go to prison for a short time. I would have to accept it and find some other way to cope with the enormity of the injustice that he had committed.

It doesn't change who you are, I told myself. *It doesn't change who your mum was.*

Soaked and cold on the outside, thinking about Mum made me feel warm and proud on the inside. Wasn't the worst already over? That first night, the funeral, the grief, the trial. I had navigated the confusing attitudes of my family, supported my siblings, birthed and mothered two babies. I had faced my father, gone on the record. Two excruciating years had happened, and I was still functioning.

You have done everything possible.

With hundreds of spirits and thousands of raindrops as witness, I promised that whatever happened the next day, I would do my best to continue telling Mum's story.

You can heal, no matter the outcome.

*

That night I stressed about what I would say to the microphones and cameras waiting outside court the next morning, expecting a statement. I couldn't predict the outcome, so I couldn't imagine how I would feel. Mum was gone either way, and Dad was already nothing to me. When the babies were tucked into bed with their soft toys and milk bottles, I flipped my laptop open and typed up two short statements:

MANSLAUGHTER.

While we accept the Court's decision we believe that if our mother were here to tell her story, today's outcome would have been different. She knew what he was capable of. Nothing will change that and nothing will bring her back. Our focus will now be to make sure our mother's wonderful legacy lives on.

MURDER.

Nothing will bring our mother back or make up for the infinite ways in which our father's actions have affected our lives. However, we are pleased that today's decision reflects reality. Our focus will now be to make sure our mother's wonderful legacy lives on.

I stared at the two paragraphs on my laptop screen. The text cursor blinked expectantly. The words fell flat and empty, but I printed the page out – just in case I couldn't come up with anything else. Two years had passed and language still couldn't wrap itself around this crime.

*

Normally, my sisters and I chat nonstop. We talk over each other loudly. We can have three different conversations going at one time and still be able to follow. Sometimes I forget that other people don't interrupt or speak over each other in the way we do. That it's considered arrogant and rude. My sisters and I can be arrogant and rude around each other and it doesn't matter. If we fight one minute, we laugh the next. Nour and Ola laugh at me and call me a pushover because I do whatever they ask of me even though I am older. Ola and I laugh at Nour's fingers because they're bony and we can't hack that she gets to be the skinny one. Nour and I laugh at Ola because she's actually funny.

Our mum raised us as one: we wore matching clothes and shared Barbies and ate Nutella sandwiches from the same tray. There aren't many rules between us.

Nour and Ola were cranky and quiet when we arrived at King Street Courts for the judgment. So was I. It was still wet and windy. Today we had access to a little room inside the courthouse so that we wouldn't have to stand outside where the cameras were.

We waited in there with Jann, Khalto Jinan, Khalto's daughters and some of Mum's other relatives and friends. We all carried fragments of Mum's story, and each of us was invested in the verdict in some way.

I'd brought my printout in my handbag but, ultimately, my sisters and I decided not to speak to media about the verdict. It was too much pressure on an already impossible day. Instead, we decided to provide a written statement with details of the fundraiser we'd organised in Mum's memory. I typed it up in my phone and Ola nodded in agreement as I read it out for their approval. Nour went outside and passed it on to the reporters, giving them permission to publish it. This was a small reclamation of our agency in the face of an uncertainty; our words and actions didn't have to hinge on the outcome of the trial.

*

When it was time to enter the courtroom, Dad's family crowded around the door. My sisters and I pushed our way through their frowning, unforgiving bodies. Some of Mum's loved ones were separated from us as Dad's nieces, nephews and brothers filled the pews closest to the front.

It seems like such a petty thing, but I was livid. I couldn't believe that there was no designated area or priority for the people whose lives had been most severely impacted by the crime. The courthouse treated victims and secondary victims the same way it treated the accused's sympathisers and the general public. The architecture, the way the room was like a theatre, said, 'You're all just here to watch.'

We settled into our seats, Ola to my left, Nour on the other side of her. I was facing the backs of my cousins' heads. Side by side they formed a wide curtain of long black hair. Dad was escorted towards the dock, all sepia-toned like an old memory. He was wearing the pumice suit from my wedding again. He smiled at the row in front of me. I rolled my eyes and looked across Ola, at Nour, feeling an overwhelming but inappropriate urge to laugh. Khalto had said that the female cousins were encouraged to come to court by Dad's lawyers. Apparently, young, long-haired female relatives attending in support would be good for Dad's image – even if they weren't his own daughters.

In the past, Dad would have reprimanded me for wearing low-cut dresses or turning up at a place where I had no business. But because they were on his side today, his nieces could do whatever they wanted. They would help him look more like a highly educated, well-assimilated, hard-working migrant father, and less like a religious Muslim Arab who attends mosques all day and murders women by night because a god tells him to. He had always been the former, but so much is assumed about Arab men based on the bodies of the women around them. In this case, a woman's body was dead, but someone – most likely a man – had decided that decorating the room with silky hair and modern skirts might help us forget that.

What upset me most was knowing that the same cousins, like most women, must have witnessed, heard about or even experienced abuse by men in their lives too. Their secrets can't be so different from mine. They'd felt the pressure to marry and have children, experienced judgments about their lifestyles and travel choices. We'd stressed together about our weight and appearance. We'd all learned that the quietest, most blue-eyed girls in the village are the most desired. We'd been told that we, with our degrees and opinions, might have become 'too much'. I'd heard them gossiped about and slandered. One uncle in Lebanon complained that he was embarrassed to be seen with them in public because they were single, wore tight jeans and laughed too loudly.

My cousins couldn't see that they were being used now, earning points at our expense.

I wanted to shake them and say, 'Your uncles loved me too until I couldn't accept murder.' We're all good girls until we want our own thing.

Dad didn't look at me at all. This, I'm sure, was my punishment for appearing as a witness in the trial. No one but my sisters could see the contradictions in his behaviour and how he inflicted pain with body language. Straight-ahead eyes, straight back, straight lips. My thumb twinged as I carved at the cuticle. The side of Dad's face was kind of saggy and dry. I wondered if my nose – which is fleshy and round and definitely from his side of the family – would end up as big as his. They say your nose keeps growing forever. I thought about getting a nose job but felt guilty. They say it's *haram* to change Allah's creation. I suspected God could forgive me in this situation, but the guilt persisted. It felt wrong to be thinking about cosmetic procedures on such an important day, but my thoughts didn't care. I concluded that I would keep the nose; *the shame isn't in my body, it is in his.*

Dad didn't notice me examining his profile. Or maybe he pretended not to notice. My mind raced. I couldn't cut my father out of me, but I could change my surname, take my husband's. I'd kept 'Haydar' after we married because Muslim women are supposed to retain their lineage and property. I'd always liked that idea.

Some colleagues found this odd and made comments about it when I got back from my honeymoon. When an expert witness in an agricultural matter I was working on called from the country, I answered, 'Amani Haydar speaking.'

'G'day Amani,' he said. 'You're still going by ya maiden name! I thought you Lebanese ladies become ya fellas' property when ya marry!'

'No,' I replied. 'That's actually a Western tradition.' I fake-laughed as I explained so he wouldn't feel too embarrassed.

With Dad in the dock, looking away from me, it made no sense to have his name. I had no idea who he was. There had to be a way to extricate myself from the big mess he'd made. But then I remembered that Mum was a Haydar before she married Dad and I'm her daughter. I'm *bint* Salwa Haydar.

I should keep the name, I decided then and there, to match my certificate of admission as a lawyer of this court.

And Mum's headstone.

*

With a few sharp knocks, Justice Garling appeared at the front of the room. 'Deus ex machina,' I whispered to myself, remembering the words from high-school Latin or somewhere like that. My sisters and I stood, bowed in unison and fell heavily back into the hard seats.

The judge started slowly and carefully, reading the details of the charges against Dad first, and then outlining the procedures and principles that he had applied in this case. The young associate sat upright. I tried to read her round, pale face for clues but it was blank. She glanced down. My stare must have made her uncomfortable. The court reporter tick-tick-ticked away.

'It is my duty and responsibility to consider whether the accused is guilty or not guilty of each of the charges, and to return a verdict according to the evidence which I have heard . . .

'In considering this verdict, I must act impartially and dispassionately. I must not let emotion sway my judgment . . .

'It is, and always has been, a critical part of our system of justice that a person tried in this court is presumed to be innocent unless and until he or she is proved guilty beyond reasonable doubt . . .'

The melody and eloquence of submissions and judgments were highlights of studying and working in the law. I had enjoyed clever banter between the bench and counsel. Observing from the back, I would re-write the submissions in my head, imagining how I might deliver long, flowery arguments in my own wig and robes one day. Arms swaying like a conductor's as I gestured and held up documents.

Today, I felt impatient. My right leg was restless, shaking like it was about to run off on its own. I needed His Honour to hurry up and tell us what the future would look like. My mind flashed back to the drops of rain on the roses at Rookwood the day before. *You can heal, no matter the outcome.*

Justice Garling then went through the facts of the case, starting with the marriage of two people – the accused and the deceased – in the village of 'Aytaroun' in south Lebanon in the late eighties. He noted the age gap, the large families, the splitting across continents. There was a paragraph for each of my siblings and a summary of life at Four-One-Six, where Mum 'stayed at home and raised her family'. My childhood played through my mind quickly as the judge recounted these events, like a VCR stuck on fast-forward.

When the tape slowed, it was 2015 and I was 'a qualified lawyer' while Mum was 'working at St Vincent's Hospital for a service known as the Quit Line'. We were so far away from the village, we hardly thought of it anymore except when we thought of Teta. But Dad did and, seeing Dad as someone inflexible, stuck in the past, Mum told a neighbour, who gave evidence in the trial, that he had 'a Lebanese village mindset' and treated her daughters differently to their brother. Mum told her friend, 'My aim is to enjoy my life with my daughters,' but, as Nour had told the

Court, Dad wouldn't divorce Mum while any of his daughters were still single. This was not because he loved his wife, nor was it because he was keen to see his daughters happily married. It was because of shame; 'he knew how society viewed a divorced woman raising single daughters.'

The Court relied on evidence from a few people to whom Mum had complained about Dad:

'She told me how all he wanted to do was watch television, but not even movies. All he wanted to do was to watch the news in Arabic. And she hated this; this is how she learned her mother had been killed. She also told me that Haydar resented her studying. Haydar told her that she did not have the ability to finish the course. Salwa was quite convinced that Haydar had a social phobia. She had started to come out of her shell. She told me that Haydar resented this behaviour.' Dad preferred an unhappy marriage to no marriage at all, so he resisted Mum's requests for a divorce, and moved into Valda 'at the last moment'. Mum permitted this on the condition that Dad contribute financially. There was no improvement in the relationship, and Dad said he was going to Lebanon. Mum told him to pack his things and leave the key. Dad packed his stuff but didn't leave the key.

I found myself nodding along while the judge summarised Dad's attitude:

'He seemed to regard this separation and living apart as inevitable, but he was not really willing to give up on the marital relationship and wished to restore it to a state which he regarded as a good one, or else he wished to control the timing and circumstances of the divorce.'

Mum was actively working out her exit. She confided in her colleagues about what she was feeling, and told them, 'I plan to get legal advice and start divorce proceedings.'

Mum had gone to lunch with one of her colleagues, Ms Kapell, the day of the murder. She'd told her that Dad resented the fact that she was coming 'out of her shell'.

Ms Kapell asked the question that needed to be asked: 'Are you afraid of him?'

'No,' Mum answered.

'Has he ever been physically violent?' Ms Kapell had probed.

'No – he was not like that,' Mum had replied.

Ms Kapell surmised that Mum 'truly saw Haydar as a non-engaging man, a weak person'.

*

Domestic violence campaigner and former Churchill Fellow Yasmin Khan of The Bangle Foundation has written about the nuance that is lost when we focus on domestic abuse as being only or predominantly physical. She says 'there are many women from conservative and migrant communities who believe a male partner who yells all the time is just letting off steam, or who doesn't give money for household expenses is being a good money manager. In effect, as a result of their conditioning, they refuse to question this behaviour.' In the opening to *See What You Made Me Do*, Jess Hill agrees with Khan's argument and includes a note about why she uses 'domestic abuse' instead of 'domestic violence'. She references Khan's assertion that her clients often say, '"he's never laid a hand on me" – but on deeper questioning and reflection, realise they have been abused for many years, in ways that have been more subtle but just as damaging and potent'.

'What's even more confusing,' Hill explains, 'is that perpetrators commonly believe with all their heart that *they* are the victim, and will plead their case to police even as their partner stands

221

bloody and bruised behind them. Their victimhood is what makes them feel their abuse is justified.'

When Dad read messages between Mum and one of her colleagues, he concluded that she was leaving him to be with someone else, and not because she had been in the process of leaving him for the last fifteen years. He ruminated on this during his time in Lebanon. His own mum didn't recognise him, he was embarrassed by his son's incarceration, and then one of his relatives in the village suddenly died. This was why he sent me the text telling me to 'look after' Mum. She was the last bit of control he had.

*

'Various actions by the accused suggested that he recognised that the marriage was finished,' said Justice Garling. 'In particular, he had packed his personal belongings up and put them in the garage at the Bexley townhouse. He had ceased paying rent there. To that extent, he went along with the fact that the marriage had ended. But other actions – such as the keeping of a key to the Bexley townhouse when it was meant to be returned, inviting his wife to come to Lebanon and entreating her to think about purchasing a home with him and ". . . be the real Salwa" – all suggest that the accused was not willing to accept that the marriage was completely finished.'

Then Justice Garling arrived at the events of that night. The night everything happened. Dad's case was that he'd come across the knife in Mum's bag before attacking Mum. But, Mum's immaculate bag had testified against him in this regard; the judge finding that the lining of the bag didn't show any damage or other evidence to suggest the knife had ever been in there. I felt relieved that my evidence had meant something here, shedding light on this important detail.

Dad had also argued that he had taken Mum's phone from her bag to his car after attacking her. Again, the judge found this could not be true. Despite the fact that his hands were covered in blood, which had transferred into his car's interior, there was no evidence of blood on the phone or the inside of Mum's handbag; it had to have been removed from the villa *before* the attack. The repeated inconsistencies between Dad's version of events and the evidence available lead Justice Garling to 'conclude that the accused is an unreliable historian who has given a partly untruthful account of the events leading up to his attack on his wife'. Justice Garling added that this was 'significant' because it showed that Dad attacked Mum shortly after taking 'the one item which he regarded as being real proof of his wife's infidelity, namely the messages on her mobile phone'. This, according to Justice Garling's reading of events, meant that Dad hadn't lost control but had decided to get up from the lounge and confront Mum in the kitchen where he accused her of 'following the instructions of someone' rather than just 'losing control of himself'.

After attacking Mum and leaving Ola behind at Valda Street, Dad arrived at his older brother's home covered in blood. He had asked Amo Khalil to drive him to the hospital saying he'd had a fight with his wife. On the way to the hospital he changed his mind, according to Amo Khalil, and asked to go to the police instead. His brother complied, and Dad walked – blood-soaked and barefoot – into Kogarah Police Station where he repeated to the officer on duty at the front counter what he'd said to Amo Khalil earlier: 'I've just had a fight with my wife. I just stabbed her. I just stabbed her.'

Justice Garling's judgment went over the police observations and investigations noting that Dad didn't appear agitated, aggressive or irrational. Nor was he assessed as being vulnerable. When asked about whether he had a history of or current mental illness,

Dad had responded that he did not, and over the course of the next couple of hours he'd quietly complied with requests and had discussions with his solicitor (swiftly appointed, it seems, by his family), after which he refused to answer any further questions about what had taken place. We would have been at the hospital learning of our mum's death at this point.

I watched Dad as Justice Garling weighed up the facts of the case. He didn't look at us, he just moved at the appropriate times: head up, quizzical frown, head down, nose in palm. Eye contact with a niece, smile. Stare up at the judge.

*

Going through the psychiatric evidence, the judge accepted that Dad had been suffering an abnormality of the mind, arising from what psychiatrists who were engaged to give evidence at the trial had diagnosed as an underlying 'depressive illness' or 'depressive disorder'. Justice Garling accepted that, on the balance of probabilities, 'the accused's capacity to control himself was impaired by his depression. It made him vulnerable to reacting in a way that demonstrated a loss of control if a trigger event occurred . . .'

I listened carefully as the judge considered Dad's defence, my heart swaying like a pendulum in an old clock. The court reporter tick-tick-ticks and I hold my breath. His Honour might find in Dad's favour. There is every chance. It has happened in other cases – why not now? 'In the course of his attack, he was clearly motivated by jealousy and anger over the deceased's infidelity, because he called the deceased "a slut" in Arabic – a direct reference to his perception of her infidelity.'

Every muscle in my body was pushing me to move, leave the room. I looked from the smooth associate to the judge to Dad, to the court reporter. They were all impermeable. I took Ola's hand.

'In my view, his attack, whilst involving a loss of self-control on the part of the accused, was predominantly caused by his jealousy and anger towards the deceased, which had been building up in his mind for some weeks because he perceived that she was unfaithful to him.'

The judge had now arrived at his decision. 'I have no doubt that, based on a consideration of all of the facts and circumstances revealed by the evidence, the accused intended to kill the deceased. When Ola asked him to stop, he did not do so.'

Oh my God. Ola's wide, soft palm felt a lot like Mum's except her fingers were shorter. She was sobbing with her head down, whispering prayers. 'I cannot accept that the impairment to his self-control existed to the same extent throughout the whole of the attack. I am not persuaded that by the time his wife had protested her innocence, and his daughter was screaming for help, when he paused and spoke to his daughter the words 'it's fine, it's fine', and then resumed stabbing the deceased, he was doing anything other than making a choice to continue with his stabbing attack on the deceased. In other words, his impaired capacity for self-control did not persist throughout the whole of the attack.'

I tightened my fingers around Ola's hand. She kept reciting the same prayer over and over again. I could hear the 'ss' of her *bismillahs*. Next to her, Nour stared straight ahead, tight-lipped.

'Whilst I accept that the accused's impairment was substantial, the ferocity of the attack, the intention which accompanied it – namely to kill the deceased, the persistence of the accused in the attack notwithstanding his wife and his daughter's protestations, together with all of the matters to which I have drawn attention, all combine in my view to positively persuade me –'

I nodded with every second word.

' – that it would not be appropriate to convict the accused of manslaughter. Put differently, the accused has not persuaded me that the impairment was so substantial as to warrant his liability for murder being reduced to manslaughter.'

The words swept over us. Feet shuffled. The court reporter's keys continued, tick-tick-tick. The associate stayed still. Blank.

'It follows that the accused has not satisfied me of each of the essential elements of the impairment defence, and it fails.'

A gasp, a sigh, a sob. Bottoms shifting, heads turning, knees clicking as men stirred.

'There will be a finding of guilty of murder on Count One.'

Guilty. Murder.

I'd waited so long for a relative, a publication, an institution to use the words I needed to hear. The arched windows behind the judge glimmered like a mosaic and bright light glazed the room. The space grew bigger, like the ceiling was drifting upwards. I squeezed Ola's hand and she squeezed mine back, telling me she understood.

'. . . there is no doubt that he wounded his daughter, Ola, when she intervened to try and stop the attack, it follows that I am satisfied beyond reasonable doubt that each of the essential elements of the charge in Count Two are made out, and that the accused is guilty of that offence.'

Two years of held breath came rushing up from my lungs.

Two years of clenched muscle and strained jaw unlocked. I was so used to being propped up by adrenaline and tension I thought I'd collapse with relief.

'I direct that convictions be entered for the offence of murder, and the offence of wounding with intent to cause grievous bodily harm . . .'

Before we could turn to each other, Justice Garling stood the proceedings over for sentencing, got up, bowed and swiftly left the room, leaving us standing, breathless. The shuffling of feet grew into a rumble as people started to move out of the pews.

Nour was hugging Khalto. I was still holding Ola's hand. She had tears running down both cheeks. They dropped to her chest where they grew into dark circles on the folds of her hijab.

I turned back to look at Dad, wanting to see what guilt looked like.

Two guards had come to cuff him. As they took his wrists, he stood tall and proud. He looked past my sisters and me to his brothers, lifted a free arm into the air and waved like a sports hero on a field.

'Thank you, thank you all for coming,' he declared.

*

Dizzy, I followed Ola, Nour, Khalto and our support people out of the courtroom. I passed Amo and his son. They looked down their long noses at us with their arms crossed. I admit, I muttered a few smug words in their direction. I passed Dad's nieces who were already lingering in the shadowy corridor like *jinns*, sighing and sobbing. They pouted as we walked by. The eldest ran her fingers through her hair, examining the strands as though there was something really interesting hidden between them. How different would things be if they had been there for the right reasons?

We were led into a room where we could close the door and debrief. Jann asked me how I was feeling.

'I just feel relieved,' I said. 'Exhausted and relieved and like I've just put down this huge thing I've been holding.'

Ola, Nour, Khalto and our friends were hugging each other. This justice, bittersweet and delayed, felt like opening a window in a stuffy room and letting the air back in. Like those quiet minutes when you lay there after giving birth, returning from the drugs and adrenaline, unaware of the extent of your injuries.

We exited the courthouse from a side door on St James Road. We were met with cameras and microphones and a strong gust of wind.

When I watched the footage that night, I saw a tired, dazed version of myself, but she was walking with her head held high and her sisters and her partner by her side. They looked like they knew where they were going.

I called Mum's sister in Germany and told her what happened, how the judge said the words we needed to hear, how indifferent my dad appeared to be, how the courtroom expanded and how the windows glowed.

'It was just so bright all of a sudden,' I said.

She cried and thanked God and said, 'Those were your mother's angels, *habibti*. They came to claim her *haq*.'

TWENTY-NINE

It would be a long time before I would sit down and actually read through Justice Garling's 75-page judgment. And when I did, I found parts of it almost indigestible. There was a section in the judgment where Justice Garling described the nature and depth of the principal wounds Mum received to her face and body during the attack. I'd known from the first post-mortem report that we received in the days after the murder that the overall number of wounds exceeded thirty. But Justice Garling described them in more detail, one by one. Eight of them involved the entire length of the blade, at times the handle. His Honour took this as an indication of Dad's desire to cause maximum harm.

'I have no doubt that, based on a consideration of all of the facts and circumstances revealed by the evidence, the accused intended to kill the deceased . . . He persistently stabbed the deceased in circumstances where, as the photographs of the lounge room show, she was bleeding profusely. He did so by thrusting the knife upwards from below and downwards from above. The ferocity of the attack, the diverse locations of the knife wounds, the depth of those knife wounds, his failure to cease and desist when requested to do so by Ola, his ignoring of the deceased's protestations that she had done nothing wrong, his failure to cease and desist when Ola physically put herself between the accused and the deceased, his persistence in the attack in more than one room of the house, his persistence in the attack over a prolonged period, his pausing during the attack to enable him to speak to Ola to dissuade her from seeking help, and then resume the attack, considered together, point convincingly to, and satisfy me beyond reasonable doubt, that the accused's intention at the time of this conduct was to kill his wife, as he succeeded in doing.'

It is very difficult to make sense of words like these. I wonder, as I paste them into my manuscript, whether there is any point including them at all. But these are the facts I live with. And I acknowledge them daily. Sometimes they are the first thing I think of when I open my eyes in the morning.

*

In considering the facts leading up to the murder, Justice Garling's judgment mentions Mum's decision to stop wearing hijab in 2012. 'In the course of 2012, the deceased stopped wearing her hijab.' Mum had told a work colleague that Dad 'was not pleased by this decision'.

It surprised me that Mum's decisions around wearing hijab had featured in the trial because it had been more than two years since she'd stopped wearing it. Maybe it shouldn't have come as a surprise.

The judge referred to this as an 'example of some of the cultural differences between the accused and the deceased' and noted that Mum had complained to colleagues and neighbours about Dad's 'Lebanese village mindset'.

It is true that Dad and Mum had different mindsets. But the binary way in which this was discussed in the proceedings erased a lot of true things about Mum, her beliefs, phases in her life, her struggles with Dad, her experiences with grief and depression and more. The Court did not see how the language used in the proceedings fed into Dad's victim-blaming and gave him the tools with which to alleviate his culpability among his family. While Dad's so-called 'traditionalism' might have prejudiced a jury against him, it did not necessarily prejudice him within his family and community. He wanted the best of both worlds and this language gave him that.

Dad may have been conservative, but he wasn't religious. The only time he went to the mosque was if someone had died. I had a pretty secular upbringing for a Muslim. We ate Maccas without checking if it was halal, and put up a Christmas tree 'for fun' until we grew out of it. It made a pretty backdrop for photos, which we sent back to Lebanon. One year we even went to the Sunday school program at a local Anglican Church. Many of the other Sunday School kids were also little Muslims whose mums needed a break and had nowhere else to go. The mums would socialise over coffee in the courtyard while we learned Bible stories. My favourite part was, of course, arts and crafts. I also liked the re-enactment of Moses's story; the youth leader wore a blanket as a cloak and shouted, 'Let my people go!' then used a broomstick to split an imaginary sea.

The first fight I remember my parents having was about what my mum was wearing. She always dressed carefully and took pride in her appearance. We were sitting in our old beige Holden Commodore eating ice cream from Ibrahim's Pastry. We used to park along the seaside around Ramsgate and Dolls Point to watch the planes take off and land from the airport across the bay. Somehow that made us feel closer to Lebanon. Dad made a comment about Mum's sleeve being too short. I didn't understand why this particular sleeve was different to any others she'd worn. He said it should have been to her elbow. They argued back and forth and Mum ended up crying. I sat quietly in the back, licking my ice cream.

Much later, at the beginning of Mum's career as a community worker, she worked at an organisation called Al-Zahra Muslim Women's Association. They were a group of religious women who supported other women, organised events for youth, and wore hijabs down to their eyebrows and up to their chins. Their offices were near the mosque in Arncliffe. There, Mum had the opportunity to grow her Islamic knowledge, and then she passed that knowledge on to me. One day, when I had reached puberty, she came to my bedroom and handed me a piece of lined paper with handwritten steps on how to perform prayer. She said, 'You're not so young anymore, you should learn to pray.' She put a finger to her chin and added, 'I should have started sooner, but we didn't learn much about religion when I was a child. It was war and the Israelis didn't allow big gatherings.'

Mum started taking me to occasional ceremonies like those held to celebrate the birth of Fatima, the daughter of the Prophet. They were held in the concrete area under the mosque, the same place we'd later pray over Mum's body. I don't remember my siblings joining us for these things; I think Mum just liked introducing me to people and getting me involved. Religion had resonated with me from a young age and I had received awards from my scripture teacher. I didn't excel in the things that required discipline but I liked the mystical stories and the warm feeling I got in my belly when I heard adhan or Quran being recited, the way it expanded my imagination and made the little hairs on my arms stand on end. At the ceremonies, girls were given presents in recognition of their decision to wear hijab. During that period, Mum decided to start wearing hijab and introduced me to women who encouraged me to wear one too. They said, 'Do not hide who you are! Be strong! Don't worry about the racists, just worry about Allah!' I was fifteen and worried about neither. For me, survival was to be cool enough to be liked at school and smart enough to pass my next maths exam.

Dad didn't like hijab on Mum, or generally. He said that it was possible to be modest without *standing out* in a hijab. He saw himself as the perfect moderate. To him, moderation meant doing religious things in a way that was as close as possible to not doing them at all. And, like the elbow-length sleeve, his expectations were arbitrary, subjective and unpredictable.

Mum encouraged him to come to events and lectures with us, but he wasn't interested. Nevertheless, Mum persisted with her *hawza* classes and wore hijab for nine years – through a period in which it was the subject of constant suspicion and hostility. I admired her layered and patterned clothes. When I think of her now, I see her in the brightest greens and purples, in swirling silk, standing tall and proud, slightly larger than she was in real life. Dad made fun of her when she wore bright colours. If she stood out in public, he became visibly embarrassed to be near her; he'd look at the ground or walk a few metres ahead. Sometimes I'd feel a little embarrassed too, because I noticed when old white people stared and frowned. I couldn't understand how such nice clothes bothered them, and yet I wished we would blend in for a minute.

When Teta was killed, Mum wore black for a year, maybe longer. Still, Dad never said anything positive. He never said Mum was strong in the way she handled her grief. He never said she was resilient or brave to go into the world and work and learn in a way that was bold and unashamed.

I realised that on my own.

*

In the months before I got married, not long after the injury to her eye, Mum stopped wearing hijab. When I spoke to her about this, she said she had so many problems at home and was tired of going out and pretending to be secure and confident. She said she no longer felt like herself. She didn't feel encouraged or supported in the face of hostility from the public. Dad never made her feel good about herself. 'He only knows how to put me down!' she would say. Her outer world was out of sync with her inner world. She didn't have any control as a wife or a mother. She was just tired.

Despite having never encouraged her to wear a hijab, Dad disapproved of this change. He shamed her, saying it was inappropriate for a woman of her age to still care about her appearance. She would be a grandmother soon and people would talk. There was no winning.

*

Justice Garling's judgment combs through the communications Dad had with Mum during the final weeks of her life. Dad had used the same shaming language in his text messages to her before he left for Lebanon suggesting that she was being immature, that it was unbecoming of someone her age to be leaving her marriage. Even though Mum had repeatedly asked for a divorce in the past, and even though they had separated, albeit in an incomplete and unresolved way, he believed that Mum was leaving him on someone else's instructions. He refused to accept the authenticity of Mum's decision, reminding her that she needed to return to being the 'real Salwa'. He thought the real Salwa was the seventeen-year-old he brought here from the village.

But the real Salwa was an adult and a mother and a counsellor who could identify emotional abuse and gaslighting, who had used these exact words to describe his behaviour. The real Salwa owned her own home and car and was in the process of getting a degree. The real Salwa was smart, forward-thinking and brightly spirited. Mum was reclaiming the real Salwa. These tricks, the shaming and the manipulation, didn't work anymore.

I find myself returning to what Mum had said to her neighbour: 'My aim is to enjoy my life with my daughters.'

*

The judge pointed out that there was no affair. Dad's conclusion was erroneous.

But so what if there had been? Safety is not something you should have to earn.

*

When an abuser is not able to reach his victim, he may manipulate and convince others to sustain abuse on his behalf. Having given evidence against my father, I worried that his hatred and anger towards Mum was being transferred to me, as the eldest and most vocal of his daughters. I don't know what conversations had taken place between Dad, his lawyers and his family, but I felt suspicion and animosity from his family. Did they blame me for the verdict? Even though the judgment explicitly stated that Dad had been an 'unreliable historian' and Amo Khalil 'not a particularly impressive witness', who 'only gave evidence of what it was that he thought would assist the accused, his brother' and 'many of his descriptions of the accused exaggerated the state of the accused'.

For all the blame and accusations Dad made against me, it was his own narrative that had established Dad's guilt. *Hoist with their own petards*, I thought as I read these lines, remembering the Shakespearean phrase that my boss at the law firm always quoted when the other party stuffed up.

*

The night of the verdict, I received a call from one of my amtos in Lebanon who had urged, 'Help your father' after Mum's funeral. The kids were asleep, Moey was out and I wasn't sure what to expect from this conversation. Could she be calling to finally admit that she'd been wrong about Dad? Was she calling to check on me? I was suspicious. Amto started by asking me how things were.

'*Kel shi tamam*,' I said, even though not everything was fine.

Amto was silent for a second. Then she said, 'You shouldn't talk about this anymore. It's over. Delete your Facebook posts.'

'Why?' I replied. 'I'm only speaking the truth.' I'd only shared a few things about the outcome of the trial on my page. All of it was public knowledge.

'BECAUSE YOU SHOULD BE ASHAMED OF YOURSELF AND YOUR MOTHER!'

My body jolted at the sudden shift in her tone. 'I – I'm not ashamed of anything. You're ashamed – you're ashamed because you took the wrong side,' I answered. My ear was so hot it could have melted my phone. 'My mother was murdered. She's a martyr.'

'YOUR MOTHER WAS A –'

Amto yelled words I never imagined I'd hear from a grown woman from the village. She's dead now so the proper etiquette is to say *Allah yerhama* and not repeat what she said. But her words still give me goosebumps. I hope no one ever remembers me the way I remember her.

I managed to shout back an offensive Lebanese analogy about feet or shoes – slightly impressing myself – before hanging up.

My hands and belly were shaking. It was dark outside and Amto's screams were ringing like sirens in my ears. What had I ever done to her?

I took a breath, put the phone down and jumped off the couch to make sure the doors were locked.

Then I wrote down everything Amto said so I'd never forget.

THIRTY

I started working on my mental health again while we waited for Dad to be sentenced. Not everyone has luck with Victims Services referrals, but I liked my new counsellor, Natasha, as soon as I met her. Her clinic was in Bankstown, and nowadays I made a point of leaving the babies at home when I went to my appointments.

I sat in a chair opposite Natasha in a pale blue room that smelled like lavender. There was a cup of water and a box of tissues within reach.

Natasha sat with my file in her lap and asked, 'So what brings you into counselling?'

I started with, 'Um, okay, so . . .'

Then the events tumbled out: the murder, two sisters moving in, a brother in prison, back-to-back pregnancies, the trial, the verdict, the harassment, the victim-blaming, the upcoming sentencing proceedings, the fact that I didn't know who I would be once all this was over because it was all I had thought about for two years . . . As I spoke, I realised I had never listed these things in any order before. I backtracked to fill in details I'd missed: my grandmother, my parents separating, my marriage, Mum's funeral, and the disturbing experience of giving evidence at trial.

Natasha didn't flinch, look away or interrupt when I talked about murder and two babies and trials. Once in a while she nodded.

'I was so relieved when Dad was found guilty, but his family's attitude soured that relief for me. They don't support me – they want me to be silent. They were like, "Isn't manslaughter enough? Wouldn't four years in prison be enough for you?" Now I don't know how I can trust them, you know? If you support someone who has committed a murder, then what's off limits? Where are the boundaries? I told them all along – I was like, this man wanted to kill her. He could never hack her leaving him. They said, "Just be patient, just wait for the trial." And I was patient. And when I saw him it was a shock because I thought he'd look sorry or something, but he just had this disappointed face, like *I* had done the wrong thing.

'I don't really care about things like the family reputation. People seem so willing to protect abusers but in doing so, hurt all victims. That's the scary part – the disconnect, the lack of empathy – it leaves me feeling unsafe. I feel blamed for the verdict because there's this expectation that a good daughter should support her dad. In my family's case, I can understand that they would love their brother more than they love my sisters and me. Whatever. I just feel that people only want to see one type of victim; someone sad and weak and helpless and crouched in a corner, shaking. People empathise with that. A victim who's silent and afraid is not as threatening, it allows people to be the saviours, to control what we say and what we don't say. But it's not right. I'm never going to be okay with my mum being murdered and if I don't say anything, who will? What kind of person would that make me?

'Now I'm just so nervous all the time. I'm jumpy, I can't sit still and my thumb is swollen because I pick it non-stop.

I put a bandaid on it today so that I wouldn't be able to pick it. I know I'm not okay because I keep forgetting what I'm doing. If I don't write it down, it's gone. Like, completely gone. I have two babies – two under two – they need me, but I can't think about anything to do with babies because I'm so angry all the time. I'm fighting, fighting all day in my head. I feel physically and mentally exhausted. I thought I'd be okay because I did all this counselling before but, because of the trial, I'm back at square one. It's like the murder just happened. Like we buried Mum yesterday. I feel like I drove here straight from Rookwood. And when I think about it, I feel like I have heartburn again and my arms get heavy like they're full of hot sand. I want to be able to function. I need to function because I have a family, but there's so much to do and I need to be the person to do it.

'The other day I found myself standing in this aisle at Bass Hill Woollies just staring at this box of tea. I had no idea why I was there or what I was supposed to buy, and in the end I went home without the milk. And another time I reversed from my driveway with the car door wide open. Would you believe! I didn't even realise until I heard it crunch against the fence. And another time I went out all day and came home to find that I had left the front door of the house open. It's a wonder we didn't get robbed! Actually, someone stole my Nikes off the front porch recently. They were still white. Ha! Sometimes you just have to laugh, eh? Where was I? Ah yes! I know all this is happening because I just can't think, because in my head I'm somewhere else. I can't shake this feeling like something bad is going to happen even though the bad thing *has* happened – one of the worst things that can possibly happen has already happened! But I'm paranoid. I drive home different ways and look out for suspicious cars. I'm double-checking the locks before bed and everything.'

I sighed.

'So yeah, now we're just waiting for the sentencing trial and I don't feel like I can start fixing myself yet. Get me? And people always talk about closure. I don't think I even believe in closure, at least not in this life, but I'm going to give a victim impact statement at Court, which might help. And I guess I'm here because I don't want to burden my sisters. One of them was there when Dad attacked Mum and was injured and called the ambulance and he just left her there. She's a real-life hero! They've been through a lot and need me to support them. Also, I can't just dump it all on my husband because he's been so good and we're meant to be in the first few years of our marriage, enjoying our lives, going on holidays and not dealing with all these problems. We were twenty-six when everything happened. So it's just been all this crap for two years straight and I haven't even had a chance to think about Mum properly and I didn't get to enjoy becoming a mother and I probably resent that more than anything.'

Natasha's eyes looked glassy. She blinked once before saying, 'Wow. How have you coped with all that?'

No one had asked me this before.

'I – I have no idea,' I said slowly. 'It all just happened and when you're in it you don't have a choice. I'm kind of spiritual so that helps in a way because I don't think this is all. I believe there's a bigger justice. For someone to kill a whole other person, that's got to violate things on a cosmic scale.'

Natasha was still nodding. 'What do you hope to get from these sessions?'

'I don't know,' I said. 'What I'm wondering is, do people even recover from this stuff or will I be like this forever?'

Natasha smiled and leaned forward as she answered, 'Talk therapy is a treatment. The treatment will give you tools that you can use. Most people find that at the end of our sessions they have what they need to cope. You have had to carry so much but, no, you won't feel like this forever.'

Then, for the first time in ages, I cried. Proper tears-and-tissues-and-snot cried.

*

I followed up with Western Sydney University about recognition of Mum's studies. In the days after the murder, a professor had called to tell me that the university would like to honour Mum with a posthumous award. I said I'd be in touch when I was ready. It had taken a long time to feel ready, but Mum's graduation ceremony was finally set; it fell in the strange April between the verdict and the sentencing hearing.

Study and work were Mum's way of reclaiming her identity and independence. By Dad's standards she could do nothing right, but she was good at her work and enjoyed learning. Realising that the public version of Mum's life didn't celebrate the things she had achieved, I decided to contact journalist Jenna Price to let her know that Mum, murdered two years ago now, would be remembered at what might have been her graduation ceremony today.

'It would be good to be able to share this part of her life,' I suggested. Jenna, who had taught Nour at university, agreed.

Nour and Ola and I argued in the car on the way to the graduation ceremony. Ola said, 'This kind of thing doesn't really make me feel better,' which offended me because I was getting into the habit of coming up with 'this kind of thing': a graduation ceremony, a memorial for Mum, a new album for our old photos. These actions made me feel better; they could fill the gaps left by the murder trial version of Mum's life.

'I understand, Olz,' I said. 'It will be triggering, but maybe we'll look back later and be glad we came.'

Walking across the stage to accept Mum's graduation certificate was one of the proudest moments of my life. It was also
very sad. This award made Mum the first in her family to attain a
university qualification. I wish she could have collected the award
in person. She would have loved the ceremony and the way one of
the speakers said, 'You make a living with what you get, but you
make a life with what you give.' She would have memorised that
line to repeat later, when the occasion suited. I hung the certificate
in my entryway to remind me of my mother as I come and go.

In the article she wrote about the day, Jenna quotes me:
'In some ways I feel I have to take charge. In a way, I do the things
my mum would want done. I try to make that happen.'

When I got home after the ceremony, I crossed off 'Mum's
Graduation' in a to-do list I'd written and shared a photo of her
certificate online captioned: 'Congratulations Mum. The first in
your family to graduate from university. A woman who overcame
barriers to better herself and her community. A woman who the
world truly and sorely misses.'

This didn't feel like closure, but it did feel good. Maybe there
is no closure. Maybe we're meant to treat the wounds with rituals
like these.

*

Moey and I decided that we would take the kids on a trip to Dubbo
Zoo before the sentencing hearing. We needed to get away. While
we were there, we visited the Old Dubbo Gaol. The gaol operated
from 1847 to 1966 and oversaw seven executions – all for serious
crimes such as murder and sexual assault. I wondered whether
they'd all really been guilty, if they had been given fair trials. Was
there any such thing as a fair trial back then? I made a mental
note to google the gaol when we got back. It's a morbid place

to go with children, if you think about it, but it was gentrified just enough to numb visitors to the cruelties and injustices that must have been committed against prisoners there. I found myself in the courtyard looking up at the gallows; a whitewashed wooden frame crisp against the autumn-blue sky. Who commits crime and who gets to punish? What are we, the victims, left with when the gaol door is slammed shut and the hangman's noose tightens?

Old Dubbo Gaol is tiny compared to operational gaols. The ones I've visited are labyrinths filled to the brim with restless people. They are cold concrete and steel. When you visit a loved one in prison, you leave your phone in the car and fill out a little slip in the waiting area. Then they check your ID, scan your eyeball and you wait again. You need to make sure you've booked the visit properly. If you don't book it properly, then your long drive to Long Bay or Lithgow or wherever is wasted. If something happens and you can't make it, you can't call your loved one to tell them. Inmates can call you, but you can't call them. You can cancel your visit with the gaol, but they might not tell your loved one. In that case, your loved one waits and waits for the visit but they do not get called and they spend the day the same way they spend every other day, reading the papers and worrying about what's happening to you and whether they'll be forgotten.

You go from one waiting space to another and line up again and walk through a metal detector. You can't have any jewellery on, and sometimes you have to take off your jacket or your shoes. Sometimes the man stares at you like he can see your insides. Sometimes the man asks you to take off your jacket and you have to politely explain that you're a hijabi and you're not properly dressed underneath your jacket. Sometimes they look at you like you've broken the law.

You walk through heavy metal doors with the rest of the visitors, over coarse gravel, uninhabited zones between metal fences where not even a weed grows. When you get to the visits area, your loved one emerges from behind-the-scenes with a row of other people's loved ones. If you're their parent, your heart drops into your shoes. They wear white overalls. The overalls are ziptied at the nape so that they can't come off. You and your loved one sit on a round metal stool. The round metal stools are spaced out evenly and arranged around a circular metal table, and all of this is bolted to the floor of a big hall. If you're visiting a loved one while pregnant, you'll swear that your back is breaking because the stool is the size of a dinner plate and there's nothing to lean on. You're allowed to take in a small clear plastic bag of coins. I can't remember the limit, but it has to be coins. The coins are for the vending machines, which contain the meal you'll be sharing with your loved one for the next hour or so. You tear the chip packet wide open and place it in the middle of the table so that the guards can see inside. So that you can't slip things into it. There are no bowls.

The room is so bare it echoes and it's hard to hear your loved one over all the other families. You drink water from a tiny plastic cup and chat about the drive and the weather and what's new with you. You miss your loved one but this conversation is boring and awkward and no one wants to talk about why they're here and if you say the wrong thing you end up fighting and no one wants to waste the visit fighting. You stare around at the other families. Some are accompanied by small children and babies who run around and roll on the floor and climb onto their father's chests and bury their noses in their beards. The mothers and wives smile at their loved ones with their mouths, but the lines in the rest of their face are long and droopy. You wonder what these boys did and how they got here. Some of them are guilty of very serious offences but sitting opposite their mums they look like boys again, hard on the surface, lost and bewildered underneath.

You don't want them to catch you staring though. Your loved one tells you about the mad dishes they cook using just a sandwich press and the 'job' he got cutting the grass for the gaol. He thanks you for the socks you dropped off because it's been getting heaps cold at night. It's so cold they leave milk out on the windowsill to keep it refrigerated.

Gaols are cruel, damaging places where most people don't deserve to be. I know that prisons do not make bad people good, but they did not seem like too much for what my father had done. There is no shame in wanting someone to be held accountable, or even punished, for hurting you or someone else. That the only repercussions available are punitive is a failure of society, not of survivors. What do we do with people who do things they can never fix? We do not individually have the tools – yet – to keep ourselves safe from abuse, especially when the perpetrators are seldom sorry.

However, this all still gives rise to a tension for me, in that the same system I am depending on to feel heard and validated after my trauma, remains a source of grief for countless families and communities – including my own. It gives rise to a tension in that I recognise the disproportionate rate of incarceration and deaths in custody for Aboriginal people within this structure. It gives rise to a tension because I feel like I have no choice but to settle for and pursue a form of accountability that does not represent the type of world I want to live in. These tensions lead me to resent Dad's violence even more.

I experienced discomfort as I wandered through the dark corridor of the Dubbo Gaol, with its cold walls and inhumane torture devices, aware that the system causes more harm than it cures, focuses on symptoms and not causes. Conscious that so far, the process had not captured Mum's experiences. Nor had it stopped new names being added to the lists of dead women. Nor had it changed the way that society expects men to be one way and women to be another. Nor had it made me feel safe. Nor had it resolved the consequences of the murder for my family.

In fact, the process had mostly excluded us. From the inter-locutory mentions to the hours spent at the front of the Court to the overcrowded pews – every part of it had been gruelling. Cross-examination was a chastisement, with Dad and his solicitor and Mr Stratton looking at me like I'd snuck out in the middle of the night with a boy. How funny that sneaking out with boys once seemed like the worst thing you could do.

THIRTY-ONE

During one of my earliest sessions with Jann, I'd asked whether I'd be able to give a victim impact statement and she'd replied, 'Yes, but only if you want to.'

Time had warped in the two years since, stretching and accelerating between bouts of depression over what had happened, and anxiety about what would happen next. I had rehearsed the things I could say in my victim impact statement while hunched over a running tap, scrubbing gunk from plates and knives. I'd gurgled ideas out loud while showering, made mental notes while driving and drafted fragments in the Notes app on my phone. All this was before the trial, when there was still a chance Dad might do something to prove he was sorry. It was before I'd seen him. Before the disturbing and disappointing experience of cross-examination, which laid bare the limitations of the criminal justice system. It was hard to tell if these limitations were flaws or features.

Even though victim impact statements were introduced as a way of giving victims greater involvement in proceedings, they're not evidence and the judges are not bound by them. There are also rules and limits to what they can include. In New South Wales, you cannot directly address the offender. You can't be offensive or aggressive. You can't talk about crimes other than the one for which the offender is convicted. You can't give your opinion about the offender or what sentence they should receive. These are the rules of the courtroom, but there's also an unspoken social pressure that victimologists have described well:

> 'Victims of crime occupy a social role, and where they are
> seen not to conform to the expectations associated with
> it, they diminish their chances of being sympathetically
> treated, and may even forfeit their occupancy of the role.'

You must be grief-stricken and meek. Not wild with rage. Certainly not vengeful. The only good victim is a helpless one.

*

The day before I was due to give my victim impact statement, I sent a message out to some friends I hadn't seen in a while, inviting them to attend court. It felt important to have their solidarity.

Moey and I decided to bring our son to court in his pram but left our daughter with my mother-in-law. My son's wide brown eyes and gold skin gave me something to admire on the train into the city. I'd felt terrible leaving him for the trial. I resented that motherhood had turned out this way.

When you have them, children are supposed to be the most important thing in your world. I'd been so distracted, there was no way I was doing motherhood right. For so long I had been dreading things: the next call, the next feed, the next court date, the next nappy change, the next difficult conversation. I was tired and it wasn't the kind of tired that can be fixed with extra sleep and a bubblebath. Parenting demands that we think ahead, gradually building a future for our kids. There was no promise that the future would be better than the past, and the past was awful. I was tired of all the things that were yet to happen.

Because of my father, I had spent my first two years as a mother in a daze, unable to enjoy my family. I hated him for taking that away from me. I wouldn't be able to get that time back, but now that the trial was over and I'd heard the words I needed to hear, things could be different. Maybe all this would finally settle into the past and I could find something to look forward to. I could go back to work or take a proper holiday. I could be more emotionally available for the kids. I could give them my undivided attention. I could take them to the good parks, do craft activities with them, teach myself to cook all the things Mum used to make.

The train rumbled through the inner west, rocking my son to sleep. I let myself get lost in the curves, bubbles and arrows of the graffiti on the walls we passed, in the chaotic lantana that creeps into unkempt spaces along the train line. I squinted as we shot through sun, shade, sun, shade.

I didn't have to read the victim impact statement out loud. It could be handed up to the judge. There was time to change my mind. This could be the last time I set foot in a courtroom. On top of everything, my father had damaged the passion I'd once felt for my job. My day in cross-examination hadn't just ruined the court and the law for me, it had ruined this whole city. The closer we got to St James, the harder I picked at my thumb. The flesh around my nail frayed and stung. My victim impact statement would be the last thing my father would hear from me, the last time I would have to see him, the last time he would keep me from my children, the last day he'd rob from me.

'Let's go.' Moey nudged me gently as we arrived at our stop.

Cameras were waiting in front of the King Street courts again. I swerved past them with my pram, towards Jann and my sisters who were already speaking quietly with Mr Barr. When I got to Mr Barr, I pulled out a plastic sleeve. It contained print-outs of messages I'd received, the things my cousins had posted online. 'This is what some of my dad's family have been doing and saying. If they're not sorry, he's not sorry. I know you can't do much with this, but I thought you should know.'

I stood next to Jann.

'Now, how are we feeling this morning?' she asked.

'Good. I think it's gonna be good to get this off my chest,' I said. 'This will be my last day here and the last time I have to see my dad. I'm having the last word.'

I'd sent her a draft copy of my statement a couple of weeks earlier, for her feedback. 'You've written a very strong statement. No matter what happens, your mother would be proud,' she replied with a smile and a nod that made her earrings sway back and forth.

*

Taking my seat in the witness box, I looked out at the room again. It was full. My friends were standing in the back. Dad was to my left. *You look so small today*, I transmitted as hard as I could across the room. His family were in the pews, as though they hadn't moved since the last time they were there. I was wearing another one of Mum's dresses. I hoped I would remind them of her. I looked back at Dad. *There's no 'allegedly' today. Today I am looking at a convicted murderer.*

'My name is Amani Haydar. I am the eldest daughter of Salwa Haydar.'

I steadied my shaking hands against the small wooden table in front of me, hoping no one would notice.

'I'm here to speak about the countless ways in which this crime has affected me. I have felt its impact every moment of every day for the last two years. In that time, I have not heard a word of remorse from the offender.

'I remember the night that I found out that my mum had been murdered. I remember feeling sick, confused and disgusted. I was five months pregnant at the time and I had just undergone a procedure to prevent a threatened miscarriage but, at once, I became infected with my mum's own protectiveness over my sisters. I made arrangements for them to sleep in my home. We slept with the lights on that week.

'I got up the next morning to prepare to take my sister to the hand specialist at Sydney Hospital. My morning sickness had completely subsided a few weeks prior, but I threw up violently as soon as I remembered what had happened. When we got to the hospital, I had myself admitted through the emergency department because of a tightening and burning sensation in my chest which made me fear for my baby.'

It felt strange giving this summary. The Court had delved so deeply into my father's state of mind with two psychologists assessing the extent to which his depression had influenced his crime. Now, here I was, reading out a one-page summary that barely touched on *my* depression, *my* isolation, *my* anger. There was no report about how my trauma had affected my mind and body or how it might excuse me from hating the people in this room.

'The next few days were a nightmare. I still wonder how I got through them and thank God for the calm he gave me in those difficult moments. But no calm could protect me from the reality of my father's actions. The funeral took a further physical and emotional toll on me. The next morning, I was admitted to hospital a second time for unexplained bleeding; again, I feared for my baby.'

I hope this makes you uncomfortable. I looked at Dad's face, square, flat, unreadable. My father would soon be given a very certain future, but I was gazing at a lifetime of uncertainty. I pushed on.

'Since that day, my husband and I have taken on not just Mum's duties but all of the responsibilities a parent should take care of. This has put pressure on me in an already difficult time in my life; financially, emotionally and physically.'

What will the trauma of these two years mean for my relationship with my husband? His solidarity had been unwavering. Would he get tired of this? Would my anger and sadness make me unlovable?

'I went from being a happy, excited, pregnant newlywed to a grieving full-time mother, maintaining a household of four, which quickly became five, and quickly after that, six. On top of that, I was doing paperwork and running errands for my brother to support his transition from prison to freedom; something which should not have been my responsibility.'

And where is my brother now that I need him?

'On 12 August 2015 I gave birth to a beautiful baby girl after a traumatic and lonely labour. As I lay there, exhausted but relieved, a kind midwife asked me, "Where is *your* mother?" She had not read my file which detailed what had happened and in which I was flagged as being at an increased risk of post-natal depression. I answered, "She was murdered in March by my father." The midwife looked at me with pity, but by that point, I'd gotten used to awkward conversations and I continued, "I am so happy to have a daughter. I am from a family of strong women."'

What incalculable impacts would all this have on me as a mother? What will I say to my children when they ask about my parents? How will I stop this from poisoning the future?

'I have spent two years trying to comprehend how someone could have such disregard for their wife and children. I find myself wondering whether anyone can truly be trusted. I have brought two children into this world doubting that it would be a safe place for them. The murder of my mother has erased every bit of security I had ever felt. The offender's total lack of remorse has exposed us to the cold and callous side of life.'

What's left to enjoy? I took a deep breath and read on.

'But you cannot take the wind from our sails. Our mother's legacy lifts us up. We have the confidence and power that characterised Salwa Haydar. We are the benefactors of her resilience and intelligence. She taught us to never settle for that which is not good enough. She taught us to value our happiness and to speak up when we have been wronged. She taught us to commit ourselves to lifelong learning and to helping others.'

Perhaps I am answering my own questions.

'So, on the date of the conviction we launched a fundraising event in honour of Salwa Haydar. We have raised five thousand dollars for the Cancer Council since that day. This is our way of turning the hurt, frustration and fear that we live with every day into something selfless and beautiful. By helping others heal, we heal. It is exactly what our mum would have wanted us to do. Western Sydney University has also honoured our mother's memory by presenting her with a posthumous bachelor's degree in Community Welfare. Walking up onto the stage to accept her award at graduation was one of the proudest moments of my life, but she should have been there herself. We should have shared that moment with her.'

Now, turn to him.

'Nothing will make up for my mother's death. No sentence will undo the permanent damage done to our lives. Indeed, the effects of your crime will continue to accrue.

'While you count down the days you serve in prison, we will continue to count memories and moments that we should have been able to share with our mother.'

Bodies shifted in the pews. Heads turned. Mouths leaned towards ears.

'But we will also be counting the many good things we will achieve in her memory. We will be counting the changes that will be made in our community as a result of this loss. We will be counting the many people who believe in us and who will support us in making the world a better place. Salwa Haydar taught us compassion and optimism, and we are repaying her every single day. She will forever have three loyal daughters who will keep her book of deeds open –'

I paused for one last look around the room.

'– and you cannot kill that.'

*

One of Mum's cousins clapped from the pews. I turned to the judge and waited for my cue to leave the witness box. His Honour was unimpressed by the ruckus but I felt like I had emerged from the stuffy courtroom into fresh air. Stepping down, I felt a little unsteady, lighter than I had been when I stepped up. Like my feet were full of helium. I went back to my seat, folding my statement neatly into my lap. It was done.

My sisters took turns to read out their victim impact statements. My dad was no longer looking at me. I was invisible now, shunned. I stared at the side of his face, reading its reactions, trying to decipher this man I once thought I knew. He was rapidly diminishing before me, becoming more and more abstract. When Nour spoke, Dad dropped his face into his palms and ignored her.

Ola's turn came next. She read out the final paragraph of her statement.

'While nothing will ever make up for what he did to her and to my family, I find some sort of peace knowing that I won't be risking running into him every time I leave my house. He has been the subject of my nightmares for two years; all I can hope for is that I never have to come face to face with him again.'

Dad lifted his head and let out a soft 'heh!' A scoff! I looked up at the judge, checking whether he'd seen it too, but he was looking at Ola. Dad glanced around the room with wide eyes, mouth pulled back on one side. Like it was ludicrous his daughter could feel that way.

His indignance made my arms pulse and my jaw tighten again. I'd been watching him as though I could hold him accountable with my eyes. It was clear now that I had to stop trying. I could not make him sorry. My presence had no effect on him. I was gazing into the abyss.

*

The gumtrees and houses were already sunset-pink when I opened the door, wondering who could possibly be coming to see us. A slender blonde girl was standing on the porch. She introduced herself as being from this channel and that show, working with that presenter. The presenter wanted to 'work together' on an episode about the murder. I nodded.

'Thank you,' I said. 'But what would you do about the Islamophobia? Because my sisters and I aren't allowed to just grieve and have opinions like everybody else would.'

Her mouth turned into a little 'o'.

'Well that usually just happens online after the show is done. We don't have to post it. It's better we speak to you than to your father's family – I saw them at Court today.' I had no idea what to say. The show itself had been part of the problem for years, and what on Earth could Dad's family have to say that would contribute meaningfully to a conversation about domestic violence?

'Hmm. Sorry, but I'm not sure what the point would be right now. We're tired, the trial has only just ended, we need to process a little. Maybe one day when it feels right, I'll get in touch, and then we can *work together.*' I smiled.

*

My victim impact statement, neither as profound nor as articulate as I would have liked, signals exasperation when I read back over it; 'Nothing will make up for what you have done. No sentence will undo the permanent damage you have done to our lives.'

I realised the power of it, however, because of the backlash it elicited from the people who had chosen to support my dad. 'You wouldn't be a lawyer if it weren't for him!' one uncle scolded outside the courthouse as I pushed past with my pram.

I loved myself a little better after reading out my statement, but it did not earn me any friends. I'd thought that maybe, by listening to my pain, my estranged family would show more empathy or realise the depth of the wound my father had inflicted. The opposite happened. When I shared my victim impact statement on Facebook, one person commented that my dad was a 'great father' and that the murder was just a 'tragedy'. When I deleted the comment, the same person rang and abused me, concerned that the family had been dragged into the limelight. 'YOU'RE A LITTLE SHIT, YOU KNOW THAT! YOU JUST WANT PUBLICITY.'

I responded in a monotone: 'I'm glad everyone's talking about it. If you or anyone else thinks that I'm going to let my mum be forgotten, you're wrong.'

THIRTY-TWO

During Dad's sentencing hearing, Mr Stratton made various submissions as to why the sentence should be mitigated even though 'the offence involving the accused taking human life is obviously objectively very grave'. He argued that Dad felt remorse 'about the death of his wife'. *Involving? Death?* Watching from the hard, wooden pew-benches, I'd felt a sting at each of these equivocations. The offence didn't *involve* my dad, it was committed by him. Mum did not simply experience a *death*, Dad murdered her.

Mr Statton submitted that neighbours, relatives and work colleagues had provided statements in support of Dad that 'his action in killing his wife is completely uncharacteristic behaviour on his part'. He argued that 'marital difficulties' may have been a 'trigger for his depression'. That his mental state was a mitigating factor in that it contributed to his 'flawed decision to attack his wife'. That he didn't represent a risk to the broader community and therefore fell into the 'low risk group for future offending'. That handing himself in to police was 'evidence of contrition'.

I disagreed furiously at every turn.

His violence was not uncharacteristic from Mum's point of view, but we can't ask her, can we?

Eating a whole packet of Tim Tams at midnight is a 'flawed decision'.

Of course he didn't represent a risk to the broader community! His abuse and his violence was linked to a sense of entitlement over his wife.

Handing himself in to police only proves he thought prison was less humiliating than ending his marriage!

I appreciate that Counsel was trying to achieve the best possible outcome for his client. Everyone is entitled to competent legal representation as a matter of procedural fairness, and it's an important part of keeping the law and the judiciary in check. But what's the line between robust advocacy and that which minimises crime or neutralises violence? What are the consequences of centuries of legal proceedings in which violent attacks against women have been justified as a legitimate response to 'provocation' and publicly characterised as 'a momentary snap' or, indeed, a 'flawed decision'? What are the emotional and psychological consequences of these words on victims?

Mr Stratton referred to a letter written by my dad to the Court in which he apparently 'very clearly accepts responsibility and blame for what he did'. I have never seen this letter nor was a letter of remorse ever addressed to me, my husband or my sisters.

In response, Mr Barr pointed out: 'In this particular case, you heard from the daughters of the offender, who have expressed their upset that the offender has not apologised to them for what he has done and how that has had an effect on them.'

'He has not had that opportunity –' started Mr Stratton before my father interjected from the dock in a defensive tone, his hand raised into the air in a high five, 'I sent five letters!'

*

It is true that Dad communicated with us a handful of times from the date of his arrest up to the date of the trial. None of his communications contained an apology for the crime he'd committed.

The first was the letter he sent in the first weeks after the murder in response to Nour's request for a visit. He informed us that *he* was 'too emotional' to see anyone and that 'Allah is with those who are patient'. As though it were *his* emotions that mattered. As though *our* patience was in question. My husband eventually (and reluctantly) visited my dad in an attempt to sort out some paperwork. Dad didn't express remorse in that visit; instead, he expressed disbelief at having to be in prison 'with these junkies'.

One or two equally meaningless letters arrived after that. There was a letter in which my father congratulated my husband and I on the birth of our daughter, and another instructing my husband to 'look after' my sisters and me (a disturbing parallel, given that he'd used the same words about Mum in the message he'd sent me while he was in Lebanon). At the end of 2015 he sent a 'Happy New Year' card with fireworks on the front. He said he hoped that 2016 would be 'better'.

Dad's letters generally have a few things in common; they are usually addressed to my husband, very brief, and never refer to or acknowledge Mum or the murder. I searched them for remorse every time, only to be disappointed and angered. My father's tone is always as though something has happened *to him*. Each one is self-centred and cryptic. They are as creepy as they are casual, as infuriating as they are mundane. Objectively, they look like an attempt at communication, but their effect is always one of denial and erasure. They do not give, they take.

*

In Australia and other Western jurisdictions, remorse is a mitigating factor in sentencing. In New South Wales, judges are legally required to take it into account during sentencing, if there is sufficient evidence for that purpose. Interestingly, in classical Islamic jurisprudence, remorse is seen as a personal and spiritual matter that does not mitigate the punishment or compensation able to be sought by victims of violent crime. It is seen as metaphysical, particularly in homicide, since the primary victim is not present to receive an apology anyway and no one truly has the right to accept one on their behalf.

In Dad's case, His Honour Justice Garling was 'satisfied that the offender has shown remorse for his actions' because of his 'offer to plead guilty to the offence of manslaughter'. This was seen to demonstrate 'that he accepts that his conduct caused the death of his wife and that he is legally responsible for those actions'. My brother had also provided a letter in support of Dad, which the judge accepted as having 'sufficiently acknowledged the injury, loss and damage caused by his actions'.

While this is legally sound, it is another example of the disconnect between legal proceedings and reality. *Don't confuse justice with the law.* Dad may have expressed remorse in a letter to the Court – which we never saw – but wasn't that just another step in the process? Walking away from the murder scene without calling for help, securing legal representation through his large and well-resourced family, fuelling the victim-blaming, failing to provide for my sisters who had lost their home and sense of security because of him, obtaining a character reference from his son, who is also a secondary victim of the same crime, offering to plead guilty to a lesser charge in a cultural context where reputation is paramount, seeking a judge-only trial to avoid the risk of prejudice, continuing to earn a rental income while in prison, seeking a mitigated sentence . . . White-knuckled and unrelenting, Dad had taken advantage of every legal and social opportunity available, even when it was at the expense of our health, safety and wellbeing. This did not look like remorse to me.

But what does remorse look like?

I took a deep-dive into Wikipedia to work out whether my expectations were misplaced. The word 'remorse' originates from the Medieval Latin word '*remordere*', which literally means 'to bite back'. There are famous works of literature and art dealing with the idea of remorse. The 1866 painting *The Remorse of Judas* by Edward Armitage depicts a Biblical scene in which Judas seeks desperately to make up for his betrayal. Judas is portrayed shirtless and bare, his arm and neck muscles appear tense as he thrusts a handful of silver coins towards three well-dressed long-bearded men who ignore and reject him. Judas's eyes are wide and unfocused. A vulture flies in the gloomy sky overhead, ready to pick off whatever is left of his soul, perhaps. The same wide-eyed torment is apparent in the *The Remorse of Orestes* by William-Adolphe Bouguereau, where Orestes clasps his hands to his ears while being tormented by 'Furies', goddesses representing vengeance in Greek mythology. In Ilya Repin's *Ivan the Terrible and His Son Ivan,* Ivan has just murdered his own son and appears aghast at his own actions. He cradles his son's head, fingers gripping the wound in a futile attempt to stop the blood that trickles out from between his fingers anyway.

I recognise remorse in the Islamic teachings I absorbed as a child. From a young age, I understood remorse as the emotion children should feel after doing wrong; what you feel when you say sorry and really mean it. Growing up I witnessed theatrical re-enactments of remorse over the Ummah's failure to sufficiently protect the Prophet's grandson Husayn ibn Ali Talib from the brutality that was inflicted upon him during the Battle of Karbala in 680 AD. This is an annual tradition that centres contrition as an important part of the pursuit of justice and, in turn, an important part of an individual's relationship with God. The ethos is: we make mistakes because we are imperfect but, so long as we are alive, we are able to mend them, and every time we mend, we draw nearer to God.

Although frowned upon and even banned in the Shia communities I've interacted with, re-enactments in some parts of the world go as far as public self-flagellation, resulting in infamous images of processions of men whose backs are dripping with blood as a symbol of their remorse.

In an article for *The Conversation* titled 'How do you measure remorse?', Australian writer Kate Rossmanith states that 'the courts are, or can be, theatres of remorse'. Rossmanith describes murder proceedings she observed at the Supreme Court of New South Wales, where 'the woman in the dock [. . .] kept tugging the edges of her black suit jacket towards her middle as if the fabric alone was preventing her insides from spilling out'. The body language of this convicted murderer is strikingly different to the way my father behaved as we read out our victim impact statements during the sentencing hearing. He didn't cry or hold himself when we spoke of how he had affected our lives. He didn't gasp or droop when Nour spoke of Mum's cold cheeks. Instead of sobbing or apologising, he had scoffed audibly when Ola said she would always be afraid to see him again. His behaviour was confident and indignant, not the 'ashamed, fearful, tight sort of a thing' Rossmanith describes.

Curious to know whether there is an objective way to test remorse, I asked some lawyers in my network for their insights. The criminal lawyers do not hesitate to say that they see it as their role to advise clients about how to express remorse. This includes steps that go above and beyond a letter to the judge, such as making sure to mention feelings of guilt to the psychologists who assess

them, to appear sorry around prison officers and even encouraging
them to 'put on the waterworks' in court. Now that I have been
a victim and a witness in a courtroom, this all seems detached
and methodical. Academic research on the topic acknowledges
that the 'the justice system may reward well-executed fakery'.
I am left feeling even more skeptical about the role of remorse in
criminal accountability.

Why did I need to see that he was sorry? What would it
have changed? Like the stories I had heard and the images
I had seen, I believed that remorse was a natural consequence
of murder. I wanted to see it because it would make the world
seem safe and predictable again. This desire is not unique to me.
I read that victims begin to search for remorse almost immediately
after a crime is committed, as part of their 'attempt to achieve
closure'. Traumatised victims are neither passive nor reaction-
ary. Instead, they engage in a 'cognitive investigation to find out
whether the perceived wrong-doers could have controlled their
errant behaviour' and, later, 'whether there was any justification
for the offender's behaviour and whether the harm was intended'
before they 'attribute responsibility'. I wanted ours to be a story
with a restorative outcome. I wanted to salvage some meaning
from what had happened.

THIRTY-THREE

On 19 May 2017, I busied myself with my usual routine. Morning tea, biscuits, daytime television in the background. Daytime television is horrible for your mental health. Advertisement after advertisement; cleaning products and life insurance. A morbid cycle preying on the insecurities of stay-at-home mums and the elderly: your visitors will hate you for your dirty toilet, your family will hate you for dying and making them pay for your coffin, and so on.

I sat on the couch with my bundled-up son, bouncing on my knee as it jiggled with nerves. My daughter was in the playpen. I checked the time and refreshed my Facebook feed, waiting to find out what would happen in the series finale of my own soap opera.

My phone buzzed with a message from Nour who was also following the news. She'd sent me a link. I clicked it nervously. A window opened and an embedded video began to play. It was Justice Garling in red. I started listening as he acknowledged the seriousness of murder and the importance of punishment, but my phone pinged with another article from Nour as the video played. Distracted, I scanned the headline and then the article:

'Haydar Haydar jailed for murdering wife', 'jealous rage' and '16½ years'. I went back to the window where Justice Garling explained the sentence: Twenty-two years imprisonment with a non-parole period of sixteen years and six months for the murder and, in respect of the wounding to Ola's hand, a fixed term of four years imprisonment. He wouldn't be eligible for release until 29 March 2033.

Nour sent another text. 'He shouted out that he was "totally insane" at the time of the murder. The judge cut him off.'

I texted back, 'What.'

My head was spinning. Dad was never going to acknowledge what he'd done. I went back to the article Nour had sent. It was from the *Sydney Morning Herald*.

'A man who murdered his wife in front of their youngest daughter stood in the dock and shouted, "I adore you my daughters, I love you so much," after being sentenced to eighteen years in jail,' the article began.

'"The stance of my daughters who I used to adore and I still love is as bad as my stance when I was insane,"' Dad had announced before the judge intervened to stop him.

In my distraction, my son had freed himself and was crawling towards a pot plant. My daughter was rattling the edge of her playpen, trying to get my attention. My home suddenly felt too small for us, too cluttered.

As bad as his stance?

Another text arrived from Nour. 'How dare he say we're as bad as he was!'

'My house is a bomb now. Dad's fault. I just let the kids destroy everything while I was finding out what was happening,' I texted back, now wrangling a shoe from my son.

'I don't understand,' she replied. 'We have done the bare minimum. Gave our VISs and distanced ourselves from his family.'

'I know.' I picked my son up and climbed into the playpen with him and my daughter. I sat at an angle and folded my legs so I'd fit.

'We haven't done or said anything unexpected from people whose mother has been murdered.'

Both babies were now piled in my lap. I had to hold my phone up above their heads to write back: 'Yep.'

Nour's final text was a picture of a Basquiat painting. It had just sold for $110 million. 'I want this,' she said.

I zoomed in on *Untitled* (1982). The lines were rough and thick. It was a painting of a skull, bare-toothed and hollow-eyed.

*

At the beginning of 2017, I decided to resume study. I *needed* to resume study. There were things I wanted to understand and think about. Maybe study would help me discipline my mind again. Before everything happened, before babies, I could think so clearly. I elected to start the research component of my masters and I knew what I wanted to write about. I wanted to know why we were expected to behave in ways that make murder comfortable for everyone else. I wanted to understand the pressure to accept the pain gracefully and quietly. Why did our legal system tacitly endorse these pressures? Why did people assume that we should help or forgive our father? Why wasn't everyone as angry about this as I was? Why did it feel wrong to be angry? I was in Auburn Library planning my research proposal when I discovered Judith Herman's *Trauma and Recovery*. Restless, I'd left my chair and drifted towards the closest shelves. *Trauma and Recovery* was only a few metres away from where I'd been sitting. Judith Herman's work is widely cited, but I hadn't heard of her yet. I'd been too busy reading about breastfeeding and sleep training and baby food. I'd never even thought of the words 'trauma' and 'recovery' together. It hadn't crossed my mind that there could be a recovery from something as big as 'my mum was murdered by my dad'.

I pulled the book from the shelf and flipped it open.

> 'To study psychological trauma is to come face to face both
> with human vulnerability in the natural world and with the
> capacity for evil in human nature. To study psychological
> trauma means bearing witness to horrible events. When
> the events are natural disasters or 'acts of God,' those who
> bear witness sympathise readily with the victim. But when
> the traumatic events are of human design, those who bear
> witness are caught in the conflict between victim and
> perpetrator. It is morally impossible to remain neutral in
> this conflict.'

'Wow,' I whispered to myself. *Where has this been all this time?* The murder was an unbearable thing. It would have taken a long time to feel okay after the trial. Insensitivity and harassment by some members of my extended family and inaction by the public made every stage – grieving, testifying, healing – infinitely more lonely and complicated than it needed to be. Dr Herman helped me understand why they were doing this.

> 'It is very tempting to take the side of the perpetrator.
> All the perpetrator asks is that the bystander do nothing.
> He appeals to the universal desire to see, hear, and speak
> no evil. The victim, on the contrary, asks the bystander
> to share the burden of pain. The victim demands action,
> engagement and remembering . . .'

Up until the trial, I had held on to these relationships, believing the behaviour stemmed from ignorance, not malice. I believed they might understand better when the trial was over. I had tried the nice route, but explaining and persuading only wore me down. I understood now, not all the family wanted us remembering. They didn't want us reminding. They didn't want to share our burden.

Throughout the trial and after the sentence was handed down, I received messages and missed calls from unknown numbers – some of Dad's overseas relations berating me, victim-blaming and slandering Mum. They said Allah would punish me someday because I was a dishonest daughter in breach of religious obligations to her father. When I used religious logic to demand support or invoke my rights as a victim, Mum's rights, they said I was too religious. One cousin even called me *daesh*. Another shared online that Dad was the wisest person he knew. 'You'll be free soon,' he wrote. 'I can feel it.'

The most absurd harassment I received was a barrage of old photos through Facebook. One of the photos was of Mum with early-nineties bangs, holding my baby brother. Another – which made every muscle in my body constrict – was a photo of my dad holding me. I would have been about three when that photo was taken. Underneath was a one-line message, 'We all love you.' I forwarded screenshots to a detective involved in Mum's case. He agreed that this was 'using a carriage service to harass' and paid a visit to one of the families involved.

When Dad was finally sentenced, social media was replete with headlines including 'A wife murderer shares chilling words for his daughters in court' and 'Haydar Haydar cries out in court as he is sentenced to 22 years for wife's stabbing murder'. The news was reported around the world, including on the LBC in Lebanon. I saw the activity the headlines generated. Islamophobes re-emerged with tired clichés. Overseas relatives from Mum's side clashed with some overseas relatives from Dad's side. Some of Dad's nieces and nephews – some of whom never even lived in the same country as Dad – lamented that my father had been a good person and was now being judged based on one 'incident'.

Some even engaged with the public. In response to a comment on an article in which a member of the public observed 'these girls have lost both their mother and their father', a relative replied, 'It is indeed sad about their mother, but as for their father, that was their choice.' This person went on to become a psychologist. I wonder whether she'd say the same thing to a client. I wonder how her own mother might feel reading those words. I wonder what choices she imagined we would have. I took screenshots of the harassment and abuse, saved them on my computer, then, one by one, I blocked the offending social media accounts and phone numbers.

Some of the people I grew up with did and said nothing. Some people I haven't seen or heard from since Mum's funeral. This was just as offensive. They ought to have known that my sisters and I would need to see or hear their support.

All the perpetrator asks is that the bystander do nothing.

THIRTY-FOUR

When Borce Ristevski was finally arrested for the murder of Karen Ristevski at the end of 2017, I read the reports and felt the familiar ripple of chemicals through my body. He was a pall-bearer at her funeral. He had comforted her family. Statistically, he was always the most likely to have killed her. But the lies and denials that had swollen around the crime made it all the more grotesque. Once they've done it, they have nothing left to lose.

Sarah Ristevski, the couple's only daughter, gave a television interview in 2020. It was the kind of interview I'd never feel safe giving.

'He's my father. I have one parent left . . . I loved him before, I love him now and I'll love him in eleven years when he's home,' she said.

I have learned not to judge the way a victim reacts to or copes with violent crime, but Sarah's words slid down my back like an ice-cube. I know that the mind does what it needs to do to protect itself. Violent crime presents you with a fact; it says, 'People are dangerous and capable of doing horrible things to one another.' The inclination is to search for a logical reason for why someone has done what they have done and, in the absence of a logical reason, we look for an exception. It is less challenging to continue loving your father, to avoid thinking about what he has done to your mother's body, than to pivot in the ways that reality demands.

This reluctance to accept the reality of violence is linked to victim-blaming. While working on my masters' research, searches of my university's library catalogue had led me to a book called *God and the Victim*. The authors, who combine Christian theology and victimology to provide chaplaincy to victims of crime, had explained that people may be dismissive towards victims of crime because 'crime victimisation makes us uncomfortable and fearful'. Although the book doesn't go as far as interrogating how patriarchal attitudes feed into this (and contains some musings on forgiveness that I couldn't relate to at all), it describes the experience of victimhood in a way that clarifies why I'd struggled to find people to connect with after Mum's murder and provides insight into why victim-blaming is such a common reaction to victims of crime:

'A victim's pain and questions too easily remind us of our own vulnerability, our own fears, and our own unanswered questions. We might offer condolences or a hug but our own fear and desire for safety keep us from reaching out fully to embrace another's pain.'

In her TV interview, Sarah Ristevski explained that she was unable to think about how her mum had died. 'It's not on my . . . I just can't go there.'

I thought about how vivid Dad's crime was in my mind. Maybe it had been easier for me to go there because I had been there before, with Teta. Maybe it was easier for me to go there because my sister was an eyewitness and had told me just enough immediately after the murder for me to be able to visualise it. What might I have been able to tell myself if I didn't have this undeniable account of my father's actions?

Sarah Ristevski opted against providing the Court with a victim impact statement for the loss of her mother and instead offered a glowing character reference for her father to 'highlight the man she knows'. The same night, I received a message from a cousin who used a number I didn't recognise to send me a link to an article about the Ristevski trial. They didn't have to say what they meant. In the eyes of some people in my family, Sarah is the good kind of victim. The kind that is loyal to her father, the kind that can be pitied because her anger is not demanding any space or action. I don't blame Sarah, but I knew her story was being weaponised against me.

There are many sentences I could have written that would be true and factual about Dad. He did not have a criminal record. He was highly educated and respected among his peers. He worked the early shift. He had taken steps to make sure we each embarked on a tertiary education. He picked mulberries with my siblings and me in the gully and gave me money to start a tutoring business. Sometimes he bought the groceries. Sometimes I felt sorry for him for not having achieved any of his big dreams.

Not once during the time between the murder and the trial did I think of offering a character reference for my father.

*

In an analysis of court transcripts from fifty-one homicide prosecutions between 2005 and 2014, researchers from Monash

University found that more than half had a history of domestic violence, but not all homicide prosecutions used and relied on 'evidence of prior violence'. The findings of the research were reported in an article in the *Sydney Morning Herald* in which Associate Professor Bronwyn Naylor points to the fact that the law does not capture the 'red flags'; 'some of this information was there but couldn't be built into the trial process'. This creates the impression that the homicide is 'hard to explain' or a 'one-off awful' incident 'even in cases where there was a history of violence, coercive and controlling behaviour'. This gap – the assumption that homicides are anomalies rather than a series of choices – allows men like Dad to claim that their actions were inexplicable and out of character. In the absence of any formal records of their 'red flags' it also allows them to be believed.

Further, according to an ACT government review of deaths resulting from domestic or family violence, a large proportion of domestic violence homicides occur with no prior reported history of violence. However, media reports invariably indicate that there is some form of abuse during the relationship between the offender and the victim and in the lead-up to the homicide. The law hears evidence of the offender's good character, but the person most qualified to give that evidence is dead. In many cases the offender's perceived good character has contributed to his ability to disguise and deny the abuse or discredit the victim. Their reputation is often instrumental in their abuse and enables them to get away with it for a longer period. There is no reference to any emotional abuse or other invisible forms of abuse that they may have inflicted, even though these can be as harmful as physical violence and contribute to long-term PTSD in survivors. By repeatedly asserting that our father was of 'good character' without 'any record', our father's family and

friends attempted to guilt and shame us for cooperating with
prosecutors, giving evidence and reading out victim impact
statements.

*

Dad didn't appeal.

THIRTY-FIVE

Haydar Haydar could have done things differently. He had a choice.

He was upset and humiliated when his wife asked him to pack his things. Who was pulling her strings? Was she thinking of someone else? All those early mornings and long shifts he'd worked, and now he'd been told to leave and never return. *I've been a good man*, he told himself. *I don't deserve to be treated this way*, he thought as he piled the last of his belongings, his books, into a tub.

When Haydar arrived in his village with his younger brother, they found their mother folded up on the floor of their childhood home. The air smelled of stale tobacco and *mazyoot*. The matriarch was draped in a blanket. She only recognised her younger son.

'*Kiifak ya ayni*! How are you, my eye?' she said and pulled him towards her. Then she turned to Haydar and offered a stiff, '*Salam alaykom.*'

He leaned in and said, 'You don't recognise me?'

She squinted, then looked away. They'd told him she was starting to forget things, but could she have already forgotten her son? How could she? He'd been the smartest and strongest of the lot! Haydar took her hand and tried to lift it to his lips. It was rippled and fragile, like wet paper. The old lady pulled her hand from his and tucked it into the blanket. In the village, women don't shake hands with strange men.

After *Asr* prayers, Haydar's brothers and cousins gathered in the garden. The men spoke of life and marriage and how well their children were doing. They took turns boasting: 'My son *professor de mathematique*'; 'My son *is an ingénieur*!'; 'My son is about to have a son!'

Haydar shifted in his chair, feeling small, *ad el namli*. 'And my son is graduating from prison!' he remarked.

It was a feeble attempt at a joke. The other men scratched their necks and gazed at the surrounding hills to spare Haydar the embarrassment. Someone changed the subject and asked, 'Did you hear what the president said last week?' Dad knew that an unsuccessful child was more shameful than corruption in the village.

A few days later, Haydar's uncle dropped dead. It was a heart attack. The men marched his body through the village towards the cemetery at the centre of the town where all the village martyrs lay. Haydar hadn't been to the cemetery in years. There lay his late father. There lay his late mother-in-law. As the men prayed for the dead uncle, Haydar wondered who his wife was seeing and speaking to in his absence. *She can't be serious about leaving me. Good men from good families don't get divorced.* He'd been trying to convince her to join him in the village. Just to talk, of course. She refused to come.

The next day, Haydar decided he was tired of the village. It was all death. He left his brother behind with his forgetting mother who simply waved and said, 'Thank you for visiting, *ya hajj*.'

He had to get back to Sydney to stop his wife from leaving him and destroying the whole family. He would destroy the whole world in order to stop her. *I don't drink or cheat or gamble. I always tell her exactly what's best for her. She makes it hard because she thinks she knows what's best for her. Why would she leave me?*

How could his wife and his mother be forgetting him like that? Maybe someday his daughters would forget him too and all he'd have left was his son and prison visits. What good is freedom if you're forgotten? *I won't let her go. I won't let her go.* There is nothing else to think about on the long flight from Beirut. He flies all the way to Sydney with both hands balled up in fists and doesn't touch the aeroplane food. *I won't let her go. I won't let her go.*

He gets to Valda Street and opens the door to his wife's house with the set of keys she'd asked him to leave behind. *Who is she to tell me where to leave her keys?* It's quiet. He takes a shower. Then he searches through his wife's things. He digs through her drawers and handbags. He doesn't even know what he's searching for. He should have asked someone to spy on her in his absence. He shouldn't have let her get a job. Now she was too smart and too independent. She didn't know her place anymore. This wasn't the nice girl he married. *Someone must be telling her what to do.*

Haydar lay back on the suede couch, his life playing in the air above him like an old cartoon. It is a long sequence of disappointing events. It's as if nothing has ever gone his way. *If people would just do what I need them to do, everything would be fine.* He needs to get back in control somehow. He does not know who to speak to. He could call his brothers. No. His brothers would be mortified to hear about a divorce. 'Divorces don't happen in families like ours,' they'd say, even though one of them was already divorced. 'Are you really going to let her leave you? What will people say!' *Ya 'ayb el-shoom!*

Haydar feels so unwell thinking about what other people might be thinking, he feels like he's going to throw up. No one has ever told him what to do with this anger. With this big hollow feeling. He falls asleep on the suede couch and dreams of a baby girl. The baby girl starts out small and starts to grow bigger before his eyes. Suddenly she is a toddler, suddenly she's a child of about five. She's familiar, with long dark hair and black eyelashes. She reminds him of his daughters but she speaks in Arabic.

She asks, '*Min inta?*' Who are you?

He answers, '*Ana Haydar.*'

The girl repeats, '*Bas min inta?*'

Haydar thinks and thinks, and he cannot come up with an answer.

The little girl smiles and holds out her hand. There is a small box in her palm. The box is lined with cotton and there is a silver key in the middle.

Haydar wants to know what this is. '*Shu hayda?*' he asks, reaching out for the box.

The girl says, 'It's not yours, it's mine!' and pulls her palm away.

Baffled, Haydar says, '*La, la*, I wasn't going to take it from you!'

The little girl starts to cry and big tears, bigger than raindrops, flow from her eyes but instead of falling to the ground they turn upwards and start falling into the sky.

'Don't cry,' Haydar pleads.

'You're a scary man!' The little girl sobs. The stream of tears gets wider and heavier and the drops keep gushing upwards into the sky.

'*Wallah*, I'm not scary,' he protests. 'I'm a good man!' But the little girl only cries harder.

'You're a bad man! You're a bad, bad man!' she screams.

'I'm not! *Wallah*, I'm a good man! I'm just sad! I'm a good man! I'm just sad!' He shouts, but the girl isn't listening anymore. Her tears are flowing like a river into the heavens, and the heavens are rumbling like thunder in the summer.

Haydar wakes up with a start.

He looks around. He's afraid and alone. His books are in a tub. His shoes are by the couch. There is nothing else left in this house for him. He gets up, knowing what he must do. He slips his feet into his shoes, picks up the tub of books and heads towards the door.

This time, he leaves the keys to the villa on the dining table and doesn't come back.

*

Dad could have done things differently. He had a choice. He could have walked away.

At some point, you have to stop trying to understand the abuser.

They want your world to revolve around theirs. You will not beat them because they will go to lengths that you are not prepared to go.

You must realise that they will not give you the ending you need.

THIRTY-SIX

By the end of my father's trial, I had set in motion three different things that would be crucial to my recovery: counselling for PTSD, resuming my studies, and the process of making sure Mum wasn't forgotten.

Good counselling, I learned from Natasha and Jann, doesn't feel like counselling. It should feel like a conversation.

Natasha told me about a book she'd read about how women are taught to ignore their gut instinct. 'You know that feeling when you get into an elevator along with a man and you tense up?' she quizzed and I nodded. She continued, 'That's our instinct alerting us to a possible danger. We've been taught to ignore that and to be pleasant and friendly instead.'

I thought of every time I'd experienced that feeling and what a lonely and anxious child I was. Perhaps I was attuned to a danger all along.

Natasha taught me to allocate a specific period of the day, each day, to think my angry thoughts, rather than allowing them to disrupt my activities throughout the day. After tucking the kids into bed each night, I'd prepare a coffee, pull my journal out and sit with my angry thoughts and they would tremble through me; *I CAN'T BELIEVE ANY OF IT, HOW DARE HE, MAY ALLAH NEVER FORGIVE THEM.* After twenty or thirty minutes in this wilderness, I'd be filled with impulse and urgency and ideas. I brainstormed and listed and worked and imagined my way out of PTSD.

Anger is not a thing of shame.
Anger is not a thing of shame.
Anger is not a thing of shame.

Al-Ghazali said Allah gave us anger so that we could identify injustice and work to remedy it.

*

I wonder what would have happened if Mum survived.

She would have been hospitalised. Sixty per cent of hospitalised assaults against women and girls in Australia are perpetrated by a spouse or domestic partner. Sixty-nine per cent of those assaults take place in the home. She would need several major surgeries. A police officer would stand by Mum's bed and tell her she was lucky to have lived. The statistics show that, if this happens again, she might not be so lucky. We would need to make a plan. Dad would be charged. An AVO would be put in place. He might be let out on bail.

I imagine my mother's wounds stitched shut, healing. Sixty-three per cent of assaults against women and girls include injuries to the head and neck. Mum's injuries included injuries to her head and neck. I imagine Mum recovering. She might have been among the forty per cent of family violence victims who sustain a brain injury. According to a report by Brain Injury Australia, she might have lived with paralysis, memory loss, chronic pain, seizures, vision and hearing disturbance, speech and cognitive impairment.

Mum might have lived with a disability. The New South Wales Department of Communities and Justice recognises domestic and family violence as the leading cause of illness and disability for women aged under forty-five. According to the Domestic Violence Resources Centre Victoria, 'Broken bones, PTSD and anxiety can each be the foundation of longer term disabilities.' Mum might have struggled to find the right support because people with an acquired disability are often 'referred to a disability service rather than the violence being addressed as the primary issue'. Over time Mum might have adjusted. Lots of women do. But she'd still face the 'secondary experiences of discrimination, social revulsion, poverty, marginalisation, exclusion, rejection and victimisation' that come with disability.

Mum would require lifelong counselling for trauma. She would have a higher risk of addiction, depression and other mental illness. She might be irritable and struggle with parenting. She would have a reduced capacity to work, reduced hours, reduced income, mortgage stress. Domestic violence is the biggest cause of homelessness for women in Australia.

Mum might have recovered but the long-term impacts of the attack would remain unknown. Things might go undiagnosed and untreated. There could be health complications down the track. There are studies linking the psychosocial stress of abuse to the incidence of cancer among women, later diagnosis and poorer post-diagnosis outcomes. There are links to eating disorders, sleep disorders, suicide. There are links to asthma, heart problems, digestive problems, problems with the immune system, sexual health problems.

What if the trial had been for an *attempted* murder?

We would have given our statements. Maybe it would be easier to believe that Dad had committed a serious assault than it is to believe he is capable of murdering someone. Mum's not anywhere near as shocked as we are. She would say she told us so. She told us he was *la-iim*, cruel. We'd say we were sorry it had to get to this before we understood. Mum would want her husband to go to gaol. Yet she wouldn't want her children's father to go to gaol. We would talk about it, plan and prepare, find our allies.

We'd go to court. I imagine Mum pursuing her rights, giving evidence against Dad. Nervously, bravely, deep breaths between sentences. I'd be there for her. I would remind her of the time that she told me about the fake suicide note, and tell her to write it down. 'You've gotta put that in your statement, Mum, it's important.' I imagine her apologising for sharing that with me when I was too young to comprehend it. I wouldn't be angry at her anymore, I'd understand. She'd tell me the things she didn't tell me then. She'd be embarrassed and anxious talking about her marriage and our dad, but we know now that this is a matter of life or death.

Mum would be upset but not surprised that some people take Dad's side. They'd slander and backbite and gossip and victim-blame, but they wouldn't have the guts to do it to her face. She's smarter than them and she's angry. She'd tell them to eat a shoe. '*Fasharto!*' She'd do an interview with the news and the radio, just like she did in 2006.

Mum would know that, deep down, other women understand. They've told her their secrets. They, too, fled wars and loving families into the arms of trusted men. Some of them came here still babies, gangly like fifteen- and sixteen-year-old girls often are. I've seen the old photos of stick-figure brides with big ears. They gave birth, worked in factories, left their war wounds untreated. Judgments and insults accumulated over the years; half of them are on antidepressants now. They're too tired to fight and leave like Mum did. It's too late. They've seen what happens if you try.

Slowly, slowly, things would settle down. Scars would heal and Mum's cheeks glow pink again. We wouldn't clash as much as we used to because I am a mother too now.

I'd get back into painting while the kids played. Mum would come over and bake her lasagne just how I like it – with mixed spice on the mince and bechamel from the jar. The kids would rummage through her good handbags and tug at her pockets, hungry for Chiclets and chocolates. She'd ask me to paint her portrait. I'd groan and fuss but, eventually, I'd get around to it.

*

Just as I started to feel like I was recovering again mentally, I started to feel weaker physically. My bones collapsed like a house of cards. My hip slipped out of place as I tried to lift my chubby son from the floor. I set him back down on the tiles and dropped to the ground as pain shot through my leg and spine. I crawled to my phone and called Moey home from work. 'I think I slipped a disc or something,' I said. He took me to see the doctor who said I had injured my sacroiliac joint. Women who have recently given birth are more susceptible to this.

'The good news is that this isn't as serious as the pain would suggest,' the doctor said.

After two days without improvement I went to see a local woman who people swore by. '*Wallah*, she cured my baby's colic!' they said. Her rooms were at a medical centre, where the seats were always full and there was always a long wait, even if you had an appointment.

I stood in front of her and she pushed my bones back into a straight line using her palms and body weight. Then she gave me a massage, and wherever she touched hurt like a bruise. I flinched and said, 'Ouch,' as she pressed knuckle into muscle. It was useless, like trying to soften the kids' dried up playdough. She laughed and said, 'You're so sensitive, most people enjoy this!'

She didn't ask how my body got this way. Instead she said, 'You need to drink more water, your thigh muscles are stringy like spaghetti,' and 'You need to lose weight, it will help with your knees,' and 'You're in pain because you don't stretch.'

In my third session, she put acupuncture needles down my back and connected them to a machine that sent a shock through each needle, straight into my nerves. I clenched my fists throughout the treatment. The zaps forced my flesh to untie itself and I felt like a wet sponge afterwards.

I knew my body was hurting because I had been under so much pressure for so long. But this attempt at healing had failed to recognise the emotional and psychological dimensions of my pain. Instead of feeling validated and supported, I felt embarrassed at how I'd let my health deteriorate; blamed for the consequences. I never went back.

THIRTY-SEVEN

I had met Mariam Mourad, the CEO of the Bankstown Women's Health Centre, at the memorial I held for Mum at the end of Dad's trial. I held the memorial at a community hall instead of the mosque so that it would be a women's only event. I organised my own speaker and a spoken word poetry performance and an auction of a still life I'd painted. Ola's friends helped with catering. One of Mum's cousins had brought Mariam as a guest. A few months later, she called me and said there was an opening on the board at the organisation and that it would be wonderful to bring in someone with a legal background. She said the bulk of the work at the organisation involved dealing with the effects of domestic violence on women's lives, both at the height of crisis and years later when the longer-term damage reveals itself. Mariam called me a survivor. I'd never thought of myself as a survivor.

At the end of 2017, I joined the board at Bankstown Women's Health Centre at the annual general meeting. I learned that we were one of only twenty government-funded women's health centres state-wide. The centre sits on Jacobs Street in the heart of Bankstown and caters to one of Australia's most culturally diverse communities. It's a women's only safe space. It is estimated that fifty per cent of its clients are culturally and linguistically diverse women, and almost all report past or current experiences of abuse. When Mariam first showed me the space, she said, 'In women's health, we don't ask, "What's wrong with you?" We ask, "What happened to you?"'

Here, women recognise that your sore body is about a lot more than how much water you're drinking and whether you've been stretching. They know that there is you now and you before the things that happened to you. The sun penetrates the waiting area where there is a big painting by local Aboriginal women. The handprints remind me of my grandmother's palms. There are trauma counsellors and case workers and a doctor at the centre. Women can self-refer for advice about sexual and reproductive health, about living with cancer, about living with an abuser, about abortion.

I start to learn about the correlation between trauma and poor health outcomes. I learned that Aboriginal and migrant women experience worse health outcomes than the broader population. They are less likely than other women to identify cancer early and seek treatment. They are less likely to survive. There's a trauma-informed dietician at the centre – for women who eat their feelings, like I do. Migrant women and Aboriginal women are less likely to report domestic violence. They are not safe reporting to police and may even be misidentified as the abuser. They might have had terrible experiences with the police before; they might not want their loved ones punished or hurt. Women feel safer talking to other women, telling the story at their own pace while they share and cook and eat. If you create welcoming programs, women will come. And if you're trauma-informed, women will build trust with you. And if they trust you, they will disclose. They all have something to disclose.

Later, I attended a meeting with the peak body. There was a discussion about whether it was the right time to campaign to decriminalise abortion in New South Wales. There was a discussion about how long it has taken to explain to politicians that abortion is not a crime issue but a health issue. There was a discussion about domestic violence and how it is not just a crime issue but a health issue. There was a discussion about the refuge movement and the reforms that decimated the refuges. There was a discussion about the rate of anxiety among young women. Someone said that this is the consequence of living in a perpetually traumatic patriarchal society. Everyone in the room was nodding. I was quiet because I was new, but it made total sense to me.

Bankstown Women's Health Centre holds a large anniversary event and I meet more people from the sector. An older woman named Jo plays the guitar. She sits at the front of the big hall we are in and sings Helen Reddy's 'I Am Woman' while we follow along off a song-sheet. We're getting the words and timing wrong but we're singing at the top of our lungs. It's so cheesy I want to cry.

On International Women's Day 2018, a local campaign was launched at the Bankstown Women's Health Centre and the mayor and our local member of parliament attended. I gave the keynote address; my first speech as a survivor-advocate, although I didn't yet feel like a survivor or an advocate. We unveiled a little rose garden at the front of the centre. A plaque stood between the newly planted rose bushes; dedicated to women and families affected by violence, in memory of Salwa Haydar.

*

There are difficulties that come with self-advocating, let alone becoming an advocate for a cause. I had to better understand the sensitivities and nuances around domestic abuse. I spent a lot of time researching, reading, chatting to mentors and identifying safe spaces. I've also had to learn my limits, how to space out speaking engagements and manage triggers through effective self-care. I am conscious that being able to advocate for myself doesn't necessarily make me the best advocate for others.

Within my advocacy, I've been asked whether my experience with the officers handling my mother's murder was positive and whether I would suggest any improvements. My answer is this: whether I had satisfactory experiences as an individual is neither here nor there. The process may have brought me relief, it may have made me feel safer, but we already know from domestic violence advocates that that safety is not guaranteed through police or even the criminal justice system. This is especially the case for Aboriginal women, who, as Dr Hannah McGlade writes, are overrepresented as victims of abuse and also twenty-one times more likely to be incarcerated than non-Indigenous women. Writing for the *Guardian*, Latoya Aroha Rule points out the paradox we find ourselves in when our fight for gender parity does not consider structural racism: 'Women's liberation marches have been growing since the 1960s in Australia, just as the incarceration rates and deaths of Aboriginal women in custody have steadily increased.' Latoya urges advocates to expand their work beyond interpersonal violence, to 'say no to state violence' so that the needs of all women are heard.

Ultimately, no matter how well trained the police officers who respond to reports of domestic violence are, if women's experiences with police have been abrasive or even harmful on our better days, can we be blamed for not trusting them on our worst days? If we've witnessed racism or cruelty from them towards people who look like us, can we really feel safe in their presence when we are vulnerable or traumatised? These, as we have learned from abolitionist feminists and the international #BlackLivesMatter movement, are the bigger questions. Questions that go beyond my personal experiences as a victim of crime. Questions that, in the context of domestic violence and other violent crimes, require us to see victims as multi-dimensional people who will find themselves at a crime scene or standing in front of a courthouse carrying the weight of past trauma, race and religious identity with them.

Despite the limitations and structural barriers, self-advocacy through storytelling provides a powerful tool both on a personal and political level. When done in safe places, the storytelling process is an effective tool for combating the shame and taboo that victims are often made to feel about their experiences. Jess Hill, with David Hollier, writes a whole chapter on shame in *See What You Made Me Do*. They say, 'when abusing people are confronted with feelings of shame, they take the path of least resistance'; they attempt to avoid or shift the shame to others through their violence. Storytelling cracks the crust of shame imposed on victims and shifts the burden to where it rightfully belongs: spitting and smouldering in the palms of the abuser.

At the core of storytelling is a desire to reconnect with the world and to do so safely. In *Trauma and Recovery*, Dr Judith Herman describes reconnection as the third stage of recovery from trauma. Violence destroys connections. Through storytelling, victims and survivors build new relationships, develop a new sense of self, create meaning out of their experiences and 'in accomplishing this work, the survivor reclaims her world'.

The best storytelling is that which builds a community and it is, in turn, a communal responsibility to make the space – in courtrooms, media, schools, society – safer for stories. That way, victims know that they are welcome and supported to reclaim their narrative and thereby reclaim their world.

THIRTY-EIGHT

In late Ramadan 2017, about a month after Dad's sentence had been handed down, I was having a sleep-in when I received a message from the cousin who had banged his hand into my coffee table. I had blocked his number, so the message arrived from one of his social media accounts. Seeing his photo in the icon immediately filled me with dread.

The message started with an abusive preamble, and concluded with this:

'Your father is suffering immensely, and being *Laylatul Qadar*, *inshallah* you can open up and forgive him. The court has sentenced him, and now it is time to move forward and forgive *inshallah*.'

I read and re-read the message, then nudged my husband.

'Hun, listen to this, my cousin hereby requests that we forgive him and my dad because, according to *his eminence*,' I drolled, 'tonight is *Laylatul Qadar*.'

The demand was so absurd I giggled even though my heart was thumping with rage. How dare he use one of the holiest nights of the month of Ramadan as an excuse to contact and guilt me.

Different schools of thought have postulated about what the exact date of *Laylatul Qadar* might be, hoping to pinpoint it and reap the thousandfold spiritual rewards promised in the Quran, but no one can say for sure when it occurs. As a child I imagined it; an inky blue sky streaked with glitter and a waning moon shaped like a mango. The rustling of leaves was the trees chanting their prayers. I imagined two gigantic angel wings arching over our house in an invisible dome of inter-meshing feathers and moon-dust, protecting us from everything outside. I was too young to know that evil is, more often, on the inside.

My husband read the message. 'So he says it's a religious obli-gation to look after your dad, but no mention of his obligation to look after his daughters?'

'Yep.' I rolled my eyes. 'Not that we'd want anything from any of them anyway. And what's with 'even if he was wrong'? *Even if?* How can you demand forgiveness when you can't even identify and acknowledge that you've been harmful?'

'Are you going to message him back?' Moey asked.

I stared at the screen, itching to respond with all the ways the message was wrong and abusive and a list of reasons why he and my father were not entitled to forgiveness. I knew, however, that this would simply drain me of the energy I had been working so hard to get back.

'If these people do not understand by now, there is nothing I can say to make them understand,' I said as I slid my phone onto the bedside table, relaxed my shoulders and burrowed back into my pillow. 'Plus, this is spiritual abuse. He is trying to manipulate and drag me into a conversation.'

I have lost sleep from the symptoms of grief and PTSD. I have lost sleep worrying about my babies, and the future. I have lost sleep thinking about how to approach challenges in my work and in my writing. I have lost sleep caring about my family, missing dead women, arguing with people on social media.

I have never, not once, lost sleep over ending my relationship with my dad.

*

I couldn't imagine that my dad would bother getting in touch after everything he'd done and said at the trial, but there have been two letters since then. They are different from the first few in that they are addressed to me and not my husband. Although I always kept my maiden name, my father uses my husband's surname. 'Maybe I've finally been disowned,' I joke. The correspondence is disturbingly cheerful. Somehow, in my father's mind, our relationship had moved into a light-hearted place. This makes me feel even more sick than I felt being stared at with disappointment in the courtroom.

This one arrived within a few days of my thirty-first birthday. The purple 'postage paid' stamp was immediately familiar. I turned it over and saw the return address, *H. Haydar, Macquarie CC.* As the words registered, my head felt like it was inflating, pressure building up inside my skull. I could just toss the envelope in the bin; all of his correspondence had been self-centred and cryptic. But, even though the trial is over and my life has moved forward, I feel like I am waiting for something. Closure? An apology? I am embarrassed to still want these things as I open the envelope, tearing it along the short edge to avoid touching the sticky seal where I imagined he might have placed his saliva.

I pull out a sole piece of brown paper – a scrap torn from another envelope. The words 'I wish you a very happy birthday' are scrawled in red ink, big and jagged across the paper. Dad has put a degree of effort into this; I can see the pencil markings indicating a draft underneath the text. There is a smiley face in the 'Y' at the end of birthday. It looks like a bat. Or a demon.

Underneath, in smaller black cursive, he's written an instruction: '*Smile Please!*'

*

As a junior solicitor I read a book called *Nice Girls Don't Get the Corner Office: Unconscious Mistakes Women Make That Sabotage Their Careers*. I was experiencing culture shock, having moved from working with youth in Western Sydney to practising in a commercial law firm run by much older men. The only much older man I'd had any kind of relationship with was my dad. My new environment was triggering anxiety and perfectionism in me like no other place I'd worked before.

Nice Girls contains a huge list of behaviours that women are conditioned into that don't serve us in workplaces where decisiveness and productivity are rewarded. It contains a list in the front where the reader is invited to tick off traits she feels are holding her back in the office. The subsequent chapters elaborate on where those behaviours originate (generally in childhood) and how they prevent us from excelling in professional spaces. I flipped through to the parts I could relate to and worked through them.

I felt empowered by the text, although I am now very aware that women are not self-sabotaging anywhere near as much as the world is deliberately structured to hurt us and minimise our influence. Because of *Nice Girls*, I started to reflect on how women are taught to appear pleasant and approachable from a young age because this aesthetic is more in line with the roles we're supposed to take on, as attentive carers and lovers in adulthood. We end up wearing smiles when there is nothing to smile about, as a defence mechanism and to avoid conflict. To a degree, I was able to unlearn this and other behaviours, and felt a real difference in my confidence at work.

Later, when I decided to start practising hijab daily, the pressure to smile manically and constantly returned. I felt it when I was walking down a street, waiting on a train platform, requesting something at a reception desk. Maintaining this pleasant facade conflicted with the grief and frustration of my inner world. Noticing this pressure, I wondered how it had come about. Perhaps it was a way to disassociate myself from scary-Muslim-terrorist tropes now that I wore my religion on the outside. It also seemed to stem from a general sense of fear and distrust of the world around me; I didn't have the capacity to take on any more conflict or face any more trauma. Niceness is a disarmament. A way of saying, 'Please don't hurt me.'

Over the past few years, discussions about workplace harassment, street harassment and #metoo have excoriated the politics of men telling women to smile. As I write, there are over 139 million hits for 'men telling women to smile' on Google. In a piece from late 2016, a contribution by *Fabulize Magazine* published on HuffPost.com talks about men telling women to smile on the street. *Fabulize* writes, 'Telling a woman to smile, even if your intent is purely innocent is dictatorial and it shouldn't happen.'

A piece in *The Atlantic* explores the same phenomenon in the workplace, multiple women share stories of being pressured to wear a smile in the workplace and suffering consequences when they don't. Another piece on APNews.com states that 'plenty of women just smile because they're afraid of provoking the man who asked.' A piece by Karen Banes on medium.com explores the 'sexist connotations behind a simple imploration' pointing out that 'women have serious shit on their minds, almost permanently. With many women still working what sociologists call the second shift, they likely have twice as much serious shit on their mind as most men.' An artist named Tatyana Fazlalizadeh, the creator of stoptellingwomentosmile.com, created an entire series of portraits and a street art project addressing gender-based street harassment.

Notwithstanding all of this criticism, it might still be tempting to dismiss the command to smile as a minor infringement in comparison to physical and structural violence. However, standing in the kitchen with my father's birthday card in my hands, reading the words '*Smile Please!*' over and over again, the link couldn't be more tangible. Only a week or two earlier, my photo had appeared in *The Australian* alongside an important article by Nicola Berkovic about the implications of domestic abuse for migrant women. When the photographer arrived at my home to take photos of me in my studio, I was thinking about the gravity of these stories. My work doubles as an expression of grief and love. I was feeling nervous about being in the paper and harbouring a healthy skepticism about the role of mainstream media in stories about migrant women. I was self-conscious about my appearance and keeping an eye on my children who were present throughout the photo-shoot.

There was *a lot* of shit on my mind. I was not smiling.

My guess is that my father saw that photo in the paper. But even if he didn't, there is no way his words could be read as genuine concern for my wellbeing. The last time I'd seen him was at court, remorseless. The last thing he'd said was that my sisters and I were *as bad as* he was. Of all the things he could have written in this card, all the ways he could have said sorry, all the ways he could have enquired after me, he chose, '*Smile Please!*'

This, like everything else my father has done since the murder, is another denial of my anger and grief. It is gaslighting. Like trying to convince Mum to join him for a holiday in Lebanon, even though she had told him it was over; like telling Ola to stop screaming during his attack and shaking his head in disappointment as I gave evidence. It is a command that I mitigate my feelings towards him and make it easier for him to erase the reality of what he has done. It is abuse.

It is how I know he still isn't sorry.

*

My daughter asks about my father.

'Where's your baba?'

'He lives far away,' I answer.

'Why don't you visit him?'

'Because I am not friends with him anymore,' I answer, carefully. 'Sometimes big people do really bad things or make us really, really sad. When they do, it is okay to stop being friends with them.'

*

It's late 2018 and I'm at a Western Sydney girls' high school delivering a talk for a White Ribbon Day event. I don't mind speaking to high school students. I spent three years in Western Sydney schools tutoring, mentoring and supporting young people while I was at university. Today my audience are Year 10 girls from a mix of backgrounds: Turkish, Afghan, Arab, African and Pacific Islander. I know from experience that, for many of these students, this will be their final year of school.

I have heard white teachers at schools like this one say things like, 'We can't wait 'til their gone!' and 'I don't know how you put up with those animals!' Next year some of these students will have to work to help their families. Some won't be allowed or supported to attend university when they leave. Some of them will be married with children within a year or two. A majority are from migrant and refugee families. Why should they care about trigonometry or what Mrs Johnson thinks of them?

The teacher coordinating this event, however, is kind and warm. She leans in as the students take their seats. She says, 'Now, we have a few girls who have had trouble at home, so this will be good for them to hear.' I confirm that they have the school counsellor on standby and I start my talk with a content warning, reiterating that I won't be offended if anyone needs to take a break or leave the room.

I always start with an explanation of the global dynamics of gender-based violence. I want the girls to understand that this mess will follow us no matter where we go. I explain the link between casual sexism and gender-based violence using a pyramid-shaped diagram. They are not convinced because sexist remarks happen every day at home and on television and in the songs they listen to. They assume rape and murder are rare scandals. I tell them that both crimes are much more common than they think.

Then I click through my slides and tell them my story. There's a photograph of my grandmother, taken when she visited us in Sydney and a photograph of my mother from her last trip to Lebanon. We watch a news interview I did about Mum and my entry to the Archibald Prize, which I include in my presentation for two reasons: it saves me having to go through everything myself and it stops them from thinking I made the whole thing up. I explain the effects of losing my mum, taking time to talk about the way it affected my mental and physical health in case one day they, too, find themselves with bodies and minds marked by trauma. I tell them about what it was like having PTSD, about not being able to stop eating, and about picking my thumb until it was raw and crooked.

One or two girls smirk and whisper to their friends. I don't mind because my heart is already heavy for them. I try not to be cynical, but I see the statistics in my slides projected over this room of young women; the inevitability of the data. One in three, one in five. I talk to them about emotional abuse and red flags but this knowledge will only go so far because we haven't made the world safe for them yet. I can't promise them anything. All my story does is tell them this is real. When you see it, recognise it. When a friend confides in you, believe her. When it happens to you, seek help. When they try to silence you, remember you have a right to speak. You have the right to place boundaries.

'You have the right to be safe.'

There is time for questions at the end and hands drift into the air, hesitantly at first, more energetically as the conversation builds. I get three different iterations of the same question: Have you forgiven your father? Will you have a relationship with him someday? Do you feel bad for cutting him out of your life?

They never ask about Mum or my plans for the future. The forgiveness questions are triggering for me, but these questions are important and need to be addressed. I answer each one with a clear 'no'.

'I do not forgive him.'

'I don't want a relationship with him.'

'I don't feel bad at all! In fact, I sleep very well at night, thank you.' I smile.

They are captivated by these declarations because no one has ever told them that it is okay to unapologetically remove men from your life. No one ever told me. Some of the girls nod in agreement and others appear frozen in thought. Maybe even slightly disgusted. I don't mind. I've been there.

'If you take anything away from this today, I want it to be this,' I say slowly and deliberately. 'No one has the right to hurt you, *not even* your parents. You are *never* obliged to forgive someone who has hurt you, but you have the choice to do so if it feels safe and right for you. It is never, *ever* your job to fix someone who is harmful, and it is never your responsibility to carry another person's mistakes.'

The girls are still and silent. I am exhausted. I want to be in a world where this is not a conversation we need to have.

THIRTY-NINE

'Muslim Burial Section 8' at Rookwood Cemetery is by the tele-
graph tower and the train line. As I pull over, I notice other people
conversing quietly with God by the graves of their loved ones. It
looks like a funeral has just finished; a small group stands around
a fresh mound of clay. I remind myself, *inna lillah wa inna illayhi
raji'un*: we belong to God and it is to Him we return.

I greet the sea of identical modest headstones – *assalam
'alaykum* – under my breath, expecting no reply. Arriving at my
mother's resting place, I empty the vases that flank her tombstone and fill them with fresh water and blooms before turning to
her neighbours.

In an adjacent row, sixteen-year-old Mahmoud Hrouk is
buried. I take my spare flowers to him. Mahmoud was sexually
assaulted and murdered in May 2015 by Aymen Terkmani, who
left his body in an abandoned house in Villawood. Terkmani was
subsequently found guilty and sentenced to a maximum of forty-
five years in prison.

Mahmoud's youthful face is never far from my thoughts; his
funeral happened soon after Mum's and the sadness of their two

stories seems to have fused in my mind. The last place Mahmoud was seen alive was at my local McDonalds. I often imagine him on his bike in the car park as I drive through. At Rookwood, I notice the lilies by his tombstone are still in the bud. I think of his mum.

I then wander towards the back of Section 8, where, right by the fence line, lays baby Omaira: 'Born without breath, but not without love.' Omaira died at five months' gestation when her pregnant mother was attacked by her abusive male partner. Omaira's tiny, humble grave has been decorated with pebbles and rainbow windmills. I remind myself to bring more flowers next time.

A breeze tugs at hairs that have strayed from my hijab. Children without parents, parents without children.

Who else is here because of male violence?

*

When Mum was murdered, Islamophobes wrote articles that ignored the reality of violence against women in Australia and reduced the incident to a caricature. The Australia First Party proclaimed on its amateur website, 'Muslim immigrant to Sydney murders his wife because she wouldn't pass the salt', while another source referred to the murder as an 'honour killing'. In these spaces, Mum's faith rendered her distinct from most of the eighty other women who lost their lives to violence that year. Already contending with trauma and grief, and conscious of this broader context, I was paralysed at the thought of engaging with the media.

It was frustrating to watch everyone other than the people who really loved and knew Mum participate in a conversation that didn't just shut us out but hurt us. Even though I had been able to give a speech at the mosque for Mum's *arba'een* – an empowering moment – my family, my community and wider society had become increasingly unaccommodating of my grief.

At a service held for Mum a year later, I walked out of the mosque, with a baby on my hip and another in my belly, in protest against an uninformed and harmful sermon in which the speaker shamed women who initiate divorce or 'embarrass' their husbands by involving police. The sheikh blamed women for increased divorce rates with that tired old line: 'The women are imprinted by the Western society.'

Such is the double-bind Muslim women survivors and activists find ourselves in. Between the screeches of Islamophobes and the booming voice of patriarchy within our own community, there is little room left for Muslim women to share their truths freely. Many of us want to critique patriarchy, to talk frankly about how rigid gender roles and inequality fuel violence and abuse. But we're also worried our stories will feed the racists or invite family disapproval, victim-blaming and slander. So we self-censor and contain our struggles to private spaces, where our power and influence is limited.

When I finally wrote a long complaint to the organisation that runs the mosque, they responded with a one-line email telling me to telephone one of the sheikhs directly. What if I don't want to talk to a sheikh? Why can't they respond in writing, with the same care and attention it took for me to write a letter while attending to two babies? Why not even an apology for the harm they caused at an event that was held specifically to remember Mum? Why is there no process for handling complaints and implementing feedback? Who do these places exist to serve if not the most vulnerable people in their communities? Do they want us to disengage completely? Why didn't anyone other than my sisters and I complain? The women who knew Mum had remained frozen in their seats as we walked out. Some said, 'This isn't the time or place.' I don't agree. Women are dead everywhere. The wounds are everywhere. Everywhere is the time and the place.

*

I have found creative and empowering ways to share my mum's story since then. But spaces for Muslim women to talk about sexism and abuse are too often limited by the hostility we face on the grounds of gender, race and religious identity. Empowerment can only come if we feel safe enough to share our stories without being blamed and vilified.

In 2019 I was invited to speak at an event at the Canberra Islamic Centre, alongside the Imam. We took turns; I shared my lived experience and the Imam shared the things he'd witnessed in his role. He talked about the long-lasting effects of abuse. The way it violates Islamic principles, both jurisprudential and spiritual. He emphasised the rights of victims of all forms of abuse to speak out and seek protection – contrary to cultural expectations that demand *sabr* and shun divorce. This was a healing moment for me – the harm that had been done at one podium had been healed at another.

*

In the wake of the #MeToo movement, a culture of accountability has emerged whereby problematic teachings and teachers can be challenged publicly. There are opportunities for women to find each other and express their concerns in safe spaces. We exchange ideas, readings, rulings and experiences. Men can't just throw words around in courtrooms, at the podium, in the media, or at work anymore. We're onto them. A growing awareness of the effects of abuse and trauma is emboldening women to speak more openly. Our experiences are evidence of why change is needed and, with so many survivors sharing their stories, I have hope that the narrative is slowly changing.

Recently, I spoke on *The Drum* alongside Jess Hill about the proposed Coercive Control Bill, which would see abusive 'patterns' in the 'arc of a relationship' recognised as a crime. My contribution to this conversation was that, perhaps, if we were having these conversations earlier, if the law recognised abuse as more than just one-off incidents, victims would be more empowered to identify abuse, report it, seek advice, and implement more robust safety measures when they decide to leave.

In a comment under the video of this conversation, one 'Michael' wrote:

> 'A woman who deletes from her own personhood by
> wearing coverings for religious reasons cannot be taken
> seriously regarding women's rights. Her "religious uniform"
> is tacit support for a religion that has created more victims
> than any other . . .'

There is no amount of experience, qualification or hard work that will change what strange white men are prepared to read into your work. It doesn't matter, because they're not who my work is intended to serve, but it does make the work heavier.

It reminds me that there's still so much left to do.

*

Religious coping may not work for everyone – and harm has occurred for lots of people in religious settings, committed by religious people. I've experienced spiritual and religious forms of abuse. However, we need to recognise the complexity of faith and culture, the agency women exercise within religious practice and the documented benefits of religious coping strategies for survivors of trauma.

I had relied on faith when I got home from the police station on the night of my mum's murder. Shaken and drained, I calmed myself by reciting quietly under my breath, *Subhanallah, alhamdulillah, la Illaha illa-llah*. An expression of praise, an utterance of gratitude, and an affirmation of the one-ness of God, these words were a crucial reminder for me of what I had previously been given, what I still had, and what I could depend on. I later found reflections on crime, punishment and accountability in Islamic texts and tradition. I found validation for my grief and anger, and learned about how these emotions could be harnessed and directed towards positive deeds and advocating for change. I found solace in descriptions of a grander justice that I could be a part of, and was uplifted by verses of resilience and hope, *Inna ma'al 'usri yusra:* Verily, with every hardship there is relief.

Patriarchy has taken so much from women. It has deprived us of freedom, personal safety and political agency. It chips away at our confidence and muffles our voices. It undervalues our time and talents. Those of us who rely on religion or spirituality to navigate these challenges do not want to be told that we should also let patriarchy take our faith. To suggest that our faith makes us complicit in our own oppression and that we should therefore abandon it is victim-blaming.

So to the men who are annoyed at outspoken women like me, who tell me my faith is holding me back, that I cannot be a feminist: you cannot have my story.

To the Muslim men I used to know, those who are silent and complicit, and those who see religion only as a validation of their desire for power and control: you cannot have my story.

I stand for neither of you. Whether you are my brother in faith or only in humanity, if you are not ready to listen, to help change the story, you cannot have mine.

*

In a report by Our Watch, researchers stated that it was unclear whether mentions of Mum's cultural background in media reports about her death were of benefit to the broader conversation about violence against women in Australia. On one hand, it would be incorrect to suggest that violence is culturally specific. On the other, we do not want to erase the different ways in which women experience patriarchy in different contexts.

One of the reasons Mum was reluctant to leave Dad was for fear of the disapproval and gossip that she believed would ensue. Mum was afraid of being labelled a bad wife and mother and, at the same time, embarrassed about how the abuse would be perceived and racialised by outsiders. Her concerns for how her extended family and community would judge her and the way this would impact her children kept her trapped in an abusive, unhealthy marriage for twenty-eight years. As the public response to Mum's murder has shown, those fears were not unfounded.

Women like Mum are less likely to report violence, and they experience more barriers in accessing support services, making them less likely to leave an abusive relationship than other women.

One of the main reasons for under-reporting is the shaming or family disapproval faced by Culturally and Linguistically Diverse (CALD) women (to use the description employed in government policy).

There are several ways this can be tackled. At Bankstown Women's Health Centre, 'soft-entry' options are used to attract clients who may prefer not to report to police or who are reluctant to disclose their experience of abuse for cultural reasons. For instance, a community kitchen health and nutrition program run by the centre attracted twenty-two women, more than half of whom ended up accessing other services offered at the centre and disclosing past or current abuse. For many CALD women, such initiatives are a far more attractive way of accessing support because they do not carry the real or perceived threat of going directly to authorities and they alleviate some of the pressure associated with legal proceedings.

For all the worry about what we wear, how we marry, how we divorce and our supposed lack of cultural and religious agency, little concern is being converted into dollars and practical protections for CALD women. Frontline workers and advocates want the conversation shifted towards a practical and intersectional response to domestic violence that includes better accommodation options, and legislative change so that women can access adequate protection that is culturally sensitive. For CALD women, it can literally mean the difference between life and death.

*

I'm cynical about men. That's not my fault; it's theirs. But, in doing any kind of activism, it's important to believe that something better is possible. I have witnessed that men can be better because I have a partner who I am not afraid of and who doesn't try to shrink me. I have found the gentleness and friendship in him that I have wanted to see in other men. This is an incredibly basic place to start. Safety and room for growth should be at the core of any relationship.

I know that a better kind of masculinity exists because my partner has filled the empty shoes left by multiple men in my life without hesitation. While men on the internet continue to dismiss and laugh about murder and rape, Moey went to identify Mum's body when her children couldn't. He didn't wait a day before inviting my sisters to our home and organising for their furniture to be delivered so they'd be comfortable; even while people whispered behind our backs that it was inappropriate for unmarried women to live with their brother-in-law. He stood in place of my father, brother and uncles at Mum's funeral. He helped lower Mum into her grave. He has witnessed the undeniable and direct link between casual sexism and violent crime. He called out the misogynists who tried to silence me, and he refuses to be a bystander. He has confronted sheikhs about sexism in their sermons. He's given evidence in court for a vulnerable neighbour who was attacked by her male partner in her own driveway.

While other men make violent jokes about their mothers-in-law, Moey says he feels robbed. 'I would've loved to have more coffees with your mum,' he tells me. We grieve the time and joy my father took from us. The murder affected our relationship in so many ways: our health, our parenting, our financial circumstances. Even now our house remains partly owned by my father, who refuses to relinquish his quarter, knowing that we can't sell, refinance or even access affiliated bank accounts without his signature. We can't finalise Mum's estate because of these legalities. We must sue him if we want to resolve this. A legal system that sees incarceration as the only solution to crime leaves victims in all sorts of messes.

The week before the murder, Moey and I were celebrating our second anniversary and expecting our first child. We've been hurtling forward since then and only now have we started to catch our breaths. We are in a process of breaking cycles, and we are imperfect. The exhaustion of the past few years makes us bad at routine and maybe a little too soft as parents. We still argue about the housework, and we're still stubborn lawyerly types who will debate a point until the sun rises the next day. We still eat too much ice cream and stay up late only to regret it the next morning.

I do not feel like I am too much for my husband, even though my art, my books, my plants have gradually taken over our living spaces. I write in our open-plan living room, swivelling my chair every now and then to measure my memory of events against his. He knows that my work and my advocacy is for both of us and for our children.

I know that there are ways to co-exist. We can unlearn the things that won't serve the next generation and grow towards a common vision. Men are capable of being in our lives in a way that doesn't hurt. There's enough love and space on Allah's earth for both of us.

FORTY

I still get anxious when I share my story, even when it goes well. Not enough has changed. Under the guise of 'feedback' there is push-back against my testimony at the end of almost every engagement. There are the young men who think my story makes them look bad. They say, 'But you didn't mention the fact that men can be victims too.' They refuse to sit with the fact that they may be complicit in the very sad and personal story I have just told them. There are people who want to recommend a course on 'forgiving and letting go'. Perhaps they struggle to sit with my anger because it asks them to be angry too.

The perpetrator demands nothing from the bystander.

*

I gave the keynote speech at an International Women's Day event in Melbourne a couple of years ago. I showed pictures of my grandmother, and talked about what was done to her. I showed photos of my mother, and talked about what was done to her.

I then explained how gender and violence are intertwined both in the home and in war.

Afterwards, members of the audience congratulated me, hugged me, gave me flowers, and warmed me with their condolences. They gave me their email addresses and business cards. A woman with short curly hair stood just outside the huddle. I smiled to acknowledge her as other people moved to the long table at the back of the room to eat *manoosh* and satay skewers. I was looking for a place to put down my flowers when the woman spoke.

'That was very good,' she said. The words were a compliment, but she stretched and rolled them in her mouth so that there was no kindness left in them when they finally came out.

'Thank you.' I smiled. Her mouth was a short straight line.

'It is very good what you are doing, but why did you have to mention about Israel?'

I blinked a few times. 'Oh, um, you mean about my grandmother?'

'Because I am Israeli and that was kind of triggering for me.'

'Sorry – are you saying *my* grandmother's story was triggering for *you*?'

We were at the Islamic Museum of Australia in Melbourne and the event was hosted by the Australian Muslim Women's Centre for Human Rights. Even here, in a space built to hold our stories and our art, my narrative was too much reality for this member of the audience. This was not the kind of violence, not the kind of human rights, she expected to hear about.

'Why do you bring it up? I do not know why it is related to violence against women,' she added.

When I'm triggered, I see my thoughts as pictures and words; they flicker and shout without structure. The fragments won't get in line. I had just told her the story. Now the story was a cluster of metal and barbed wire stuck in my throat, too big to spit into a clever response. My mouth was already dry from speaking. Her eyes were wide, waiting for answers.

'This is my story, and this is an event about violence against women and human rights. My mum's context matters, my grandmother mattered. As I mentioned, women with war trauma might experience more complex PTSD as a result of abuse, they might find it harder to trust authorities, the abuse can trigger those memories . . .'

Why am I justifying myself? She's not really listening.

The woman's mouth was slightly open now. Before she could interrupt, I asked, 'Do you know about intergenerational trauma?'

The woman adjusted her shoulder bag and shifted her body from one side to the other and said, 'Yes, I do but –'

In the same moment, another woman stepped between us, clasped my hands and pulled me towards her like an aunt would, even though I had no idea who she was. 'That was beautiful, *habibti*,' she said.

The woman with the short curly hair retreated into the crowd at the back of the room, talking and mingling with other people, every now and then glancing in my direction.

*

Why are you comfortable with my story when my father is the perpetrator, but uncomfortable when the state is the perpetrator?

The question crystallised a few hours later while I was sitting alone on a bench in the Khalil Gibran exhibition at the Immigration Museum. The room was dim and the walls were magenta, like a womb. *Khalil* means 'friend' in Arabic. I hid there, thinking about the way that the woman with the short curly hair had denied my experience. I felt ashamed for not having the right response and allowing her words to wound me. I wondered how she could have sat through my story and still remain so detached from me at the end of it.

In *Rage Becomes Her*, Soraya Chemaly talks about the ways in which people are careless with others' stories, and the erasure that occurs as a result. She refers to the two defining features of 'epistemic injustice', drawing on the work of philosopher Miranda Fricker. The first is 'testimonial injustice', 'in which a speaker, because of prejudice on the part of the person or persons listening, is not considered trustworthy or credible'.

The woman who had accosted me that morning had not accepted the credibility of my knowledge, even though my knowing resulted from both lived experience and formal education. Not only was this a denial of my right to tell my story as I had experienced it, it was a denial of the real issues that women activists before me have sought to highlight in terms of the gendered effects of war. The fact is, 'gender inequality is magnified in situations of war, refugee situations and rebuilding efforts after armed conflict'. Researchers on gender and war, such as Golie G. Jansen of Eastern Washington University, have observed:

'Women bear the brunt of these measures as they cope
with a decline or absence of welfare spending and the lack
of access to credit and often suffer from an increase of
domestic violence owing to the availability of more arms.
Other prewar conditions are increased militarization,
with high expenditures for arms, at the expense of health
care, education, and public services. These conditions also
engender a strengthened rhetoric of patriarchal roles in
which men's roles as protectors of women, children, and
the country and women's roles as mothers are reinforced.
These patriarchal reinforcements often coincide with a rise
of violence against women, when men turn to killing their

315

own women when they perceive that their honor has been offended by women who escape patriarchal codes of 'purity' . . . Women are not just caught in the cross-fires but are increasingly victims of violence in war situations. There are widespread atrocities; in war, women's bodies become a battleground – rapes, forced pregnancies, kidnappings, and sexual servitude are common . . .'

I can't even write about how these things played out for my grandmother because, as a consequence of armed conflict, I've been denied a right to know her well, and then, as a consequence of intimate partner violence, I've also been denied the right to access observations Mum might have made about her mother's experiences.

This ties in with the second feature of epistemic injustice which, Chemaly writes, is 'hermeneutical injustice': 'the injustice of having one's social experience denied and hidden from communal understanding'. As a result, 'people who experience the effects of the injustice themselves have no framework for understanding what is happening to them. When a society wilfully looks away from injustice, it fails to develop language to describe it, to communicate what is happening, or to prepare the individual to adapt'.

Feminist activism, the #MeToo movement, and ongoing discussions about abuse have provided a language with which survivors are able to describe the injustices that have taken place in their lives. As a result, I can communicate my mother's story in a way that is consistent with communal understanding. I am able to conduct my advocacy within the frameworks that have been established because enough people now refuse to look away. I am able to adapt because there was enough indignation and understanding in 2015 that Mum was counted in Destroy the Joint's 'Counting Dead Women' project, that her death was reported as domestic violence, that what happened to her was treated as a preventable crime, rather than as an inevitable tragedy or something that existed outside of mainstream Australian culture.

On that very first day, the law stepped in, police took action, social workers provided advice and the media took notice. These responses have had to be fought for and still don't guarantee every woman safety.

Writing for *Women's Agenda* the day after the murder, Lucia Osborne-Crowley explained how increased coverage in the media had led directly to political leaders pledging action on domestic violence across party lines:

'There is no question that the issue's raised profile signals
that we are one step closer to solving the problem – but it is
the steps that come next that are crucial, and they need to
be taken immediately. As it stands, the increase in coverage
of domestic violence has been matched by an increase in
deaths resulting from it.

'Awareness is essential in the ongoing battle against
domestic violence. But it is not enough.

'We know this because all of the coverage and pledges
made in the early months of 2015 were not enough to
keep those 26 women safe. Those 26 women constitute
a national emergency, and we need to treat them as such.
We need to do more than just talk about ending violence
against women. We need to take the next steps, and we
need to take them fast.'

At around the time Mum was murdered, the violent deaths of women had started receiving immediate national attention. This was owing to the mounting pressure from survivor-advocates, feminists and specialist organisations demanding that these crimes be taken seriously. It's difficult to quantify what effect this had on Mum's case. How many similar crimes had quietly churned through the system before ours? How many cases of violence against women have barely received a mention let alone accountability because the victim is Aboriginal or an international student or disabled or transgender? If there were fewer eyes on what was happening, if the press had been quieter, if Mum were less 'us' and more 'them', if my sisters and I had not had access to education, to a language and framework, if we'd been less assertive about our concerns, the ODPP might have accepted Dad's plea. To have transgressions against you recognised and prosecuted shouldn't be a privilege, but for a lot of women it remains so.

Without a communal understanding and a society that was paying attention, Dad might have got what he wanted, as many men before him have and still do: his wife's complaints and desires silenced in exchange for a few years in prison. Had my sisters and I been young children, we might have been more susceptible to gaslighting and manipulation by Dad or his family. We might have been handed over to relatives or foster care only to be returned to him when he was free. He might have moved us overseas, got a new job, maybe even a new partner. We might never have seen the matter go to trial. We might have never known what happened to Salwa Haydar.

*

When my mum was murdered, someone in my family had already been murdered in an equally violent and deliberate manner, albeit in very different circumstances. That someone was my grandmother. Physiologically, I experience the two events as one wound. They are linked for me in a way I should not have to articulate. Both events have shaped me. Neither is acceptable.

However, Teta's is an injustice that has been denied a language and a response. There is no movement and no hashtag for this kind of dead woman. Her experience is not rare, but it is not part of the communal understanding because too many of us wilfully look away. My cousin Zaynab says it so clearly:

'There is no way to get justice for what war does. War just happens to you and you can do absolutely nothing about it.'

With Teta there was no process to hold on to. There was no trial and no accountability. The news reports engaged with our sadness but not with the politics of why civilians are able to be killed in their own homes. I have never visited Teta's grave because I am too afraid. I am ashamed of this fear. I worry that, even in her grave, Teta is not safe. Every now and then planes transgress the airspace over the village. People film it with their phones and post the videos to Facebook. Then they turn their palms to the sky and make *dua*. But bombs are not rain; they do not fall from the sky because God or nature has decreed it. Someone builds the weapon, someone buys it, people are recruited, someone gives a command, buttons are pressed, triggers are pulled. Bombs are not rain.

FORTY-ONE

On my ninth birthday, my mum gifted me a small collection of gold jewellery. That she was entrusting me with something sentimental made me feel grown up, close to her. I'd heard older women talk about gold as a way of preserving and passing on wealth. They'd say things like, 'This bangle was part of my brides-gift,' and 'This ring is made of all the old pieces I had melted down,' and 'Look at this chain, see how it flashes like lightning!' I'd seen them take rings straight off their fingers and gift them to one another. Even as a young girl I wanted to be a part of this love-language.

My mum handed the pieces over one by one, reminding me they may be small and delicate, but they are *tha-al* – heavy. She gave me a small gold *khatim*, which barely fits around my pinky now, and a twinkling chain with a rectangular pendant inscribed, *Ya Rab ihfad li baba wa mama* – 'Oh God, preserve my father and mother'. My new treasures were not fashionable or cool or even particularly valuable, but I wore them with pride. More than once, teachers pointed out that my dangly earrings didn't comply with the dress-code. They said it was a matter of safety, 'they'll tear right through your earlobes if they get caught on something!'

Now I have a daughter and she stands and watches me as I get dressed. I pull out the little music box my husband bought me when we were engaged and my daughter points with a small upturned palm.

She says, 'I like your jewellery, Mummy.'

I say, 'Good. One day *inshallah*, they'll all belong to you.'

'When I'm big?'

'Yes, *mama*.'

I try not to pre-empt the circumstances in which my daughter might inherit my grandmother's gold bangle.

*

Teta starts the crochet by tying a little loop in the thread. She calls it a khamsi, *which means five. The Arabic numeral for five is 'o'. Through the 'o' the silver* sannara *goes, in, latch, out, up, through.*

As I worked through the paperwork for Mum's estate, I realised that I didn't have essential documents like evidence of Mum's marriage and citizenship. These had been stolen by Dad, presumably before the murder, along with other important documents. How would I retrieve the information I needed?

Teta says we start with one simple stitch, then we build on it. Her fingers are thick but her work is delicate.

Then it hit me. Mum had prepared me for this. In the bottom of a basket full of letters, notepads and payslips, I found the copies I had taken seven years earlier.

I sent them quickly to the lawyer. 'Are these helpful? Can you believe Mum had the foresight to get me to secretly copy these?'

You have to count, count the stitches for an even finish.

Once I had made headway with Mum's affairs, I could turn my attention to my own. Making art is a language that comes more naturally to me than anything. More naturally than writing, more than mothering. I decided that this was how I would start sharing the parts of our stories that Dad's family, the legal system and the media had not made room for.

The terms of the Archibald Prize require the sitter to be alive. An image took form in my mind: it couldn't be Mum, but it could be me telling my mum's story and her telling her mum's story.

The first sketches for the self-portrait were done in black biro on yellow sticky notes. I stuck them into my diary and finally let the law firm know that I wouldn't be coming back. They'd been holding my position for over two years. Even though I hadn't returned after the murder, I'd struggled to call it quits. Letting go of something you've worked hard for, succeeded in, and have been encouraged to do is not easy. I wrote a script of what to say: 'I have decided to resign at this stage in order to pursue other things.'

Teta holds the little lace floret in the air. There! That's the first circle done.

For a week straight I painted. Stopping only to roll back in my chair to check how much of the imposing white canvas remained. And to feed the kids, of course. My sisters and husband cheered me on when the self-doubt emerged.

For the artwork to say what I wanted it to say, I needed the photo of Mum holding the photo of her mum which was first taken in 2006 and re-circulated in 2015. You have to order and pay for good prints of press photos and I was only ten days from the submission deadline. I decided to print the photo straight from the internet using my home printer, with the Fairfax watermark over it. I decorated myself in clothing featuring intricate designs like those found on the tiles of a mosque. Each tiny, careful stroke of paint felt like a tribute to the lives Mum and Teta lived. I titled the work 'Insert Headline Here' because my trauma seemed always the subject of headlines. This painting was my way of reclaiming the story and telling it my own way. To my shock and delight, the work was selected as a finalist and hung in the Art Gallery of New South Wales.

Light shines through the soft architecture of the floret.

A journalist asked me about my painting, 'Was it cathartic? Did you cry?'

'Yes, it was cathartic. No, I did not cry.'

There have been studies into the role of visual narratives in depicting gender-based violence and its legal and medical consequences. Researchers have observed that 'legal approaches' require traumatised individuals 'to provide "valid" and "measurable" evidence of trauma upon which judgments about justice are made' whereas images can go beyond 'moral binaries' and 'clear-cut distinctions'. My catharsis was a sense of satisfaction at what I had placed onto the canvas. The sense of order I had constructed. It did not arrive as sadness. It arrived like a puzzle piece shifting into place. My painting had allowed me to say something about my experiences and my grief that I had not yet been able to put into words. The most vulnerable parts of my story had to come out of my body in pictures before I could phrase them clearly. I felt a sense of order and triumph about what I had constructed: three generations of stories spanning two continents and ten years, distilled into one piece of work that could speak on my behalf to thousands of people.

Teta puts the floret in my hand. 'Yallah, *your turn now.*'

I got a call from Jason Clare MP. He had heard me speak at an event and called to ask if I was interested in providing information

323

about the problems I had accessing my Parental Leave Pay. He delivered a speech on the issue at the Federation Chamber in late 2018 and again in early 2021. This one small change could mean a lot for the next person. I've recently followed it up with the Minister for Women. I continue to await a response as the Australian government grapples with allegations of violence against women by some of its highest officers.

I've drafted submissions to the NSW Sentencing Council on sentencing, I've volunteered, made art, spoken to lots of people, drawn on my lived experience to shed light on the pros and cons of criminalising coercive control, consulted with organisations. In early 2020, I was one of three finalists for the New South Wales Premier's Women of the Year awards. I was declared 2020 Local Woman of the Year for Bankstown. I received a Community Recognition Statement, tabled in Parliament by Tania Mihailuk MP. I accepted these with mixed emotions: proud that I had done what Mum would have wanted, what other women seemed to want to see, yet suspicious about being celebrated and rewarded when I have achieved so little.

Be careful lest it unravel! Lest the cotton comes spilling out of itself like blood from a wound.

There are days I still feel hopeless. The work is repetitive and slow and there's still so much work to be done. I doubt that I have the tools or the skills for the task. I recognise my own limitations, my contradictions. But I know that without action, the wound persists.

I've listened to lots of 'thought work' podcasts, to help rewire my thinking so that I'm not always so anxious, or people-pleasing, or feeling like an imposter. I treat my trauma one neuron at a time. But the wound is not just inside me; it cuts across society. I can't treat one without treating the other. So, I am trying to build on what I have learned, to make sure that I am considering perspectives other than my own. I try to imagine a society with an expanded sense of justice, wide enough for everyone. The podcast host says, 'Hope does not come from external circumstances.' She quotes abolitionist feminist Mariame Kaba who says, 'Hope is a discipline.'

Start with one simple stitch and build on it.

EPILOGUE

I am trying to find a way to end this book with the right balance of hope and reality, when Beirut is blown apart. The wound is over two hundred metres wide and forty-two metres deep. It is a series of concentric circles of shredded metal and shattered glass. It is felt across the ocean in Cyprus.

I feel the wound here in Sydney, watching 2,750 tonnes of ammonium nitrate rapidly expand until it no longer fits my phone screen. Until the audio is lost and the image is incohesive. I do not know if the person who filmed this video is dead or alive. It occurs to me that I should call Khalo Hussam and Zaynab and ask if they are okay, but I am afraid of the emotions suspended in the airwaves between us whenever we try to communicate. *Inshallah kheir*. No news is good news.

I watch the video again – play, pause, play, pause – trying to pinpoint the exact moment when everything blows up. The exact moment when the people see the barely visible force coming, unable to stop it or escape. That tiny moment of total powerlessness against this big, irreversible thing. In the next video, wires are wrapped around buildings like abandoned crochet.

The next day is the seventy-fifth anniversary of Hiroshima and there are renewed calls to ban the bomb. No one with the power to end these things will do it. A few lines from Khalil Gibran's *The Prophet* come to mind:

'And as a single leaf turns not yellow but with the silent knowledge of the whole tree,
So the wrong-doer cannot do wrong without the hidden will of you all.'

I've watched the Beirut explosion so many times, I don't think I can see it again. Instead I watch people protesting in the streets for hours, yelling, '*Thawra, thawra, thawra!*' I watch, trying to understand with my limited Arabic and the biased politics I inherited. I understand enough to know that this is part of the problem.

*

I read somewhere that if trauma can be inherited then so can strength, resilience and joy. From both Mum and Teta I learned that resilience is not a thing that you are born with but something you do. I think perhaps both are true.

Teta's crochet needle sits next to her mother-of-pearl prayer beads and a folded napkin she hand-embroidered with a blue thread when she was sixteen. I keep them next to a pinecone I found in the park one day. They are more than physical forms. In this curated collection, I find some of the tools I need to survive. My grandmother taught me how to use my palms and fingers to shape my world, to turn them upwards and pray, to make something beautiful out of nothing, stitch things back together when they needed mending. She taught me to take the hammer and use it to extract the nuts because sometimes the work is tough and lonely, but the rewards are sweet. Teta gave me aunts and cousins on every continent who watch and support my work.

From my mum I inherited the courage to speak. The desire to follow things through. I learned to assert myself and take up space, even in a world that is hostile towards women who do these things. I meet people who knew her: a radio host who once interviewed her, a teacher who taught her, a colleague she befriended at a workplace, a person she helped quit smoking. She taught me to pray, and when I pray now, I wear a set of robes we bought when we were in Lebanon together. I inherited Mum's silk hijabs and colourful dresses. I inherited her sociology books and her wanting to know and keep learning. My mother gave me sisters who walk with me. I have watched them grow into women she would be proud of. When I switch on the news nowadays, there is a chance I will see Nour reporting. Ola lives nearby and has just graduated from university. Sometimes my daughter's smile reminds me of my mother's.

*

About a year after my self-portrait tours with the Archibald Prize, I am offered a space at Fairfield City Museum and Gallery to exhibit my work. I get nostalgic and develop a body of work inspired by kitschy migrant décor and the music I grew up listening to as Mum chauffeured us to and from school. I rummage through some of my mum's old things; photos, documents, objects and even clothes I salvaged from her home. There is a photo of my mother taken in Lebanon in 1987. In it, she is wearing a hot-pink outfit, with her face nestled between the branches of an oleander bush.

I stitch things together like my seamstress grandmother once did. I reflect on the intergenerational effects of trauma and abuse.

My artworks include references to home and homeland, but both places have been disrupted and fragmented by violence. My intention is to interrogate whether any space is safe for women – to be all that they want to be, to actualise their ambitions and to express their spirituality.

I consider the wounds caused figuratively and literally to women in my family as a result of male aggression, armed conflict and migration. My memories of childhood, my identity and my sense of security have all been affected by trauma. Without proactively searching for ways to recover from those wounds, it is easy to feel overwhelmed by the darkness and cruelty of those experiences, and by the knowledge that people all over the world continue to be displaced physically and psychologically by violence every day.

The exhibition I put together is a personal and political exploration of my family background with recurring themes of violence, loss, innocence and aggression. There is an underlying question throughout all of these works; are some traumas too deep and too abstract to fully heal, or is there hope that the cycle can be ended through self-awareness, creative practice and activism?

I dust off the two drawings I did on my lounge room floor in 2014; the one with the childlike body, swaddled in a white sheet, and the landscape with the lemon tree. They've spent almost five years rolled up and tucked away in a cupboard, I reclaim them, touch them up, get them framed. I make a short film about Mum and Teta and record myself repeating Teta's words: 'Everything starts out small and grows bigger over time . . .' I paint a big self-portrait. In it, I am holding Teta's silver needle, crocheting. I title the exhibition *The Mother Wound*.

That's it, we're knitting one layer onto another.

Stitching the wounds shut.

*

When I encounter people who are sympathetic to my story, they say, 'Your mother would be so proud of you.' I like hearing this. I know she would be proud. My mum was proud of me when she was alive. When I was named dux of my primary school, she bragged to all the other mums that her daughter was 'the duck of the school'. My sisters and I laughed about it for weeks.

But there were also wounds in my relationship with my mother. There were teenage 'I hate yous' and secrets kept. I was so angry I threw a bucket of *laban* onto the carpet one time. Swiftly, Mum had me clean it up. And, as quick as that, we'd move on. I see the ways in which these tensions and outbursts were mutual exchanges of frustration and grief.

Author Bethany Webster, in explaining the concept of the 'mother wound', states that 'mothers may unconsciously project deep rage towards their children in subtle ways. However, the rage really isn't towards the children. The rage is towards the patriarchal society that requires women to sacrifice and utterly deplete themselves in order to mother a child.'

I watch my children as they play. They're drenched in giggles. I notice how soft and warm they are, curled up next to me when we're watching a movie. I try to compensate for being absent-minded and busy by making an extra effort to give them my time and attention; we end up at the shops or the play-centre, holding hands, skipping, eating *gozleme* and picking dandelions in the park.

I want to be the shield between what has happened and what will happen next. I acknowledge that I am, to some extent, powerless to do so. I read an article that says trauma can affect babies while they are in our bodies. If the baby is a girl, she already has all the eggs she will ever have, and those eggs contain the genetic makeup of any offspring she goes on to produce. By this logic, my grandchildren have already been exposed to the chemicals that flooded my body on the night of my mother's murder. By this logic, I've already lived through Teta's wars and Mum's abusive marriage.

I don't have an answer ready the first time my daughter asks me where my mum is. 'Where's your mum?' she asks.

I reply as casually as I can, 'My mum is not here *mama*.'

'Then where is she?'

'She is in heaven already,' I tell her.

My daughter wants to know if there are unicorns in heaven. We talk about that instead.

The wound throbs.

AUTHOR NOTE

The Mother Wound takes its name from the theory that the relationship between mothers and daughters is affected by unhealed traumatic experiences passed down matriarchal lines. The term was originally coined by an Australian, Dr Oscar Serrallach, who describes it as both an ancient and modern phenomenon, whereby our male-dominated society denies women access to 'ongoing matrilineal knowledge and structures'.

The mother wound carries feelings of comparison, shame and guilt. It can manifest as not being your full self because you don't want to threaten others; demonstrating a high tolerance for poor treatment; and conditions such as eating disorders, depression and addictions.

If you would like to learn more about the mother wound, visit: www.bethanywebster.com/about-the-mother-wound/

ACKNOWLEDGEMENTS

Alhamdulillah. This memoir is a thankyou to Mum and Teta, who faced immense injustices but left me with gifts that continue to serve me. Nothing will make it okay, but to be able to document their stories is an immense honour and is my gift back to them. It is the least I can do.

To my children, who tapped me on the shoulder many times as I wrote this book, I want to say thank you for being a source of cheer and wonder during some of my worst days. I hope that by the time you are old enough to read this there has been revolutionary change, or at least enough change that some of what I have recounted here seems unbelievable and outdated. I hope that you find courage in your identities and ancestry, as I have. I hope you are part of a more just, equal and visionary society.

Moey, marrying you was the best decision I ever made. Thank you for being the antidote to so much ugliness. I love you and I am grateful for every day we have – may there be plenty of good ones ahead!

To my best friends, my sisters, Nour and Ola, I would be both bored and boring without you. Thank you for the feedback and

335

the criticism and the laughs. You are both heroes. You each make me proud.

This book would not have come together the same way without the members of Mum's family who have supported me. Thank you, Khalto Jinan, for cheering me on. To Zaynab, thank you for trusting me and sharing parts of your story with me. I am proud to be related to survivors like you and your family. I pray that we find ways to be closer and that we remain in touch no matter what.

Thank you to Jann who, even in the very early days, said that I would be able to go on with life and do the things I wanted to do. This was so hard to believe then, but it was so important to hear.

Mariam Mourad at the Bankstown Women's Health Centre, thank you for doing the work for so many years, for seeking me out and providing me with the opportunity to learn. Thank you for believing in me as a leader and an advocate. I am proud to be able to contribute and I am in awe of the women who came before me and what they have managed to achieve. I know we can do more and be better. To the allies and organisations that I've had the pleasure of working with over the past few years, thank you. I have found so much meaning and recovery in this work.

Sarah Malik, I am glad to have met you in the buffet line at an event a few years ago. You were the first editor to notice my work and publish my writing. That experience marked the start of my writing career – thank you!

Jenna Price, thank you for turning up as more than a journalist, for taking my writing and advocacy seriously when I had barely started, and for making sure that I would go on to write a book.

Thank you, Julia Baird and Hayley Gleeson at ABC News for supporting my work. I am proud to have worked with you both as an illustrator and a writer. You gave me the space to authentically express myself when I said I wanted to write something – look how far it has come!

To my agent, Grace, thank you for seeing this book in me and believing in it. I'm grateful to be able to call you when feeling doubtful and imposter-y and overwhelmed. I can't wait to see what's next! To my publisher, Cate, thank you for helping me shape this work and bring it into the world. You made this process – which seemed huge and daunting at times – as smooth and positive as it could be.

Thank you to the team at Pan Macmillan, who have valued and respected both my story and my craft. You've been incredibly gentle with me and have helped me transform some messy, at times disparate, misshapen ideas into something I am very proud of. Thank you Danielle, for your expertise and attention to detail throughout the editing process and Clare, for being the most caring, sensitive publicist I could have hoped for.

Thank you, Dr Michael Mohammed Ahmad and Winnie Dunn at Sweatshop Western Sydney for providing me with a safe space where I could contribute both as a visual artist and writer (even when I was still a 'Bad Writer'). Some of my most magical breakthroughs happened in the space you've created.

I was blessed to be partnered with Carly Findlay through the *Kill Your Darlings* mentorship program while I was working on the early stages of my manuscript. Carly became one of the first people to read chapters from my work. Thank you, Carly, your advice and support have been so empowering. I learned from your work before I had the chance to meet you, and I am lucky to now count you as a friend.

Randa Abdel-Fattah, thank you for reading my manuscript in its earlier stages and providing immensely valuable feedback and encouragement. I am proud to be a part of a rich sisterhood and to have learned from Muslim women like you.

To my friends, who mourned and attended court with me, who have tolerated, celebrated and entertained me through my various phases and moods and changes of mind, may we continue to discuss life and love and politics over many platters of cheese. I'm proud to know women like you.

To the people in my community who offered care without judgment while we were grieving, thank you. To mum's friends and colleagues who have remained in touch, thank you. And finally, thank you to the women and allies I have connected with over the past few years and everyone who has contacted me to say they find empowerment or healing in my work. This means so much.

HELPLINES AND SUPPORT

If you or someone you know is experiencing or is at risk of domestic abuse, call 1800RESPECT on 1800 737 732 or visit www.1800respect.org.au for resources and information.

The following 24-hour helplines are also available for information, crisis support, and counselling:

Australian Capital Territory	Domestic Violence Crisis Service (DVCS) (02) 6280 0900
New South Wales	NSW Domestic Violence Line 1800 656 463
Northern Territory	Catherine Booth House (08) 8981 5928
Queensland	DVConnect 1800 811 811
South Australia	Domestic Violence and Aboriginal Family Violence Gateway services 1800 800 098
Tasmania	Safe at Home Family Violence Response and Referral Line 1800 633 937

Victoria	Safe Steps Family Violence Response Centre 1800 015 188
Western Australia	Women's Domestic Violence Helpline 1800 007 339

Men who are experiencing abuse or who are concerned about their own behaviour can call MensLine Australia on 1300 78 99 78.

Immigrant Women's Health Service: (02) 9726 4044 or (02) 9726 1016.

More information and additional helplines are available at www.respect.gov.au/services/

CREDITS

This Book contains excerpts of court transcripts and judgments that are the property of the Crown in the right of the State of New South Wales (Supreme Court of NSW) ©

Parts of this book were originally published in SBS Voices and ABC News online articles and have been reproduced with kind permission from © SBS and ABC News online.

Radio interview on pages 67–68 reproduced with kind permission from ABC's AM Radio.

Quote on page 221 used with kind permission from Yasmin Khan.

Quotes on pages 221–22 and 291 from *See What You Made Me Do* by Jess Hill used with kind permission from Jess Hill.

Quotes on pages 268 and 291 from *Trauma and Recovery* by Dr Judith Herman used with kind permission from Hachette Book Group.

Quotes on pages 315 and 316 from *Rage Becomes Her* by Soraya Chemaly used with kind permission from Simon & Schuster UK.